KU-363-158

SHAKESPEARE AND THE
TRUTH-TELLER

EDINBURGH CRITICAL STUDIES IN SHAKESPEARE AND PHILOSOPHY
Series Editor: Kevin Curran

Edinburgh Critical Studies in Shakespeare and Philosophy takes seriously the speculative and world-making properties of Shakespeare's art. Maintaining a broad view of 'philosophy' that accommodates first-order questions of metaphysics, ethics, politics and aesthetics, the series also expands our understanding of philosophy to include the unique kinds of theoretical work carried out by performance and poetry itself. These scholarly monographs will reinvigorate Shakespeare studies by opening new interdisciplinary conversations among scholars, artists and students.

Editorial Board Members
Ewan Fernie, Shakespeare Institute, University of Birmingham
James Kearney, University of California, Santa Barbara
Julia Reinhard Lupton, University of California, Irvine
Madhavi Menon, Ashoka University
Simon Palfrey, Oxford University
Tiffany Stern, Shakespeare Institute, University of Birmingham
Henry Turner, Rutgers University
Michael Witmore, The Folger Shakespeare Library
Paul Yachnin, McGill University

Published Titles
Rethinking Shakespeare's Political Philosophy: From Lear to Leviathan
Alex Schulman
Shakespeare in Hindsight: Counterfactual Thinking and Shakespearean Tragedy
Amir Khan
Second Death: Theatricalities of the Soul in Shakespeare's Drama
Donovan Sherman
Shakespeare's Fugitive Politics
Thomas P. Anderson
Is Shylock Jewish?: Citing Scripture and the Moral Agency of Shakespeare's Jews
Sara Coodin
Chaste Value: Economic Crisis, Female Chastity and the Production of Social Difference on Shakespeare's Stage
Katherine Gillen
Shakespearean Melancholy: Philosophy, Form and the Transformation of Comedy
J. F. Bernard
Shakespeare's Moral Compass
Neema Parvini
Shakespeare and the Fall of the Roman Republic: Selfhood, Stoicism and Civil War
Patrick Gray
Revenge Tragedy and Classical Philosophy on the Early Modern Stage
Christopher Crosbie
Shakespeare and the Truth-Teller: Confronting the Cynic Ideal
David Hershinow

Forthcoming Titles
Making Publics in Shakespeare's Playhouse
Paul Yachnin
Derrida Reads Shakespeare
Chiara Alfano
The Play and the Thing: A Phenomenology of Shakespearean Theatre
Matthew Wagner
Conceiving Desire: Metaphor, Cognition and Eros in Lyly and Shakespeare
Gillian Knoll

For further information please visit our website at edinburghuniversitypress.com/series/ecsst

SHAKESPEARE AND THE TRUTH-TELLER

Confronting the Cynic Ideal

◆ ◆ ◆

DAVID HERSHINOW

EDINBURGH
University Press

Edinburgh University Press is one of the leading university presses in the UK. We publish academic books and journals in our selected subject areas across the humanities and social sciences, combining cutting-edge scholarship with high editorial and production values to produce academic works of lasting importance. For more information visit our website: edinburghuniversitypress.com

© David Hershinow, 2019

Edinburgh University Press Ltd
The Tun – Holyrood Road
12(2f) Jackson's Entry
Edinburgh EH8 8PJ

Typeset in 12/15 Adobe Sabon by
IDSUK (DataConnection) Ltd, and
printed and bound in Great Britain.

A CIP record for this book is available from the British Library

ISBN 978 1 4744 3957 2 (hardback)
ISBN 978 1 4744 3959 6 (webready PDF)
ISBN 978 1 4744 3960 2 (epub)

The right of David Hershinow to be identified as the author of this work has been asserted in accordance with the Copyright, Designs and Patents Act 1988, and the Copyright and Related Rights Regulations 2003 (SI No. 2498).

CONTENTS

ACKNOWLEDGEMENTS

Diogenes might stand alone, but this book is a testament to the fact that I do not. This project began as a dissertation written at Johns Hopkins University, and it's impossible to overstate how formative those years of training proved to be on my sensibilities as a scholar and intellectual. This book simply would not exist without the support and guidance of Richard Halpern, whose course on 'The Continental Renaissance' first introduced me to the figure of Diogenes, and whose mentorship and feedback helped me to shape rough ideas into the material this book would eventually become. Frances Ferguson taught me to think about form and Amanda Anderson taught me to evaluate the *ethos* of an argument. While he arrived too late for me to take coursework with him, Drew Daniel was, and continues to be, an invaluable interlocutor and cheerleader. I thank my classmates for making a small programme feel so replete. Special thanks go to Tara Bynum, Elisha Cohn, Robert Day, Cristie Ellis, Rob Higney, Jason Hoppe, Claire Jarvis, James Kuzner, Ben Parris, Andrew Sisson, Beth Steedley and Dan Stout. I am especially grateful to Rebecca Brown and Sam Chambers for being such incredible friends and role models. Finally, I have to thank the members of my Accountability Group: Stephanie Hershinow, Dave Schley, Jessica Valdez and Maggie Vinter. For the past decade, their willingness to celebrate even the smallest accomplishment has been essential.

I had the great fortune to work with a number of brilliant colleagues in the Princeton Writing Program who offered me a supportive intellectual community in which to turn my dissertation into a book. Between drinks, meals, hallway conversations, and more formal discussions of each other's projects in our Works-in-Progress colloquia – which grappled with an earlier version of my *Timon* chapter – Sara Bryant, Gen Creedon, Rachel Gaubinger, Steven Kelts, Pat Moran, Jennifer Schnepf, Keith Shaw, Amanda Wilkins and Shannon Winston have helped me in ways both big and small. At Baruch College, CUNY, the support and friendship of a number of colleagues have helped me see this book through its final stages. I am particularly grateful to Lisa Blankenship, Allison Deutermann, Matt Eatough, Laura Kolb, Jessica Lang and Mary McGlynn. I've also benefited immensely from the friendship and collegiality extended to me by members of the Columbia University Seminar on Shakespeare, especially Heather Dubrow, Gavin Hollis, András Kiséry, Alexander Lash, Zoltán Márkus, Steve Mentz, Vim Pasupathi, Tanya Pollard, Debapriya Sarkar, John Staines, Richard Strier and Matt Zarnowiecki. My chapter on *Hamlet* is immeasurably better for having portions of it presented and discussed at seminar. I am thankful to the Schoff Fund at Columbia University for their help in publication.

Earlier versions of Chapter 3 and Chapter 5 appeared in *Criticism* and *Modern Philology*, respectively. My gratitude to the anonymous readers who commented on these essays, and to Wayne State University Press and the University of Chicago Press for permission to reprint.

My family has been a balm throughout this process, most particularly during the dark summer in which I formed the serious conviction that I wasn't cut out to write a book and that winning the Mega Millions would be the best – albeit not the likeliest – means of gracefully exiting academic life. I thank my parents, Lorna and Shel Hershinow, as well as my sister, Kim LaRocca, for surrounding me not only with love but also with three amazing models of the English professoriate. For their support and good company, I also thank David, Ruby and Star LaRocca, along with Kathy and the Rickeys Wood. For their unpredictable and always-welcome affections, I am grateful to my feline children, Lolo and Ira, who view this book (or, at least, the computer on which I wrote it) as a sibling with whom they've had to compete all their lives. More recently, my son Harvey has taught me to feel entirely new shades of love and devotion; I could not have asked for a better dose of perspective during the final year-and-change of finishing this book.

Like me, this book would be a shadow of itself without the influence of Stephanie Hershinow. The twinned paths of our lives have charted two different graduate schools, multiple moves and jobs, a baby, countless TV binges, and a constant back-and-forth of reading and commenting on one another's work. She has read every word of this book and its many, many drafts. Diogenes has his lantern; I have Stephanie. She is the giver of all good titles and punchy last lines. She is the light of my life. This book is dedicated to her.

SERIES EDITOR'S PREFACE

Picture Macbeth alone on stage, staring intently into empty space. 'Is this a dagger which I see before me?' he asks, grasping decisively at the air. On one hand, this is a quintessentially theatrical question. At once an object and a vector, the dagger describes the possibility of knowledge ('Is this a dagger') in specifically visual and spatial terms ('which I see before me'). At the same time, Macbeth is posing a quintessentially philosophical question, one that assumes knowledge to be both conditional and experiential, and that probes the relationship between certainty and perception as well as intention and action. It is from this shared ground of art and inquiry, of theatre and theory, that this series advances its basic premise: Shakespeare is philosophical.

It seems like a simple enough claim. But what does it mean exactly, beyond the parameters of this specific moment in *Macbeth*? Does it mean that Shakespeare had something we could think of as his own philosophy? Does it mean that he was influenced by particular philosophical schools, texts and thinkers? Does it mean, conversely, that modern philosophers have been influenced by him, that Shakespeare's plays and poems have been, and continue to be, resources for philosophical thought and speculation?

The answer is yes all around. These are all useful ways of conceiving a philosophical Shakespeare and all point to lines of inquiry that this series welcomes. But Shakespeare is philosophical in a much more fundamental way as well. Shakespeare is philosophical because the plays and poems actively create new worlds of knowledge and new scenes of ethical encounter. They ask big questions, make bold arguments and develop new vocabularies in order to think what might otherwise be unthinkable. Through both their scenarios and their imagery, the plays and poems engage the qualities of consciousness, the consequences of human action, the phenomenology of motive and attention, the conditions of personhood and the relationship among different orders of reality and experience. This is writing and dramaturgy, moreover, that consistently experiments with a broad range of conceptual crossings, between love and subjectivity, nature and politics, and temporality and form.

Edinburgh Critical Studies in Shakespeare and Philosophy takes seriously these speculative and world-making dimensions of Shakespeare's work. The series proceeds from a core conviction that art's capacity to think – to formulate, not just reflect, ideas – is what makes it urgent and valuable. Art matters because unlike other human activities it establishes its own frame of reference, reminding us that all acts of creation – biological, political, intellectual and amorous – are grounded in imagination. This is a far cry from business-as-usual in Shakespeare studies. Because historicism remains the methodological gold standard of the field, far more energy has been invested in exploring what Shakespeare once meant than in thinking rigorously about what Shakespeare continues to make possible. In response, Edinburgh Critical Studies in Shakespeare and Philosophy pushes back against the critical orthodoxies of historicism and cultural studies to clear a space for scholarship that confronts aspects of literature that can neither be reduced to nor adequately explained by particular historical contexts.

Shakespeare's creations are not just inheritances of a past culture, frozen artefacts whose original settings must be expertly reconstructed in order to be understood. The plays and poems are also living art, vital thought-worlds that struggle, across time, with foundational questions of metaphysics, ethics, politics and aesthetics. With this orientation in mind, Edinburgh Critical Studies in Shakespeare and Philosophy offers a series of scholarly monographs that will reinvigorate Shakespeare studies by opening new interdisciplinary conversations among scholars, artists and students.

Kevin Curran

INTRODUCTION

Early on in Shakespeare's *As You Like It*, the melancholy Jaques, having just made the acquaintance of Touchstone, declares himself 'ambitious for a motley coat', explaining his interest in foolery in terms of the freedom its practitioner can exercise in criticising others

> I must have liberty,
> Withal, as large a charter as the wind,
> To blow on whom I please.[1]

This is not simply a matter, for Jaques, of getting to be full of hot air; rather, he imagines that being a fool would entail his practicing a way of life with real political consequences:

> Invest me in my motley; give me leave
> To speak my mind, and I will through and through
> Cleanse the foul body of th'infected world. (II, vii, 58–60)

Jaques's ambition for motley is ambitious indeed, for he attributes to foolery the capacity to speak a new, healthier world into being, as if the critique a fool delivers holds the power to overcome and thus transform all others with its truth. At least, Jaques entertains the desire for such a power, a desire he belatedly – and I think mournfully – acknowledges to be out of his reach. Were he to be invested in motley, Jaques promises to 'Cleanse the foul body of th'infected world', but only on the condition that others 'will patiently receive [his] medicine' (II, vii, 61). Jaques's world-making critical impulse is checked by the pragmatic realities of argument and debate, under which interlocutors can always refuse to listen. Yet rather than modulating his vision for critical outspoken-ness in order to conform to these realities, Jaques completely abandons his ambition for motley in favour of turning her-metically inward. If the world will refuse his ministrations, then he will refuse the world in order to contemplate a better one of his own.

A failed fool before he even tries, Jaques renews his com-mitment to melancholy, which he now views as the antith-esis of the critical impulse that drew him to licensed foolery. We see this when, in the play's second half, Jaques mounts a defence of his melancholia, insisting that he 'love[s] it better than laughing' (IV, i, 4), thereby opposing Rosalind's view that she 'had rather have a fool to make [her] merry than experi-ence to make [her] sad' (IV, i, 25–7). Here, Jaques entirely disclaims his earlier commitment to social critique in order to instead endorse an antithetical position: 'Why, 'tis good to be sad and say nothing' (IV, i, 8). In contrast with his earlier partisanship for a fool's communicative and socially minded ethics, Jaques subscribes here to an ethics of muteness. By this view, his travels in search of 'sundry contemplation[s]' amount to a cultivation of the self in which experience and the acquisition of critical insights advance an exclusively per-sonal enlightenment. They serve to enclose Jaques in a kind of mental cocoon, or, as he puts it, 'my often rumination wraps me in a most humorous sadness' (IV, i, 7–9).

There is something undeniably comic about Jaques's careening from one extreme of social engagement to another, yet Shakespeare characterises him in this pendulous fashion not only for the sake of comic contrast but also for the sake of serious comparison. Of course, the precise nature of the comparison I understand Shakespeare to be thinking about does not entirely come across in the figure of Jaques, whose return to melancholy marks a total withdrawal from the project of social critique. The comparison between artificial foolery and melancholia that Shakespeare builds into the character of Jaques does not seem to satisfy Shakespeare, for he goes on to explore the overlap between the two orientations in his subsequent characterisation of the melancholy Hamlet. Though critics have generally cast Hamlet as a failed revenger, it would be more correct to say that Shakespeare depicts Hamlet as a man who reframes the project of revenge and its entailments – rather than exacting revenge, he withholds it, counterintuitively offering critique by way of hermetic detachment instead of heroic engagement. Hamlet, I argue, forgoes an action-oriented effort to set his time back into joint and, instead, contemplatively seeks to further disjoin himself from time. When he imagines Alexander the Great turning to dust and that dust being used to stopper a beer barrel, or when he muses over the progress of a king's body through the guts of a worm, a fish and finally a fisherman, Hamlet ruminates his way out of his fixed place in time in order to view worldly happenings from an incorporeal vantage. Eschewing individual action as the means of achieving vengeance, Hamlet pursues his critical agenda against Claudius and a rotten Denmark by claiming to see the inevitability of things as they have been, are and are going to be – thereby fulfilling his revenge through the impersonal operations of the cosmos. The aspirational inverse of Jaques's world-cleansing foolery, Hamlet undertakes an ethics of thoughtful sadness that posits contemplative self-enclosure as public activism's final frontier.

In *Shakespeare and the Truth-Teller*, I argue that Shakespeare takes a particular interest in testing and commenting on a series of practical strategies for realising what we might call the critic's will to revolution, strategies for living and acting in just the right way to be invested with an absolute degree of critical authority and agency. These are strategies that do not work, even as they nevertheless invite our belief because of our didactic relationship to literary and para-literary charac-terisations of the radical critic. I argue that Shakespeare com-ments on the conflation between literary character and ethical character that sustains these visions of aggrandised critical agency and that he produces this commentary in and through his depictions of several wise fools, Hamlet, and Timon of Athens. What links these disparate examples? In each case, Shakespeare's engagement with the character of the radical critic is more specifically an engagement with his period's mixed reception of Diogenes the Cynic – the Greek (anti-) philosopher and contemporary of Plato who, in the sixteenth century, becomes a central figure in debates over the possibil-ity of giving voice to radically effective critique. An irritat-ing iconoclast who rejected creaturely comforts, humiliated Plato in front of his students and masturbated in the agora, Diogenes had no interest in making himself easy to love. And yet, both in ancient Greece and over a long reception his-tory, he gained an admirer for every detractor. Suspicious of schools of thought, uninterested in disciples, Diogenes nev-ertheless proved to be a powerful (if troublesome) model for critical engagement.

It may at first seem odd to cast a Cynic like Diogenes in the role of revolutionary critic, for the term 'cynic' has come to name a person of worldly disenchantment, a person who sees the dirty reality of things as they are and doesn't believe in the possibility of change. However, this particular understanding of modern cynicism[2] has only been around for some two hundred years, and its emergence is but one salvo in a millennia-long interpretive struggle over the figure of the Cynic, a figure that has been viewed both as the most formidable truth-teller that the world has ever seen and as a crackpot whose perverse behaviour renders anything he says

self-evidently dismissible. Indeed, as we will see, the interpretive conflation of literary character with ethical character
that Shakespeare works to address plays a hand in provoking
these differing views not only in his historical moment but
also in subsequent ones, including our own. Consequently,
Shakespeare's efforts to confront the problem of character
posed by the Cynic ideal continue to be as valuable now as
they were in his own day.

Diogenes and His Early Modern Reception

We have no direct knowledge of Diogenes the historical
person. Born in Sinope, an Ionian colony on the Black Sea,
late in the fifth century BCE, Diogenes put none of his views
into writing and, by many accounts, refused to take on any
students. Our knowledge of Diogenes thus comes to us indi-
rectly through the many anecdotes about his sayings and
doings that have been told and retold through the centuries.
A span of three hundred years divides Diogenes of Sinope
from the earliest extant accounts of him, and another three
or more centuries separate these accounts from Diogenes
Laertius's *Lives of Eminent Philosophers* (*c.*300 CE), which
contains the first comprehensive collection of diogenical
anecdotes, and which therefore plays an influential role in
this figure's later reception history.[3] A work of doxography,
Laertius's chapter on Diogenes gathers together the many
stories about the Cynic philosopher that had accumulated
over the previous centuries, stories that were variously
inflected by the admirers and detractors of Diogenes who
took part in the telling of them. These anecdotes tell us
as much about the people who partook in their transmis-
sion as they do about Diogenes himself. In particular, they
reveal the thorniest and most evaluatively uncertain aspect
of Diogenes' reception to be his critical mission. Some of
the most unflattering accounts of Diogenes – like the story

of him masturbating in public as a demonstration of his self-sufficiency, or of him begging alms of a statue in order to 'get practice in being refused' – deal with his efforts to criticise the phoniness of the people around him.[4] At the same time, the anecdotes that present Diogenes in the most ennobling light – like the stories in which he stands up to Alexander the Great, or the one in which he claims that freedom of speech (*parrhêsia*) is the most beautiful thing in the world – also deal with the theme of the Cynic serving as a deliverer of critique.[5]

These competing pictures of Cynic critical activity prove to be a persistent and vexing feature of Diogenes' reception history, and two of the origin stories Laertius attributes to Diogenes offer some preliminary insights into the cause of this interpretive dilemma. In one origin story, Diogenes, the son of a Sinopian banker, visits an oracle and is instructed by Apollo to 'alter the political currency'. Initially misunderstanding this mandate, he returns home and adulterates the city's coinage, and it is only after his banishment and subsequent relocation to Athens that he comes to understand that the prophecy was allegorical: his true purpose is to challenge the social and political values in which everyone around him fraudulently trades. In another origin story, Diogenes becomes a Cynic philosopher when he arrives in Athens and sees a mouse 'not looking for a place to lie down in, not afraid of the dark, not seeking any of the things which are considered to be dainties' and discovers, in consequence, 'the means of adapting himself to circumstances'.[6] In the first story, we have the beginnings of Cynicism understood as a form of truth-telling; in the second, we have the beginnings of Cynicism understood as an ascetic practice that eschews social and material niceties in order to obtain personal happiness and peace of mind, the kind of Cynicism that Crates learns from Diogenes and in turn passes on to Zeno, the father of Stoicism.[7] Read separately, as some people assuredly have done, these two anecdotes paint very different pictures of diogenical Cynicism. However, this book takes interest in the vexed reception history that coheres around the figure of Diogenes precisely because people have so often read them together, understanding him to undertake an extreme regimen of ethical self-discipline as the means of legitimating his acts of truth-telling. More than anything else, it is the proposition of a causal link between Diogenes' ethical and critical projects that provokes divergent assessments of his efficacy as a truth-teller. Does his absolute adherence to guiding ethical principles make Diogenes into a truth-teller who is singularly able to speak truth to power, or is that very extremism a sign that he is cracked, a perverted madman who pleasures himself in public as a matter of 'principle', and therefore someone whose criticisms are self-evidently unserious and dismissible?

Diogenes has, to one degree or another, been provoking this interpretive struggle for over two thousand years, but the sixteenth century stands out as a watershed moment within this span for two interrelated reasons: first, because thinkers in this period begin to cathect on the problem of the Cynic truth-teller more than ever before, and second, because they do so at a time when actual practitioners of the Cynic way of life had been lost to living memory. This is a period in which the critical practice Diogenes is understood to exemplify circulates only in the form of literary and para-literary characters, meaning that the ethics of diogenical truth-telling is embodied not by real people but by their simulacra. Indeed, as we will see, the revolutionary potential of Cynic truth-telling becomes more hotly debated in this period precisely because sixteenth- and seventeenth-century thinkers engage only with characterisations of it. This is to suggest, on the one hand, that there is a notable change in the way people read and interpret literary and para-literary character in this period, one that leads some to see more actionable potential in Cynic practice than would have been true in previous eras. On the other hand, it is to suggest that this new interpretive tendency in turn leads to a newly energised backlash.

In mid-sixteenth-century England, Diogenes quickly transitions from being an arcane figure to a ubiquitous one. In part, this rise in popularity can be credited simply to increased availability, one facilitated by Nicholas Udall's 1542 translation of Erasmus's *Apophthegmatum opus* (1531), a compilation of apothegms and anecdotes that devotes more space to Diogenes than to any other figure. As David Mazella notes, this collection – along with accounts of Diogenes peppered across a range of classical and medieval texts – was quickly incorporated into the standard curriculum for teaching students rhetoric.[8] In a curricular framework wherein students looked to the past for both positive and negative examples of argumentative and oratorical technique, Diogenes and his Cynic conception of *parrhêsia* proved to be especially valuable because his saying and doings could furnish students with both kinds of exempla. This schismatic approach to moralising on Cynic truth-telling had the effect of formalising a division between the Renaissance High and Low Views of Diogenes.[9]

On the one hand, accounts of Diogenes fearlessly cutting Alexander the Great down to size led early modern humanists and courtiers to invoke him as the period's ideal of an honest and forthright counsellor, one who is able to distinguish himself from the many flatterers at court and to command a lord's attention. As the story goes, Alexander one day approached Diogenes lying on the ground near his tub and offered to grant the Cynic any favour of his choosing, to which Diogenes replied 'Do not make shadoe betwene the sonne and me' (as Udall explains, the Cynic philosopher 'was disposed to sonne hym selfe').[10] In this anecdote, Diogenes rejects Alexander's offer of beneficence from his position of relative abjection, a condition that he deliberately cultivates and that he revalues as the ethical basis from which he can critique the comparative fraudulence of Alexander's personal and social values. If Alexander aspires to god-like status – to live up to the example of Heracles, from whom he claims to descend – then Diogenes offers a harsh reminder that Alexander can never replace the warmth and light that emanates from the sun. The implication is that Alexander's best efforts at securing power and distributing favour only amount to an interposing shadow, something that would deprive Diogenes of his true, basic needs. According to Mazella, early modern admirers of this story all sought to assimilate Cynicism into the *ars rhetorica*, viewing Diogenes as a counsellor who could productively test the outermost limits of courtly decorum while managing to stay safely within its bounds. Certainly it is true that a majority understood Diogenes' exemplarity to lie in his skill at the rhetorical game of truth-telling, a game in which the sovereign interlocutor agrees to exercise magnanimous restraint on condition that the frank subordinate maintain just enough decorum to preserve his interlocutor's goodwill. However, in this book I identify a subset of these thinkers – Thomas Wilson and John Lyly among them – who find in Diogenes a more extreme possibility. For the humanist who felt especially caught between the aspirations and the frustrations of critical activity, for the courtier who felt especially tired of playing games, the story of Diogenes confronting Alexander the Great held the promise of a specifically non-rhetorical method of delivering critique, one that imbues an advisor with enough critical authority to make unwelcome truths literally impossible for a king to discount. As we will see, in Chapter 2, this is the import of Alexander's claim that he simply 'cannot be angry with [Diogenes]' in Lyly's *A moste excellent comedie of Alexander, Campaspe, and Diogenes* (1584).[11] Lyly's Alexander doesn't admit to a fondness for Diogenes in this statement but to an utter incapacity to counter the force of Diogenes' critique.

This idea of the Cynic stance as the position from which to speak maximum truth to power – so much so that truth displaces power – deserves our attention, not only because it is noteworthy in its own right, but also because it seems to provoke several antithetical assessments in early modern England. Pointing to the many accounts of Diogenes' extraordinary shamelessness and incivility, belittlers of Cynicism sought to link Diogenes to such early modern types as the melancholic, the misanthrope, and the parasite-jester, all of whom can be disbelieved on the basis of their faulty or untrustworthy character.[12] In this context, we may recall the story of Diogenes playing sophist and palatably preaching to a growing crowd on the theme of virtuous living, then ending his uncharacteristically pleasing discourse by squatting in front of his audience and taking a shit.[13]

Mazella understands the negative view of Cynic truth-telling – that of its being utterly self-defeating – to emerge out of the curricular process that locates examples of 'bad Cynicism' in a different subset of apothegms than those associated with 'good Cynicism', yet such an account overlooks the tendency for Cynicism's admirers and detractors to read the same apothegms in completely different ways. The story of Diogenes walking the streets with a lantern in broad daylight, explaining to passers-by that he is looking for a single honest man, is but one of many anecdotes held up as evidence that a Cynic is nothing but a misanthropic railer, and a decidedly perverse one at that.[14] Yet this same story has also been invoked as an example of effective Cynic truth-telling that is aimed not at a king but at society as a whole. Samuel Rowlands takes this latter view in *Diogenes Lanthorne* (1607), an entry into the fashionable 'book of fools' genre in which Rowlands has a narrating Diogenes taxonomise the many different kinds of fools, knaves and hypocrites that populate society.[15] In a similar vein, the vernacularisation of Diogenes that reads Cynicism through the lens of melancholia produces a positive assessment of Cynic truth-telling in addition to the negative one Mazella rightly identifies. We see an example of this when Robert Burton, in his preface to *The Anatomy of Melancholy* (1621), revalues his retreat from public service into private intellectualising by likening himself to Diogenes, thereby casting intellectual melancholy as a sublimated form of critical activity.[16] In both cases, competing evaluations of Cynicism's critical potential are bound together by their shared object of analysis, the depictions of Cynic character upon which these antithetical assessments are based.

The fact that early modern thinkers could look at the same depictions of Cynic truth-telling and see them so differently caused no small amount of uneasiness. To appreciate why, think of how disconcerting we all find it to know that others see a rabbit where we see a duck (or, to take a more recent example, to know that others see a white and gold dress where we see a blue and black one) and add the socio-political stakes of having such a difference of perspective over a mode of conduct that is either the most or the least effective way to speak truth to power. The hermeneutic uneasiness that surrounds the early modern reception of Diogenes is important to note because the unresolvability at its core made the figure of the Cynic into a culturally productive object of cathexis. I say this not only because Diogenes was carted out as both icon and whipping boy for writers grappling with the means both of delivering effective counsel and of impressing upon others one's Protestant (or Catholic) religious convictions, but also because writers of the period would advance their positions in these debates by generating new literary and para-literary depictions of the diogenical truth-teller.[17] This is most obviously the case with texts like Lyly's *Campaspe* and Rowland's *Diogenes Lanthorne*, which use known anecdotes about the Cynic philosopher as a starting point for their own rendering of him, thereby modelling themselves on Lucian's and Dio Chrysostom's creative engagement with Diogenes in late antiquity.[18] Less obviously, but perhaps more importantly, writers drew on both the positive and negative iterations of the Cynic type to populate the literature of the period – drama, most especially – with a whole host of characters that might exemplify either the efficacy or the impotence of truth-telling grounded in an extreme way of life. Sometimes allusions to Diogenes are built into these characterisations; often they are not. But either way, these early modern iterations of Cynic character are held up to the judgment of viewers and readers on the basis of their critical posture and its perceived practical value.

As we will see, Shakespeare does not take sides in contemporary debates over Cynicism's critical efficacy; instead, he diagnoses the crisis of character that is provoked among his peers by the diogenical figure of the indomitable critic. Shakespeare, I argue, proves to be especially sensitive to the interpretive confusion that results from reading literary and para-literary characterisations of Cynic truth-telling as practical how-to guides, a confusion considerably intensified in the sixteenth century by the protocols of dramatic realism that were just then coming to dominate the English stage. If, as I claim in Chapter 2, realism develops as a representational form because it enables literature to be the vehicle for instruction that is practical rather than prescriptive, then Shakespeare identifies in his period's struggle with the Cynic ideal a new potential for didactic failure that goes hand in hand with realism's considerable potential for didactic success. This is to suggest, first, that the protocols of dramatic realism led viewers and readers to expect the actions and outcomes of literary characters to be instructive in ways that have practical applicability. Second, it is to propose that this assumption is especially misplaced when it comes to representations of Cynic critical practice that posit moral virtue in an ethics of extremity. Shakespeare, I argue, understands that bringing the instructional expectations of realism to bear on the figure of the Cynic provokes his contemporaries' antithetical assessments of diogenical truth-telling, causing some to mistake the ideal for the real and others to insist on maintaining their distinction. In his Cynic characterisations of Lear's Fool (a parasite-jester), Hamlet (a melancholic) and Timon (a misanthrope), Shakespeare forces his viewers and readers to confront the literary mediation of Cynic character that produces such intense cathexis on the idea of its real-world revolutionary potential.

Cynicism and the Western Critical Tradition

In tandem with its close reading of Shakespeare's plays and the early modern diogeneana to which Shakespeare is responding, this book mounts a larger argument about our complex, centuries-long relationship to the character of the radical critic, an argument that is in effect an addendum to Michel Foucault's unfinished genealogy of Cynicism in the Western critical tradition. In his final two years of research and lectures at the Collège de France, Foucault moved away from a diagnostic interest in 'regimes of truth' – in which subjects participate in ratifying their own domination – and toward a heuristic interest in the kind of truth-telling practice that aims to challenge, even obliterate, such regimes.[19] Foucault advances this undertaking by looking to the past for his answers, aiming 'to construct a genealogy of the critical attitude in Western philosophy'.[20] This work leads him to conclude, in his 1984 lectures, not only that Cynicism is the practice he is looking for, but also that it figures as 'the matrix, the embryo anyway of a fundamental ethical experience in the West'.[21] In these lectures, Foucault develops a compelling account of why Cynicism's ethics of extremity emerges as a foundational (albeit under-acknowledged) ideal in our Western critical tradition.

But in addition to identifying the emergence of this central thread in our critical traditions, Foucault also endorses Cynic truth-telling as a viable model for changing the world, thereby inserting himself into the long arc of Cynicism's reception history that has been produced by a persistent misunderstanding of Cynic character and the practical lessons it can and cannot teach us. Attending to these lectures is thus a thorny and a necessary undertaking, thorny because Foucault's valuable genealogical insights get tangled up with his own participation in that genealogy, necessary because, properly untangled, Foucault's lectures are both a starting point for my own account of the Cynic ideal's centrality to our critical tradition and an example of the interpretive mistake the causes the persistence of this centrality. While I'll discuss Foucault's reading of Diogenes at length in the next chapter, it's worth sketching out his claims in miniature here, as they capture the stakes of confronting the Cynic ideal rather than succumbing to it.

In his 1984 lectures, the last he ever delivers, Foucault makes a powerful argument for seeing Diogenes' brand of Cynicism as the logical culmination of an impulse that is common to post-Socratic Greek philosophy and that in turn proves foundational to the critical attitude in the West – the impulse to derive one's authority as a speaker of truths from living in a manner that is true to one's words. Foucault helps us to see that a logic of maximisation is imminent to this ethical turn, for it follows that the more closely one can match word to deed, the more powerfully one can convey the truth behind both. In disclosing this logic, Foucault takes particular interest in the under-acknowledged ethical virtue a person must demonstrate in order to achieve maximum communicative power, a virtue he calls 'the courage of truth'. It takes courage to fashion one's life in conformity with one's principles, but it takes courage of truth to do so absolutely. This is the difference between Socrates' moderate approach to the project of *eudaemonia*, the pursuit of the good or happy life, and Diogenes' extreme embodiment of its values. Whereas Socrates embraces the principles of self-sufficiency and authenticity by living in a modest house and wearing simple clothing, Diogenes applies these values to his daily life with unremitting rigour, sleeping not in a house but in an abandoned cistern, or tub, and under the awnings of public buildings, wearing only a blanket (or, on hot days, nothing at all), and even going so far as to seek out hardships, for example by rolling his tubular home over hot sand in the summer.[22] Foucault understands Diogenes to be the first (and only) post-Socratic philosopher to demonstrate complete courage of truth, matching *logos* to *ethos* so perfectly that he fully realises the Hellenistic ideal of 'the true life', a life that, for Foucault, is imbued with the power to change the world:

> the Cynic is someone who, taking up the traditional themes of the true life in ancient philosophy, transposes them and turns them round into the demand and assertion of the need for an *other* life. And then, through the image and figure of the king of poverty, he transposes anew the idea of *an other* life into the theme of a life whose otherness must lead to the change in the world. An *other* life for an *other* world.[23]

Foucault understands Diogenes to show his peers that their own social values, when lived truly, entail a life and a world that is scandalously other, and for this reason he concludes that Cynicism was 'the banality of philosophy, but it was a scandalous banality'.[24] Cynicism is banal because it pursues the same core ethical values as every other Hellenic school of philosophy: self-sufficiency and authenticity (which is to say, the matching of word to deed, principle to practice). Yet Cynicism is also uniquely scandalous because it assigns virtue to an extreme state rather than a mean one, thereby exposing the fraudulence of other people's watered down claims to authenticity.

Foucault takes Cynicism to name an ethical experience that belongs to the role of the social critic, the experience of seeking, or, at the very least, of desiring, a means of delivering one's critique so effectively and so absolutely that it brings about its own obsolescence. This impulse is felt most acutely by the critic who bridles against the rhetorical limits of argument and debate, who strives to improve the collective good by convincing society of a truth that most have failed to discern and would prefer not to accept. Foucault identifies Cynicism as the means for overcoming these limits; it names for him the critical practice imagined to bring about a socially transformative event, one that leaves everyone in its wake shaped by the sheer obviousness of the truth the critic sought to impart. Alain Badiou theorises the Pauline event as a purely subjective experience: at some point on his solitary walk to Damascus, Saul becomes Paul – the event of his conversion is interior and self-derived.[25] By contrast, Foucault suggests that the critical attitude in the West conceives the event as something one person can compel upon another, much in the way Jesus's rigorously self-sacrificing way of life directly effects the convictions of his disciples, or the way early Christians similarly undertook a life of asceticism and corporal humility in order to impel Christ's truth upon others. To shift from a secular to a religious register with these examples is entirely fitting, as early Christian proselytisers explicitly modelled their asceticism, principled outspokenness, and mendicant itinerancy upon the established protocols of Cynics in the first and second centuries CE.[26]

Presented as a developmental genealogy, Foucault's theorisation of Cynic *parrhêsia* necessarily imbues it with an air of climactic finality; it is, after all, the catalyst for a world-changing revolutionary event. And yet, Foucault does not see Diogenes' ethical achievement as the end of a history so much as the beginning of one. The realities of delivering a circumscribed series of lectures on what is essentially a work-in-progress leave Foucault with little space to explore and outline this history, but he manages to devote his seventh and final lecture to a consideration of early Christianity's appropriation of *parrhêsia* and the true life as an ethical basis for spreading the good word. He also offers tantalisingly brief remarks on the modern, secular perpetuation of the Cynic critical stance, which he locates in the ethical militantism of certain nineteenth-century political revolutionaries and (somewhat disjunctively) in the *ethos* of modernist art. Finally, Foucault implicitly places himself at the tail end of this history. In a January 1984 interview – given just a week prior to starting his final course at the Collège de France – Foucault explains his recent shift in direction from a longstanding interest in exposing the complicity between Enlightenment rationality and forms of domination to a newfound interest in identifying 'the ethics, the *ethos*, the practice of self, which would allow . . . games of power to be played with a minimum of domination'.[27] Foucault is looking for a practical means of unleashing the emancipatory power of the avant-garde philosopher and social critic, a means of fulfilling the project of Enlightenment that, according to his earlier scholarship, has come to be thoroughly subverted by the knowledge–power nexus and the operations of instrumentalised reason. Yet at the time of this interview, Foucault has not yet fixed his attention on Cynicism as the means for achieving this end, and so the moderation figured in the fight for a minimum of domination does not reflect the role he envisions for himself and other avant-garde philosophers some three months later.

   It is my sense that Foucault comes to care about the prospect of Cynic *parrhêsia*'s finality, the prospect of a critical agency robust enough to effect the radical transformation of others and, through them, the political world they populate. However, in moving the goalposts from Socratic to Cynic *parrhêsia*, Foucault also finds himself telling a history of *parrhêsia*'s (enduring) Cynic moment that poses a serious problem for his own critical ambitions. If the Cynic style of life, in its unstintingly courageous relation to truth, is constitutive of the true life, and if the true life is 'an *other* life' that brings about 'an *other* world', then why is Athens not remade in Diogenes' image? The very fact that we can tell a history of *parrhêsia* in which people have turned time after time to Cynic militancy suggests that this mode of veri-diction isn't as radically transformative as Foucault seems inclined to think. It also suggests that there is something about Cynic character that, time after time, invites such an inclination, and this insight can lead us to a more fruitful way of thinking about the history of Cynic *parrhêsia* and the will to revolution in our Western critical tradition. If my diagnosis of this failure seems deflationary, it is only because I share with Foucault and others an optimism about the pos-sibility of radical change; I simply find suspect the lodging of a revolutionary *ethos* in a single figure, and hence the conclusion that sweeping change might be achieved through the exercise of one individual's critical agency.

In *Shakespeare and the Truth-Teller*, I take interest in the figure of Diogenes not because Cynic critical activity produces the revolutionary effects Foucault would have us believe – it doesn't – but because huge swathes of our intellectual history have been shaped by a succession of people who, whack-a-mole-like, nevertheless entertain the hope that it does. In the sixteenth century, Thomas Wilson invokes Diogenes when defining *parrhêsia* in *The Arte of Rhetorique*: 'Diogenes herein did excel, and feared no man when he saw just cause to say his mynde. This worlde wanteth suche as he was.'[28] (In the prologue to this book's 1560 edition, the firmly Prot-estant Wilson describes his own deployment of diogenical *parrhêsia* when arrested for heresy in Rome and unapologet-ically defending his faith before a tribunal of Catholic judges: 'I tooke such courage, and was so bolde, that the Iudges then did maruaile at my stoutnesse.'[29]) Some two centuries later,

Jean le Rond D'Alembert echoes Wilson – 'Every age, and especially our own, stands in need of a Diogenes'[30] – and he does so for remarkably similar reasons; D'Alembert exhorts Europe's men-of-letters to accelerate the spread of enlightenment by emulating Diogenes, whose robust critical *ethos* seems to promise a means of escaping the rhetorical constraints of polite conversation, the dominant (and inherently conservative) mode of discourse in eighteenth-century salon culture. As Louisa Shea aptly notes, this exhortation prompts a competition to become the next Diogenes that includes Denis Diderot, Jean-Jacques Rousseau and Voltaire, among many others, and Cynicism consequently plays a foundational role in the articulation of Enlightenment ideals.[31] In the nineteenth century, Friedrich Nietzsche directly alludes to Diogenes when defining the *Übermensch*, the superman who announces the death of God, and, in the twentieth century, Peter Sloterdijk looks to classical Cynicism for modern cynicism's cure just months prior to Foucault's Cynic turn.[32]

I offer here a curated sampling of thinkers who see something worth emulating in Diogenes, and I do so in order to paint a preliminary picture of Cynicism's recurrent valorisation from the sixteenth century to the present. This picture is important, but it represents only half of the whole story. Our relationship to Cynic character has driven much of our intellectual history over the past five-or-so centuries, and it has done so not only because of Cynicism's valorisation but also because of its debasement. As I mentioned earlier, Shakespeare's contemporaries struggled with their assessments of Diogenes, and the unique problem Cynic character poses for them remains a persistent feature of Cynicism's reception history. Shea has helped us to see that, in the eighteenth century, men competing to become a Diogenes for the new age had to confront the ease with which adopting a rigidly Cynic stance could backfire and be interpreted as evidence of their pridefulness or misanthropy. At times, this practical reality led would-be Cynics to moderate their posture, essentially conflating Cynicism with a conventionally Socratic ideal, but at other times it led these same men to police against such concessions. Accusations would thus be levelled that one or another aspirant was in fact a 'false Cynic' merely posing as a principled provocateur while conforming his discourse to the conservative interests of his noble and wealthy patrons. Here we have an early articulation of counter-Enlightenment critique as it springs from the identification of the modern (lowercase) cynic, the self-serving rationaliser who willingly acts as a functionary of prevailing ideology, participating not in reason's radical advancement but rather in its covert instrumentalisation.

Thanks to a renewed scholarly interest in Cynicism and its legacy, we are just now discovering that these competing responses to the figure of Diogenes together play an important role in the unfolding of Western intellectual history writ large, especially as it concerns the countervailing movements of the Enlightenment and counter-Enlightenment, along with post-Enlightenment efforts to break free of our modern cynical malaise by returning (à la Foucault and Sloterdijk) to the radical promise of classical Cynicism.[33] Mazella, Shea and Heinrich Niehues-Pröbsting have all added ground to this field of inquiry, and, for each of them, Cynicism's guiding influence upon the trajectory of Western thought begins in the mid-eighteenth century and extends into the present.[34] In this book, I offer two correctives to the work that has come before me. First, I argue that debate over the practical value of Cynic truth-telling starts to drive our modern cultural formation in the sixteenth century, not the eighteenth century. Second, I draw out the literary dimension of these ostensibly practical debates, thereby adding another explanatory layer to our centuries-long struggle with the Cynic ideal – a layer, it should be said, that makes the tools of literary criticism necessary to the work of historical and philosophical analysis rather than vice versa.

Shakespeare is not a prophet or a seer. He does not fore-
tell that Cynicism's countervailing assessments will act as a
two-piston engine driving future developments in Western
intellectual history. I claim of Shakespeare only that he is an
especially keen observer of Diogenes' mixed reception in his
own historical moment and that his writerly engagement with
Cynic character mounts an intervention vis-à-vis this vexed
reception. Nevertheless, in this book I consistently concern
myself with Cynicism's later reception history, and I do so to
establish the ongoing relevance of Shakespeare's intervention.
To take just one urgent example: in the twenty-first-century
context of climate change – a context in which our world is
in quite literal need of cleansing and in which the diminishing
resources of oil, water and air all call upon our baser instinct
to compete rather than cooperate – critics and activists simply cannot afford to be lured by the unrealisable fantasy of
Cynic critical agency as a means of effecting radical change.
Living as we do at a time when we must truly fashion 'an
other world', and soon, the need for Shakespeare's diagnosis
is more urgent than ever before.

Chapter Summaries

This book is divided into two parts. In Chapters 1 and 2, I lay
out the theoretical foundations of my argument. In Chapters
3, 4 and 5, I perform close readings of Shakespeare's three
most prominent Cynics and I show how each, in turn, impli-
cates a different strand of our intellectual history. Readers
who consult this book primarily for its Shakespeare criticism should not feel obliged to delay their gratification. The
first two chapters clear the way for the more focused work
of analysing Shakespeare's engagement with the diogeneana
of his day, but for those willing to accept my preliminary
claims, the preview of Part I offered in this introduction provides sufficient context for skipping ahead.

In Chapter 1, 'Cynicism and the Courage of Truth', I take a closer look at Foucault's final lectures in order to substantiate my reading of his Cynic turn – a turn in which he comes to view Cynicism's extreme approach to the courage of truth as the logical means of becoming a radically effective truthteller. I then offer a revised account of Diogenes' mixed reception history that better registers the struggle being played out between the alluring logic of ethical extremity that underwrites our critical tradition, on the one hand, and the time-tested imperative to find virtue in moderation, on the other. That being said, I devote the lion's share of this chapter to the preliminary work of laying out my reading of Foucault's lectures, and I do so because my take-away from them is not particularly conventional. The very nature of these lectures, in which Foucault tests out ideas with an exploratory spirit – pursuing some through-lines, abandoning others and adopting new key terms along the way – means that any effort to draw a unified account from them is open to considerable room for disagreement. With latitude to see things another way, current scholarly discussion of these lectures has rather understandably avoided the view that Foucault first identifies and then endorses a totally nonviable critical *ethos*. Nevertheless, it is important to understand that the general arc of Foucault's thinking in these lectures tends in the direction of precisely such an endorsement.

In Chapter 2, 'The Realist Turn: *Parrhêsia*, Character and the Limits of Didacticism', I explain why the crisis of character to which this book attends emerges in the sixteenth century and not sooner, and I do so by offering a new account of literary realism and its origins in early modern drama. I argue that the proliferation of non-allegorical characters in early modern drama results from a major innovation in the role and function of didacticism in literature. This is to suggest that literary realism first emerges as a way to instruct viewers and readers in the ethics of self-care by offering up to judgment the actions and outcomes of characters fashioned to be verisimilar to people. For as long as humans have been telling stories, literary character has served as a vehicle for prescriptive instruction, but it is only in the sixteenth century – with the advent of characters that are more-or-less constrained by the same ethico-political conditions of existence under which all people must necessarily operate – that literary character begins to serve as a vehicle for practical instruction.

Moving into the seventeenth century and beyond, literary realism becomes fictionality's dominant representational mode precisely because it serves as a virtual arena in which to exercise one's prudential judgments about the ethical means and political ends of action. My particular interest lies not in telling the history of literary realism's didactic success but rather in telling the concomitant history of its nagging failure. This latter history (or, at least, one key strand of it) coheres around diogenical depictions of the ideal philosopher or social critic that valorise an extreme rather than – following Aristotle – a medial approach to ethical self-care as the best and only means of becoming a radically effective teller of truths. Read through the lens of realist didacticism, this kind of characterisation leads sixteenth-century thinkers into trouble because the positive portrayal of ethical extremity is precisely where the most problematic and incommensurate conflation of ethical character and literary character takes place. There is an enormous amount to say on this point, but the essential observation is straightforward: a positive outcome in a narrative framework does not necessarily correspond to a positive outcome in a political framework, and this is especially true regarding an ethical ideal premised on extremism. The advent of realist didacticism as a normative hermeneutic was also the advent of abiding efforts to refract various ethico-political ideals through the edifying lens of narrative and figural representation. However, the figure of the Cynic truth-teller amplified the non-correspondence between the operations of literary character and the operations of ethical character, and as a result certain figurations of the truth-telling critic became objects of intense cathexis – they became the lodestones around which larger social, political and intellectual histories formed. I argue that the striking proliferation of diogeneana in the sixteenth century takes place precisely because early modern thinkers were beginning to apply the protocols of realist didacticism to their encounters with idealised representations of Cynic character.

The three chapters on Shakespeare's Cynics follow a particular order, one intended to reconstruct the experience of someone like Jaques, someone who aspires to critical sovereignty and who seeks alternative means of achieving this state when a previous strategy for its obtainment falls short of the mark. Shakespeare's Cynic characterisations of wise fools, Hamlet and Timon show him to be keenly aware of the fact that the critic's will to revolution is like pressurised magma seeking a path to the earth's surface: when one channel is closed off, another must be found. In this sense, his various treatments of the Cynic critical stance are designed to put his viewers and readers in Jaques's shoes, to produce a sequence of aspirational identification and eventual disillusionment, and to repeat that process with multiple iterations of the Cynic critical ideal.

In Chapter 3, 'Shakespeare's Bitter Fool: The Politics and Aesthetics of Free Speech', I argue that Shakespeare responds to the most straightforward fantasy of Cynic critical sovereignty – let us call it the direct approach, as reflected in the aspirations of Wilson, Diderot and Foucault – through his depiction of wise fools. In *Twelfth Night*, *Timon of Athens* and *King Lear*, Shakespeare's citation of diogeneana gives form to a series of wise fools designed to provoke a collision between his period's antithetical assessments of Cynic critical activity: one that reckons Diogenes' freedom of speech to be singularly effective, and one that lambasts Diogenes for being utterly inconsequential, a mere parasite-jester who has renounced all claims to seriousness. This double gesture is most evident in a passage unique to the Quarto *Lear* in which the Fool defines, and simultaneously performs, the critical activity of a 'bitter fool'. Here, especially, Shakespeare's composite characterisation of the Cynic stance challenges viewers to comprehend that the 'bitter fool' offers only the appearance of a robust critical practice – that its stridently critique-oriented posture exists in form but not in substance.

Chapter 4, 'Cynicism, Melancholy and Hamlet's *Memento Moriae*', follows Shakespeare as he responds to a version of the Cynic critical stance that takes root in what appears to be a posture of political disengagement; this is a version of the Cynic fantasy that can be entertained by the sort of person who has already discovered the impossibility of obtaining critical sovereignty via the direct approach and who, however counterintuitively, now seeks to satisfy the critical will to revolution without having to be an agent of change in that revolution. As I've already intimated at the outset of this introduction, Shakespeare's characterisation of Hamlet constitutes both an exploration of and a response to the lines of affiliation between the Cynic-inspired fantasy of unstoppable critical agency and his period's romanticised portrait of intellectual melancholy. Shakespeare repeatedly has Hamlet frame his opposition to Claudius in terms of Diogenes' opposition to Alexander, but he also has Hamlet reconceive the operations of Cynic critique when, in the graveyard scene, he imagines the process by which Alexander's decomposing body over time becomes the plug for a beer barrel. (It is no coincidence that Diogenes asserts his repudiation of society by living in a barrel, nor that Robert Burton invokes Diogenes' inhabitation of a barrel when he similarly adopts a posture of Cynic melancholy.) Looking upon the ossified remains of a wise fool, Hamlet attempts to breathe new life into the project of Cynic critique by resorting to intellectual sublimation. This is to suggest that, when Hamlet ruminates over Alexander's dust plugging a beer barrel, he is imagining a broader historical process by which the politics of kingship with which he is loath to take part will eventually be succeeded by an entirely new formation of the political.

Shakespeare calls upon his viewers to be sceptical of the posture Hamlet adopts, and this note of caution is signalled most clearly when Hamlet decides to approach the gravedigger and speak with him, thereby producing a tableau in which Hamlet plays the part not of Diogenes but of Alexander. For all that Hamlet commits to an extreme ethics of melancholy rumination, thereby imagining himself to commune with the will of the cosmos, the truth is that his *ethos* of sublimated intellection is enabled by the conditions of his princely privilege, by the labour of a busy multitude about whom he does not think. When Hamlet reflects on the possibility that matter from Alexander's body will eventually become the stopper of a beer barrel, he does so in order to imagine the inevitability of a world in which the forms of power and domination that both Alexander and Claudius represent will eventually be replaced by something else altogether. However, his indulgence in this speculative philosophy noticeably overlooks a key point of continuity between his own moment and this imagined future: the underlying presence of money, labour and commerce, for he invokes a future in which people still have to make and serve beer for a pittance of a living. Hamlet takes comfort in being a conceiver of historical process, but in imagining the large-scale transformations that will enact his revenge for him, he remains blind to the more intractable and depersonalised forms of domination that subsidise his life of the mind.

The irony of Shakespeare's intervention against Hamlet's intellectually sublimated agency is that it completely backfires. As I go on to show, the posture of Cynic melancholy becomes integral to an influential branch of modern philosophy – the philosophy of history – that emerges out of the intellectual hotbed of German Romanticism, a movement that was itself shaped by its participants' intense identification with Shakespeare in general, and with Hamlet in particular. After linking both Hegel's and Marx's philosophies of history to the legacy of Cynic melancholy, I show how Shakespeare's ultimate interest in problematising this stance allows us to turn the tables on Hamlet's modern philosophical reception: instead of using modern philosophy as a lens for better understanding an early modern Hamlet, I use an early modern Hamlet as a lens for better understanding the conditions and limits of modern philosophy.

Shakespeare takes us behind the curtain of Hamlet's Cynic melancholy by disclosing his unthinking reliance on princely privilege, a reliance that recasts him as being more akin to Alexander than to Diogenes. In doing so, Shakespeare points out that Hamlet, like Alexander, cannot see past a world in which power and influence depends on the accumulation and distribution of wealth, a world in which cash, and not the person who temporarily possesses it, is king.

In Chapter 5, 'Cash is King: Timon, Diogenes and the Search for Sovereign Freedom', I argue that Shakespeare aligns Timon first with the figure of Alexander, then with the figure of Diogenes, in order to formulate a diagnostic response to two related fantasies of sovereign freedom, both of which imagine the possibility of operating entirely outside money's influence. Karl Marx famously cites *Timon* when claiming that Shakespeare understands the true nature of money to be the 'alienated ability of mankind', yet it would be more precise to say that Shakespeare – who lived during an earlier chapter of capitalism's history – understands the true nature of money to be the alienated ability of the sovereign.[35] In both his philanthropic and misanthropic modes, Timon attempts to set himself above (or outside) the requirements of an otherwise moneyed world, and while it is true that both attempts meet with failure, these failures serve to diagnose two distinct fantasies of sovereign freedom that emerge in symptomatic response to a moneyed world. Drawing on a philological analysis of the word 'frank' – in which I place considerable pressure on John II's 1360 ordinance authorising the first minting of the French franc – I argue that Timon at first understands sovereign frankness to make itself manifest as a personal state of exception, one that entitles a true sovereign (like Alexander the Great, or England's James I) to inaugurate other states of exception at no cost to himself. Just as a king can enfranchise this or that serf as a Franklin, or elevate this or that soldier to a newly created position among the landed gentry, so too (it is imagined) can he speak monetary value into being. When Timon comes to understand that his attempt to instantiate boundless generativity has only ever amounted to a condition of endlessly accelerating expense, he leaves Athens in favour of a self-exiled life in the forest; there, he pursues a particularly extreme regimen of Cynic asceticism in order to recover his self-sovereign ability to speak the truth of money's alienating effects, the ability to annihilate, not inaugurate, money's value. Ultimately, I argue that Shakespeare reveals the irony of Timon's two fantasies of sovereign freedom – fantasies I show to operate across some seven hundred years of our intellectual history: at the end of the day, no one can single-handedly reshape a world in which money talks.

Notes

1. Shakespeare, *As You Like It* in *The Norton Shakespeare*, II, vii, 47–9. Further citations will be to this edition and in-text.
2. In this study, I follow the convention of using the uppercase and the lowercase as a means of distinguishing ancient Cynicism from modern cynicism.

3. Laertius, *Lives of Eminent Philosophers*.

4. Ibid., 6.46, 49.

5. Ibid., 6.38, 69.

6. Ibid., 6.22.

7. For a useful primer on Crates, see Dudley, *A History of Cynicism*, esp. pp. 42–53; as well as Navia, *Classical Cynicism*, esp. pp. 119–44.

8. Mazella, *The Making of Modern Cynicism*, esp. pp. 48–50.

9. See Mazella, *The Making of Modern Cynicism*, p. 49. See also Lievsay, 'Some Renaissance Views of Diogenes the Cynic'.

10. Erasmus, *Apophthegmes*, M5ʳ–M5ᵛ. For another influential version of this story, see Plutarch, *The lives of the noble Grecians and Romanes*, p. 728.

11. Lyly, *Campaspe*, 5.4.95. Though shortened to the now-standard *Campaspe* in subsequent editions, the play was first printed under the title *A moste excellent comedie of Alexander, Campaspe, and Diogenes*.

12. Building off Lievsay's earlier work, Mazella distinguishes between the High View of Diogenes as a potent counsellor and the Low View of him as a melancholic and a misanthrope. However, neither Lievsay nor Mazella discuss Diogenes' reception as a parasite-jester. See Mazella, *The Making of Modern Cynicism*, pp. 47–80. On the connection between Diogenes and the tradition of 'licensed' fools, see Kinney, 'Heirs of the Dog', pp. 294–328.

13. For influential versions of this anecdote, see Chrysostom, *Discourses 1-11*, Discourse 8.36; and Julian, *Orations*, 6.202b.

14. Laertius, *Lives of Eminent Philosophers*, 6.41; and Erasmus, *Apophthegmes*, N3ʳ.

15. See Rowlands, *Diogenes Lanthorne*.

16. Burton, *The Anatomy of Melancholy*, p. 4.

17. For an account of *parrhêsia* being invoked in the context of communicating religious conviction, see Colclough, *Freedom of Speech in Early Stuart England*, esp. pp. 47–8.

18. Lucian features Diogenes prominently in nine of his dialogues (a number of appearances exceeded only by his very favourite avatar, Menippus), while four of Dio Chrysostom's eleven

discourses depict Diogenes in conversation with various inter-locutors. For additional examples of early modern texts that generate new literary and para-literary depictions of Diogenes, see Lodge, *Catharos*; Stafford, *Staffords Heavenly Dogge*; and Goddard, *A Satirycall Dialogue or a sharplye-invective conference*.

19. For Foucault's most sustained consideration of regimes of truth, see *On the Government of the Living*.

20. Foucault, *Fearless Speech*, pp. 170–1.

21. Foucault, *Courage of Truth*, p. 287.

22. See Laertius, *Lives of Eminent Philosophers*, 6.22–3.

23. Foucault, *Courage of Truth*, p. 287.

24. Ibid., p. 232.

25. Badiou, *Saint Paul*.

26. Downing, *Christ and the Cynics* and *Cynics, Paul, and the Pauline Churches*.

27. Foucault's articulation of this claim, couched as it is in rela-tive terms, appears just prior to his turn toward Cynicism. See Foucault, 'The Ethics of Care for the Self as a Practice of Freedom', p. 18.

28. Wilson, *Arte of Rhetorique*, sig. Ddii^v. Quoted in Colclough, *Freedom of Speech in Early Stuart England*, p. 47. In his study of the various ways the classical mean–extremes polar-ity gets taken up in the early modern period, Joshua Scodel persuasively shows that early modern thinkers accept the con-ventional view that mean-states are virtuous while applying this moral schema to categories unanticipated by Aristotle in ways that flexibly present what otherwise might have been an extreme state as instead being a virtuous mean. However, when it comes to the courage of truth, at least some thinkers in the early modern period appear to break from the principle of virtuous moderation and instead wholly accept the possi-bility of a truly virtuous extreme. See Scodel, *Excess and the Mean in Early Modern English*.

29. Wilson, *Arte of Rhetorique*, sig. Av. Quoted in Colclough, *Freedom of Speech in Early Stuart England*, p. 48.

30. D'Alembert, 'An Essay upon the Alliance betwixt Learned Men, and the Great', pp. 153–4.

31. See Shea, *The Cynic Enlightenment*.
32. See Nietzsche, *The Gay Science*, §125; and Sloterdijk, *Critique of Cynical Reason*.
33. I am indebted to Shea's insight that Foucault's embrace of classical Cynicism marks a closing of a circle and thus a return to Enlightenment ideals. By contrast, Mazella's genealogy of Cynicism supposes that modernity is defined solely by its descent into modern cynicism.
34. See Niehues-Pröbsting, 'The Modern Reception of Cynicism, pp. 329–65.
35. Marx, *Economic and Philosophic Manuscripts of 1844*, p. 168.

PART I

OUR CYNIC LEGACY

CHAPTER 1

CYNICISM AND THE COURAGE OF TRUTH

Foucault's realisation that 'Cynicism is the matrix, the embryo anyway of a fundamental ethical experience in the West' is premised on the remarkable insight that our Western critical tradition is catalysed by an impulse to promulgate truth, an impulse so absolute in its communicative ambition that achieving its perfect fulfilment seems logically to call for an ethics of virtuous extremism.[1] The sheer strangeness of finding virtue in ethical extremity becomes apparent when compared to Aristotle's account of virtue ethics, in which each moral virtue names a mean-state between extremes of excess and deficiency. Take, for instance, the virtue of courage, to which Aristotle turns as his first and readiest example in the *Nichomachean Ethics*. In the context of soldiering and war, a person who sacrifices his or her life to little purpose – say, by individually charging an opposing army as a show of fierceness – is rash. By contrast, the person who cannot master his or her fear of death and who consistently avoids hazard is cowardly. Set against these two poles, only the person who undertakes self-sacrifice for the instrumental purpose of delivering the greatest advantage to mother country demonstrates courage. For Aristotle, moral virtues achieve external goals in an optimal way. In other words, they are 'calculated to act upon the circumstances out of which they are formed', and it is important to understand that the calculation Aristotle sees leading to an ideal outcome in any given situation involves charting just the right path between deficiency and excess.[2]

From classical to modern times, we have accepted Aristotle's view that effective action is indexed to moderation and that moderation is in turn indexed to circumstance. Simply put, experience continually shows us that no matter the virtue we have in mind, and no matter the variation in what constitutes moderate action in a given case, it is always possible to be overzealous and thus to undermine one's virtuous objectives. As we will see, the courage of truth is just as bound by this practical constraint. And yet, as we will also see, Foucault's genealogical investigation into the problem of the truth-teller – the problem of 'determin[ing] who has the specific qualities which enable him to speak the truth (and thus should possess the right to tell the truth)' – leads him both to rediscover and to reproduce the Cynic conclusion that the virtue calculated to resolve this dilemma must by necessity be an exception to the rule.[3] When it comes to authorising oneself as a truth-teller, the thinking goes, an extreme and unending practice of conforming word to deed, or *logos* to *bios*, leads to the virtuous communication of truth in every instance, circumstances be damned.

I argue in this chapter that interpretations of Diogenes have played a formative role in our critical tradition precisely because thinkers across the ages have had to contend with the Cynic ideal. This is to suggest that a large swathe of our intellectual history, spanning from classical antiquity through to the present day, springs from an ongoing struggle to reconcile the two competing ethical logics – one finding virtue in extremity, the other in moderation – that become attached to the project of communicating difficult truths. In his endorsement of Cynic truth-telling's revolutionary potential, Foucault takes his place at the tail end of this intellectual history, meaning that he is subject to the diagnostic critique I'll be advancing in Chapter 2. However, the genealogy of thought he constructs in order to arrive at this endorsement goes a long way toward explaining his own susceptibility to the ethical extremism figured in Cynic truth-telling. Foucault offers a compelling account of how and why Cynicism in general, and the figure of Diogenes in particular, became linked to the idea of virtuously extreme truth-telling in the first place, and I dwell on this account because it forms the starting point for my own diagnosis of the underlying forces at play in our centuries-long struggle with the Cynic ideal. The bulk of this chapter is therefore devoted to drawing out Foucault's conclusion that the formation of the Western critical tradition is tied to the emergence of a virtue – the courage of truth – that is understood to be fully instantiated only through an ethics of extremity.

I rehearse Foucault's ideas at such length out of necessity, for the conclusions I see him reaching in his final two years at the Collège de France are not ones that other scholars have sought to highlight. Admittedly, Foucault treats his lectures as an opportunity to try out new lines of inquiry, and so his thinking on various topics can at times shift in ways that challenge our efforts to impose continuity on them. Yet this alone cannot explain why so many of the scholars who write about Foucault's final lectures make no mention whatsoever of his engagement with Cynicism, to which he turns in favour of Platonism as the ideal model of revolutionary truth-telling for the entire second half of his 1984 course.[4] The sheer persistence of this omission is telling. It suggests that many scholars simply cannot bring themselves to see Diogenes – who takes the courage of truth to a scandalous extreme – as Foucault's privileged example of effective truth-telling. Instead of attending to Foucault's conclusion that Attic ideas about the courage of truth follow a developmental arc that culminates in Cynic absolutism, they focus their accounts of Foucault's analysis on his more moderate (and preliminary) examples of Socrates and Plato.

Even among those scholars who do acknowledge Foucault's Cynic turn, there is a similar reticence to see that he attributes radical, world-changing powers of critical speech to the person who adopts a sufficiently extreme self-disciplining regime vis-à-vis the courage of truth. These critics avoid this aspect of the lectures in one of two ways, either by insisting that Foucault understands Cynic truth-telling to be a product of its own moment and in no way applicable to the present day, or by granting Foucault's presentist regard for Cynic exemplarity only to suppose that he makes more qualified claims about the effects that this revolutionary truth-telling has on those who are exposed to it.[5] Given that, as a matter of historical fact, no radical transformation of the social or political order follows in the wake of Diogenes or any other Cynic philosopher, these two efforts to impose a pragmatic bent on Foucault's final lectures are perfectly understandable. But if Foucault's commentators find it hard to credit that he might actually believe that Cynic truth-telling leads to such an impracticable outcome, it is in large part because they do not know about the long line of aspiring social critics who have shared in this belief. Foucault stands out, in this history of misreading the figure of the truth-telling Cynic, because the genealogy he undertakes to arrive at this misplaced belief goes a long way toward explaining why he and others have been so susceptible to it.

Parrhêsia, *True Discourse and the Logic of Virtuous Extremism*

In a series of six lectures delivered at Berkeley in the autumn of 1983 – at the midpoint, so to speak, of his two-year engagement with the problem of the truth-teller at the Collège de France – Foucault takes a moment to indulge in metacommentary, reflecting on the principle that allows him to approach this new genealogy of thought as a search for origins. We can locate the beginnings of certain cultural formations, he suggests, by identifying historical moments shaped by conceptual crisis:

> The history of thought is the analysis of the way an unproblematic field of experience or a set of practices, which were accepted without question, which were familiar and 'silent', out of discussion, becomes a problem, raises discussion and debate, incites new reactions, and induces a crisis in previously silent behavior, habits, practices, and institutions.[6]

In these Berkeley lectures, Foucault offers a more refined and compact account of his previous semester's project of locating the emergence of a certain kind of philosophical practice, one concerned not only with the love of knowledge and the advancement of philosophy qua philosophy but also, and more particularly, with the civic service that can be rendered to political decision-makers through the intervention of a dedicated philosopher. This is a kind of philosophical practice in which '[p]hilosophy's question is not the question of politics' but rather 'the question of the subject in politics';[7] it is the kind of philosophical practice that aims to teach political actors how to govern themselves such that they in turn possess both the authority and the discernment necessary to govern others. In his opening remarks at the Collège de France in the spring of 1983, Foucault is upfront about his intended object of study:

> What I would like to do this year is retrace some paths already followed, taking up again a few points, such as, for example, what I said to you last year about *parrēsia*, true discourse in the political realm. It seemed to me that this study would make it possible to see, to tighten up a bit, the problem of the relations between the government of the self and the government of others, to see the genesis,

the genealogy, if not of political discourse in general, the object of which is essentially government by the Prince, at least of a certain form of political discourse whose object would be government of the Prince, of the Prince's soul by the counselor, the philosopher, the pedagogue responsible for forming his soul.[8]

For Foucault, this is the beginning of philosophy understood as a practice of truth-telling, and he ties this beginning most particularly to Socrates and Plato.

By the time he delivers his Berkeley lectures, Foucault has reached the conclusion that philosophy's 'Platonic moment' constitutes both the fulfilment of and resolution to a crisis that first emerged in a purely political context, one induced by the difficulty of knowing whose words should be heeded when the fate of the commonwealth is at stake. Ultimately, however, Foucault revises his conclusion that Plato and Socrates solve the problem of the truth-teller, instead finding that it takes Diogenes' more extreme devotion to principled living to demonstrate courage of truth, thereby unlocking the full emancipatory power of critical speech. This happens about halfway through his final course of lectures at the Collège de France, yet it is important to understand that this perhaps startling shift in focus is the product of a larger continuity in Foucault's thinking. Though he did not see its immoderate implications right away, the genealogy of *parrhêsia* Foucault began to trace in the previous year already carried within it the logic of ethical extremity that leads to his Cynic turn. We must therefore begin with a consideration of his 1982–3 lectures at the Collège de France.

As Foucault intimates in his opening lecture of the series, the genealogy he wants to trace finds its origins in the problematisation of *parrhêsia*, a concept he initially glosses as 'true discourse in the political realm'. At first, Foucault locates *parrhêsia* in the discursive relation a counsellor holds

to a prince, but his early lectures lead him to the discovery
that *parrhêsia*'s problematisation – though eventually felt in
the context of every structure of government – first induces a
new sense of crisis in the context of Athenian democracy. It
is within the bounds of this experiment in political egalitari-
anism that people first felt the need to distinguish between
isēgoria, a citizen's constitutional right to speak up during
collective decision-making, and *parrhêsia*, a term used to
name the act not only of speaking freely (which any citizen
could do) but also of speaking truly. According to Foucault, a
purely democratic approach to political participation comes
to be felt as a problem when, near the end of the fifth century
BCE, Athenians start to worry that reaching collective deci-
sions by way of *isēgoria* can all too often mean that the influence of bad, immoral and ignorant speakers will overwhelm
the minority who advise the *demos* on the basis of experience
and reason.[9] Consequently, Athenians of the period become
increasingly aware of the need to differentiate between those
who speak either ignorantly or duplicitously and those who
engage in *parrhêsia*, or 'true discourse'. But how is one to
make this distinction? How is one to recognise a speaker of
true discourse from among the many who are not? This is the
problem of the truth-teller in a nutshell.

Foucault helps us to see that Athenians tried to answer
this problem by linking *parrhêsia* to virtue ethics and the
demonstration of good character. The power of this solution
lies in the fact that daily and indefinite training in virtues
like courage, temperance, generosity and friendliness accomplishes three things at once. First, it provides Athenians with
a way to prioritise a citizen's capacity for good judgment, for
a person who is able to follow the most virtuous course of
action in any given situation can do so only by possessing a
higher-than-average degree of *phronesis*, or practical wisdom.
Second, it ensures that the person identified as a truth-teller
will have a robust sense of civic duty, for the *eudaimonia* that

virtue ethics seeks to achieve is a form of happiness that is
not personal but collective; it names the condition of 'human
flourishing' the people can only achieve as a civic body.[10]
Third, tying *parrhêsia* to virtue ethics makes it possible to
render visible the qualitative distinctness of the truth-teller,
for becoming virtuous requires that one undertake a project
of training and self-discipline (*askēsis*) in one's daily life, a
project that is out in the open, so to speak, and thus percep-
tible to others. Taken together, these three attributes of virtue
ethics enable the parrhesiast to stand metaphorically above
other citizens when speaking before the *demos*:

> [E]ven if *parrēsia* functions within the egalitarian field
> of *isegoria*, it presupposes, it implies a form of political
> ascendency exercised by some over others. If Ion wanted
> to have *parrēsia*, it was not just so he could be a citizen like
> others; it was so he could figure in the *proton* (the front
> rank) of citizens.[11]

There is of course nothing surprising about political actors
striving for a position of dominance over others, but *parrhêsia* differs from all other 'form[s] of political ascendency' in
that the parrhesiast wields a power that does not serve the
purpose of advancing individual or factional interests. Rather,
in conformity with the *telos* of moral virtuousness, the parrhesiast engages in true discourse in order to advance the
good of the city-state as a whole. In the context of *parrhêsia*,
to claim a position in 'the front rank' of society is to cultivate
the kind of ethical character that authorises a person to speak
with a force approaching that of undeniability on the topic of
what actions will achieve the greatest collective good.

Though Foucault does not know it at the time, his account
of *parrhêsia* as it emerges in the context of political deliberation starts him on the path toward recognising truth-telling's
logic of ethical extremity, and it does so because he takes seriously the insight that political *parrhêsia* was meant to be a

mode of veridiction other than that of rhetoric, not an art of persuasion but rather a 'profession of truth'.[12] The difference lies in each mode's deployment of *ethos*. In the case of rhetoric, a speaker's persuasiveness is grounded in the character of the argument itself, or rather, as Eugene Garver explains, it is grounded in the reasoning that a given argument puts on display, for good practical reasoning is 'the discursive embodiment of good character'.[13] Rhetorical persuasiveness depends on a judgment that the speaker possesses good character, but it is a judgment made through the indirect means of considering not the speaker but the speech. By contrast, parrhesiastic persuasiveness is grounded in a more direct demonstration of the speaker's good character, a display of practical *ethos* to complement and augment the display of sound discursive *ethos*. According to Foucault, the concept of parrhesiastic truth-telling develops out of a growing concern over the danger rhetoric poses in the context of deliberative politics. While rhetoric can serve as the basis for a 'game of truth' – a game with agreed-upon rules for adjudicating conviction in what other people say – it is one in which a speaker can convince people of things that he does not personally believe to be true. Even worse, rhetoric enables a person to make an argument that is perfectly valid in terms of its robust discursive *ethos* while also being completely insincere. Picture, for example, a patrician in Athens addressing the *demos* on the need for everyone to sacrifice for the greater good while having no intention of doing so himself. Through their emphasis on discursive *ethos*, rhetorical games of truth allow speakers to lend the cover of credibility to precisely the kind of class-over-country false dealing that judgments about a speaker's good character are supposed to curtail.

It is in the context of rhetoric's ethical pervertibility that Foucault sees *parrhêsia* constituting itself as a revolutionary alternative. Because the parrhesiast commits to living in accordance with his stated principles, always matching word to deed, or *logos* to *bios*, he alone is able to engage in 'true discourse' – the only game of truth that Foucault paradoxically understands to be no game at all. Like rhetoric, *parrhêsia* requires that an argument touching the *polis* demonstrates good discursive character, meaning that its persuasiveness rests not only on its logical soundness, which is to say its *logos*, but also on the clear civic-mindedness of its *ethos*. But unlike rhetoric, *parrhêsia* holds its speaker to an additional standard: the speaker must also demonstrate a practical commitment in his own daily life to the argument's civically minded principles, he must fulfil an ongoing 'pact between himself and what he says'.[14] This is why rhetoric can function as a 'discourse of truth' without being 'true discourse', for while the rhetorician and the parrhesiast both profess to tell the truth, only the parrhesiast undertakes truth as a profession.

On the face of it, grounding a truth-teller's veridical authority in the cultivation of virtuous character seems like a perfect solution to the question of how to recognise true discourse when it occurs. Yet Foucault argues that placing evaluative emphasis on a person's practical *ethos* does not settle the matter of who speaks truly so much as set in motion a new coming-to-awareness of the problem at hand, one that reveals the need for philosophy to intervene in politics. Through readings of Plato's Socratic dialogues (along with some of his other writings), Foucault shows how Socrates and Plato both work to define *parrhêsia* as a mode of veridiction that can be wielded only by a dedicated philosopher. After all, it is not enough to practice one's principles if those principles are themselves morally flawed, and people who devote themselves to the realm of politics are likely to lack both the time and the training to parse difficult moral questions. This is the context in which Foucault understands Socrates and Plato to step forward and place *parrhêsia* under the aegis of philosophy:

Rather than being a power of persuasion which would convince souls of anything and everything, philosophy presents
itself as an operation which will enable souls to distinguish
properly between true and false, and which, through philosophical *paideia*, will provide the instruments needed to
carry out that distinction.[15]

This is not to suggest that the philosopher-parrhesiast per-
suades interlocutors by engaging in philosophy's analogue to
rhetorical discourse, using philosophical rigour to produce
arguments so exquisitely well-reasoned that their discursive
ethos alone carries the day. Philosophy as a techne for parsing true from false solves the problem of moral discernment,
but Socrates and Plato also aim to imbue their discourse with
a new degree of veridical force by practicing philosophy as
a way of life. If, in an act of philosophical *parrhêsia*, the
philosopher is understood by his interlocutor to be a person
who professes the truth, it is ultimately because he authenticates the rightness of his moral judgments by living whatever
truths he is able to determine:

> Being an agent of the truth, being a philosopher, and as a
> philosopher claiming for oneself the monopoly of *parrēsia*,
> will not just mean claiming that one can state the truth in
> teaching, in the advice one gives, and in the speeches one
> makes, but that one really is in fact, in one's life, an agent
> of the truth. *Parrēsia* as a form of life, *parrēsia* as a way of
> behaving, *parrēsia* even in the philosopher's style of dress,
> are constitutive elements of this monopoly that philosophi-
> cal *parrēsia* claims for itself.[16]

Foucault finds in *parrhêsia*'s Platonic moment an understanding of why a person would undertake philosophy as a way of
life that is entirely absent from Pierre Hadot's earlier account
of that practice.[17] Hadot, who coined the term 'philosophy
as a way of life' in 1981, understands it to be a practice

aimed at achieving personal happiness and peace of mind, the state of *ataraxia*, or freedom from emotional disturbance and anxiety, to which Stoicism, Epicureanism and Pyrrhonean Scepticism all strive. By contrast, Foucault shows Plato to consistently imbue the philosophical life with an outward-facing agenda. For Plato, the final purpose of undertaking the project of ethical self-care is to authorise the philosopher as a speaker of ethico-philosophical truths, as the deliverer of a 'true discourse' in which the truth of one's words is made manifest through the degree to which one lives up to them.

Foucault understands this mode of veridiction to be on display throughout Plato's Socratic dialogues – many of which end with the discussants convinced that they must join Socrates in further discussion and self-testing, further practice in government of the self so that they may in time be good at governing others – but he finds his most compelling evidence of Plato's parrhesiastic agenda in the *Laches*, wherein Plato most clearly articulates the cause of Socrates' success as a truth-teller.[18] The key moment occurs when, in what might seem like mere preamble, Laches explains why he will agree to have his thinking examined by Socrates, a man he has never before encountered. Laches is an Athenian general, and he has been asked by a friend to determine what kind of tutor might best instruct that friend's son in those virtues that mark a man out as an evident leader of other men. The main body of the dialogue centres on the task of defining courage, the virtue deemed most essential to the manifestation of leadership, and, at the outset, Laches agrees to be examined and guided by Socrates because Socrates has already proven himself to be courageous. Laches, it should be noted, mentions that he has heard Socrates fought well as a soldier in the battle of Delium, but Foucault insists that this is not the act that proves Socrates to be courageous in Laches' eyes. Instead, Foucault asks us to consider the set of criteria Laches presents as a basis for judging Socrates' worth in the moment of their actual encounter, and not on the basis of report:

> Whenever I hear a man discussing virtue or some kind of wisdom, then, if he really is a man and worthy of the words he utters, I am completely delighted to see the appropriateness and harmony existing between the speaker and his words. And such a man seems to me to be genuinely musical, producing the most beautiful harmony, not on the lyre or some other pleasurable instrument, but actually rendering his own life harmonious by fitting his deeds to his words.[19]

The kind of courage that Socrates demonstrates right before Laches' eyes is not soldierly courage but rather the courage to harmonise word and deed 'in the reality of his life'. For Foucault, the precise nature of the harmony Laches witnesses is crucially important, because it goes beyond his noticing a correspondence between Socrates' known opinions on virtuous living and his appearance of living up to them.[20] More importantly, Laches sees in Socrates a man who takes his philosophical discussions seriously, using each one as an occasion to question anew the nature of virtue and to apply his conclusions to his own life in an ongoing and affirmative practice of self-care. According to Foucault, Laches sees rare courage in the sheer indefiniteness of this undertaking; Socrates does not present himself to Laches as someone who has already harmonised word and deed but rather as a someone who remains ever dedicated to further self-testing and self-improvement. Here we have Plato's most overt bid to advance a new mode of philosophical practice defined by its monopoly over *parrhêsia*, a practice in which philosophers become truth-tellers by instantiating a new kind of virtue: the courage of truth. As Foucault puts it, 'The truth of courage and the courage of speaking the truth were bound up with each other and connected in the *Laches*.'[21]

Foucault performs his reading of the *Laches* in the winter of 1984, halfway through his final course of lectures at the Collège de France, and his analysis of this dialogue concludes his rather lengthy (and at times revisionist) rehearsal of the material he had covered the previous year. In his 1983 lectures, Foucault does not yet define the courage of truth as a particular kind of moral virtue, despite having already concluded that the veridical force of truth-telling is grounded in the parrhesiast's demonstrable alignment of word and deed. Initially, he conceives the role of courageousness in terms of the inherent riskiness of engaging in true discourse and the attendant bravery of accepting possible or even likely rejection and danger to self. This changes one year later when Foucault, having spent the first half of the semester retracing (and refining) his account of *parrhêsia*'s developmental trajectory from politics to Platonic philosophy, arrives at his reading of the *Laches*. Now, he concludes that the courage of truth does not pertain to truth-telling's embrace of hazard but rather names the moral virtue that allows true discourse to bypass the risk of rejection and reprisal.

What Foucault discovers in his reading of the *Laches* is the articulation of a moral virtue that purports to solve the problem of the truth-teller by breaking from the normative framework governing virtue ethics as a whole. Whereas a virtue like courage requires a person to act moderately, exercising practical wisdom to avoid being either cowardly or foolhardy in the context of a given situation, the courage of truth entails its practitioner's commitment to achieving a one-to-one correspondence between word and deed, *logos* and *bios* – a commitment from which an ethics of extremism logically follows. The more faithfully a person puts principles into practice, the greater the veridical force conferred upon that person's true discourse. This is the structuring logic Foucault imputes to the courage of truth as Plato deploys

it, and it is the reason he ultimately looks beyond Plato and
Socrates – both of whom draw a line on how far they will
follow a tenet like the importance of living simply – for an
example of a philosopher who embodies the courage of truth
in a more radically authenticating way.

Truth-Telling and the Cynic Ideal

Shortly after his reading of *Laches*, Foucault announces for
the first time that he wants to turn his attention to the relationship between philosophical *parrhêsia* and Cynicism, caution-
ing that he does so 'without knowing how far [he] will take
it, if it will last until the end of the year, or if [he] will stop'.[22]
But while initially tentative about the direction in which this
new line of inquiry will take him, Foucault concludes soon
afterward that Cynicism constitutes the zenith of *parrhêsia*'s
developmental arc, and the remaining lectures stay focused
on Diogenes and his disciples as a result. Why does this
happen? In large part, we can explain the decisive shift in
Foucault's thinking by noticing his introduction of a new
term – 'the true life' – when offering up a revisionist account
of the work he's done up to this point: 'What I wanted to try
to recover was something of the relation between the art of
existence and true discourse, between the beautiful existence
and the true life, life in the truth, life for the truth.'[23] In part,
associating philosophical *parrhêsia*'s argumentative force
with 'the true life' rather than 'true discourse' is simply a way
for Foucault to better register this veridictive mode's reliance
on personal *ethos* above and beyond discursive *ethos*. Yet in
reframing his genealogy of *parrhêsia* as an attempt to trace
'[t]he emergence of the true life in the principle and form of
truth-telling', Foucault also seeks to combine a new account
of *parrhêsia*'s philosophical antecedents with his established
sketch of its political origins – a new account that links the

rise of the truth-telling philosopher (and of the Cynic critical ideal) to the ethical project of Eudaimonism that underwrites Hellenic philosophy as a whole.

Noting that every school of ancient Greek philosophy sought to answer the question of how to how to live a good and happy life (*eudaimon*), Foucault takes interest in the fact that a conception of something like true discourse has a history of operating in the philosophical (rather than political) realm, where it is provoked into being by the problem of knowing whose philosophy of happiness actually to heed. In this context, 'the true life' functions as an ethical ideal within every school of philosophy, not just those of Socrates and Plato, and in each case its purpose is both veridictive and decidedly philosophico-centric: the philosopher proves to others the validity (and hence the value) of his philosophical system by living in a way that is entirely true to it.[24] Initially, then, the true life figures as the authenticating basis for a mode of veridiction in which a person speaks philosophical truths in order to yoke more people to the self-improving project of philosophy. Against this backdrop, Foucault understands Socrates and Plato to innovate in a precedent-setting way when they position the true life as the basis for philosophical truth-telling that aims to affect the political realm, as well. This is to suggest that 'the emergence of the true life in the principle and form of [political] truth-telling' occurs when Socrates and Plato begin to instruct political actors in the means of governing themselves properly so that they, in turn, can govern the city properly.

Ultimately, tracing the trajectory of philosophical Eudaimonism through to its moment of convergence with political truth-telling leads Foucault to see Diogenes, and not his Socratic forebears, as the first person to actuate *parrhêsia*'s world-shaping promise – a view he comes to hold precisely because he understands Cynicism to require the truest possible commitment to the true life. Foucault reaches this conclusion after observing that the attributes characteristic of something that is true (*alēthēs*) – that it be unconcealed, unmixed and unchanging – mean that anyone seeking to embody the true life must undertake an ethical project that is conceptually premised on realising a series of absolutes.[25] Here we see Foucault arriving at truth-telling's logic of ethical extremity in an undeniable way, for it can no longer be the case – as it might have been under the rubric of his earlier term, true discourse – that philosophical *parrhêsia*'s veridical force is achieved through enacting a virtuous mean-state that is extreme only in a relative sense, one that comes very close to the pole naming this virtue's excessive extreme without being identical to it. Now, however, the absolutising standards of the true life mean that moderating one's courage of truth to even the tiniest degree would be unvirtuous.

For Foucault, Cynicism does not name a distinct school of philosophy or an idiosyncratic cult of personality, both of which assume that Diogenes aims in his own direction. Rather it names the way of life that results from practicing the most basic and widely held tenets of Eudaimonism with unmitigated and unremitting zeal. Indeed, as A. A. Long points out, however much Diogenes may seem to be the antithesis of his philosophical contemporaries, Cynic doctrine can nevertheless be described in terms that capture the essential elements of Eudaimonism common to all Hellenistic philosophy of the period:

1. Happiness is living in agreement with nature.
2. Happiness is something available to any person willing to engage in sufficient physical and mental training.
3. The essence of happiness is self-mastery, which manifests itself in the ability to live happily under even highly adverse circumstances.

4. Self-mastery is equivalent to, or entails, virtuous character.

5. The happy person, so conceived, is the only person who is truly wise, kingly, and free.

6. Things conventionally deemed necessary for happiness, such as wealth, fame, and political power, have no value in nature.

7. Prime impediments to happiness are false judgments of value, together with the emotional disturbances and vicious character that arise from these false judgments.[26]

Diogenes follows conventional tenets aimed at achieving true happiness, tenets widely accepted by his society, yet he follows them to the point of shamelessly doing conventionally shameful things. Hence the story of Diogenes masturbating in the marketplace as a demonstration of self-sufficiency, along with the many accounts of his unassuageable asceticism, from discarding all superfluous possessions – even a modest wooden bowl where cupped hands will do – to finding shelter in an empty barrel and under the awnings of public buildings.[27] For Foucault, Diogenes' extreme implementation of the true life is significant because it builds on the essential insight that gives rise to *parrhêsia*'s 'Platonic moment', the insight that a serious enough commitment to living the truth of one's principles can enable a philosopher to carry out a critical mission that extends far beyond the bounds of philosophical discourse. Diogenes and his Cynic followers simply press the question of how serious one's commitment to the true life must be in order to achieve these communicative ends. Whereas Socrates – who, Foucault reminds us, 'had a house, a wife, children, and even slippers' – practices the courage of his convictions in moderation, Diogenes seeks to unlock the full veridical powers of truth-telling by taking up the familiar themes of the true life and 'pushing these themes to their extreme consequence', thereby revealing 'a life which is precisely the very opposite of what was traditionally recognized as the true life'.[28] In matters of truth-telling, Foucault understands an ethics of extremity to be the essential element that separates Socrates' stinging gadfly from the greater impactfulness of Diogenes' biting dog.

According to Foucault, Diogenes' unqualified pursuit of the true life unlocks the full veridical powers of philosophical truth-telling because Cynicism functions as the 'banality of philosophy', a banality that becomes 'scandalous' through the uncompromising degree of its fulfilment:[29]

> the Cynic life is at once the echo, the continuation, and the extension of the true life (that unconcealed, independent, straight, sovereign life), but also taking it to the point of its extreme consequence and reversal. What is the shameless life if not the continuation, the pursuit, but also the scandalous reversal of the unconcealed life?[30]

By adopting the most general and conventionally accepted principles of contemporary philosophy, and 'by making the philosopher's very existence their point of application' and 'site of manifestation', Cynicism makes apparent that the true life is something 'other than the life led by men in general and by philosophers in particular'.[31] The result, for Foucault, is scandalous, but not in the way we might expect. To be sure, his use of the term calls to mind the negative reaction many people have had to Diogenes, whose behaviour can be viewed as unseemly and repulsive, and whose philosophy of life can therefore be met with scornful dismissal. Nevertheless, Foucault understands the Cynic way of life to be scandalous in a more sweeping sense, positing that the Cynic practitioner overturns propriety not just in his own life, but also in the lives of everyone else. He sees in Diogenes' extreme courage of truth the possibility of a scandal that manifests as the absence of scandal, the possibility of everyone being so swept away by the truth made visible in and through Cynic critical practice that they are transformed by it:

> the Cynic is someone who, taking up the traditional themes of the true life in ancient philosophy, transposes them and turns them round into the demand and assertion of the need for an *other* life. And then, through the image and figure of the king of poverty, he transposes anew the idea of *an other* life into the theme of a life whose otherness must lead to the change in the world. An *other* life for an *other* world.[32]

This is to imagine that Cynicism is an ethical practice that imbues an individual, acting alone, with sufficient veridical powers to transform the world.

Foucault's initial focus on Socrates and Plato leads him to speculate that philosophical *parrhêsia* settles over time into the mode of critical activity undertaken by a counsellor addressing a king. But once he traces philosophical *parrhêsia* through to its point of culmination in Cynicism, Foucault comes to the realisation that our Western critical tradition bends toward a mode of truth-telling in which the counsellor can supplant the king, in which a philosopher's critical sovereignty can supersede a king's political sovereignty. Foucault invokes Dio Chrysostom's *Fourth Discourse on Kingship* (*c.*100 CE), in which Diogenes and Alexander the Great engage in a lengthy dialogue on the topic of kingliness, to make his point.[33] This dialogue is a retelling of an apocryphal story in which Alexander, having expressed interest in meeting Diogenes, and having tried and failed to secure a visit from the infamous Cynic, decides to visit the elusive philosopher instead. Chrysostom uses this well-known encounter as the occasion to stage a conversation on the qualities of true, incontrovertible kingliness, and the conclusion reached is that only Diogenes enjoys a state of real and complete sovereignty. Alexander's form of kingliness is shown to be precariously dependent on other people, including those who would wield more power for themselves if they could, meaning that Alexander must always protect himself against external and internal threats alike. On the other hand, Chrysostom's Diogenes claims to possess the kind of natural sovereignty that belongs to the king of bees, an animal alleged to have no stinger precisely because he has no need for it. One reading of this dialogue would see it as offering a contrast between Alexander's unsustainable effort to exert sovereignty over others and Diogenes' willingness to exert sovereignty only over himself. By this view, the Cynic needs no weapons because he makes no effort to exert his will upon other people. But Foucault sees it differently, recovering a sense of what it means for Diogenes to be a Cynic as opposed to a Stoic. While Diogenes' asceticism and embrace of shamelessness does lead him to a state of happy self-sovereignty – a state he can enjoy only by refusing to participate in Alexander-like games of power – the final purpose of this ethical project is to exercise sovereignty over others in a game not of power but of truth: 'First, Cynic sovereignty founds a blessed mode of life for whoever exercises it. Second, this Cynic sovereignty founds a practice of the manifested truth, of truth to be manifested.'[34] By this view, the proof of Diogenes' true sovereignty is his ability to disclose a tyrant's lack of real kingliness so authoritatively that he need have no fear of reprisal.

Foucault's genealogy of *parrhêsia* leads him to conclude that our critical tradition is premised on a logic of truth-telling that aspires to complete critical sovereignty, an aspiration that Diogenes is imagined to realise through the virtuously immoderate courage he demonstrates when disciplining himself to the true life. Ultimately, then, Foucault comes to see that our critical tradition's parrhesiastic ideal is that of a truth-teller who engages with the world much more directly than Socrates and Plato ever do. Rather than addressing the souls of individual political actors so that they in turn can contribute to the effective governance of the city-state, the Cynic parrhesiast cuts out the middleman and addresses the collective soul of all humankind:

> The Cynic battle is an explicit, intentional, and constant aggression directed at humanity in general, at humanity in its real life, and whose horizon or objective is to change its moral attitude (its *ēthos*) but, at the same time and thereby, its customs, conventions, and ways of living.[35]

Though Diogenes has at times been taken up as the model for a more limited form of truth-telling in which a counsellor addresses a king, Foucault understands Cynic *parrhêsia* to be the 'matrix . . . of a fundamental ethical experience in the West' because Diogenes exemplifies the most revolutionary parrhesiastic ambition to which social critics can aspire: that of addressing all of humanity with enough veridical force to reshape the world.[36] This is the critical ambition that leads Christian evangelisers of the third and fourth centuries to adopt the lifestyle of contemporary itinerant Cynics. It is the ambition that leads a number of eighteenth-century thinkers to see in Diogenes the means of hastening the spread of enlightenment, the ambition that Friedrich Nietzsche nurses when articulating his Diogenes-inspired image of the *Übermensch* announcing the death of God.[37] This is the critical ambition that Foucault rediscovers through his work on *parrhêsia* and that leads him to envision the possibility of present-day truth-tellers capable of combating reason's instrumentalisation, thereby delivering the modern world from its own sins.

If, for Foucault, Cynicism names a fundamental ethical experience in the West, it is the experience of striving for the practical means of delivering critique to immediate revolutionary effect, means to be found in a virtuously extreme relation to the courage of truth. However, this understanding of the ethical experience Cynicism provokes fails to account for the ways in which subsequent thinkers not only aspire to the Cynic critical ideal but also struggle with this aspiration. It is to this struggle that we now turn.

To Moderate or Not to Moderate: Truth-Telling's Crisis of Character

Near the tail end of his 1984 lectures, Foucault asserts more than once that he understands Cynicism's radical – and radically effective – approach to truth-telling to persist as an communicative ideal in later eras, first with respect to early Christianity, and later with respect to modern philosophy and the modern critical tradition more generally. However, Foucault's death some three months later means that his work on the genealogy of *parrhêsia* remains uncompleted. We must therefore look to his final semester at the Collège de France for an idea of what he had in mind when making these claims, and there we can find only glimpses. In the second hour of his last lecture of the semester, he briefly turns to early Christianity's reception of Cynicism, which he locates in the Christian embrace of asceticism both as a source of parrhesiastic authority for evangelisers and, somewhat contrarily, as a way of life that leads Christians not to a world otherwise but rather to another world: the kingdom of heaven. Yet even as Foucault offers these thoughts, he makes clear that they are highly provisional, insisting on 'the reservation, of course, that [they] may have to be completely reworked, re-examined from every angle, and begun again quite differently'.[38] For later iterations of Cynic militancy with respect to the true life, he offers only two offhand examples: nineteenth-century political revolutionaries

and artists from the eighteenth century onward (modern artists, most especially).[39] These references afford us the bar-
est sketch of Cynicism's afterlife, but they are sufficient to
deducing one salient feature of Foucault's unfinished history
of truth-telling in the West: he imagines this history unfolding as a series of people embracing Cynic militancy in a bid
to change the world with their revolutionary truth.

By one reckoning, Foucault is not at all wrong to hold
this view. Our critical tradition does unfold, at least in part,
as a series of people embracing Cynic militancy in precisely
this way. Indeed, there are many examples left unmentioned
by Foucault to which we can point. Yet there is also a way
in which Foucault's genealogy of truth-telling gets it quite
wrong, for the idea of one truth-teller after another following in Diogenes' wake cannot be reconciled with Foucault's
understanding of Cynic *parrhêsia*'s unparalleled revolutionary success. If Cynic critical activity were as radically effective as Foucault sometimes seems to think, then we would
already live in the world otherwise to which Diogenes sought
to deliver us. Moreover, the fact that we continue to live in
such a flawed world tells us something important about the
many would-be Cynics who model themselves on Diogenes,
for they, too, fail to bring about the radical transformations that they seek. Why, then, do certain thinkers across
the centuries form the conviction that Cynic truth-telling
works? Setting aside Foucault's own credulous assessment of
Cynic critical activity, his genealogy of *parrhêsia* provides an
answer to this question by revealing our critical tradition's
foundation in a logic of ethical extremity. *Parrhêsia*'s logic of
virtuous extremism is the reason thinkers in later eras have
been receptive to the idea that immoderate adherence to the
true life might imbue a person with untold persuasive force;
it is the reason this idea has retained an evergreen potential
to make sense at a conceptual level even as experience shows
it to make no sense at all at a practical level.

In its forever-unfinished state, Foucault's genealogy of truth-telling fails to recognise that this tension between theory and practice – between the Cynic ideal, on the one hand, and the rhetorical pragmatics of critique, on the other – is integral to the unfolding of our critical tradition as we know it. This is to suggest that a significant portion of our cultural, intellectual and political history in the West has been the product of a centuries-long struggle to reconcile the Cynic vision of producing unignorable, incontrovertible and thus world-changing critique with the practical reality that over-zealousness is precisely what delegitimises a speaker in the eyes of his or her interlocutors.

We see this tension at play in two aspects of Christianity's appropriation of Cynicism not mentioned by Foucault. On the one hand, early Christians looked to Cynicism for a model of truth-telling that delivers sweeping, revolutionary change through a devotee's absolute and unyielding commitment to the true life. Scholars like F. Gerald Downing have argued that Christians of the first few centuries CE – beginning with the historical Jesus, no less – actively took itinerant Cynics of the same period as their model for living an honest and authentic life, even to the point of adopting the same haircut, blanket-cloak and begging bowl.[40] One could argue, as Foucault does, albeit briefly, that this embrace of Cynic asceticism aims only for personal salvation, that it marks a Christian adaptation of Eudaimonism that extends from happiness in this life to happiness in the next. However, the near programmatic effort by early church fathers to ground Christological iconography in Cynic antecedents – especially when figuring Christ-on-the-Cross as a transformational 'king of misery' – suggests that they saw a meaningful connection between Cynic extremism and the transformative power Jesus Christ could have on the people around him.[41]

On the other hand, later Christians increasingly advanced a revisionist account of Cynicism premised on an ethics of moderation, and they did so in an effort to square the tradition of valorising the revolutionary effects of Cynic militancy – which required an absolute embrace of shamelessness – with their own respect for social convention in matters of modesty. This is evidenced in Saint Augustine's famous and highly influential speculation that Cynics could not possibly have masturbated and copulated in public, as is reported of them, because 'there could [not] have been any achievement of such pleasure under the glare of human gaze'.[42] Augustine supposes that the Cynics instead advanced their case for self-sufficiency and the necessary shedding of social convention by covering themselves with a blanket and 'act[ing] out the motions of lying together before the eyes of men who really did not know what was done under the cloak'. For Augustine, it is impossible to imagine critical potency accruing to a person who pursues an ethics of shamelessness in an overzealous way. In his eyes, a person who goes so far as to masturbate in public is guided not by principle but perversity, and he cannot see his way to taking such a person seriously. Consequently, Augustine seeks to temper the excesses of Diogenes and his ilk, and while this results in his rather absurd endorsement of men pretending to fornicate in the streets in order to make a point, he entertains this absurdity with complete seriousness because it allows him to envision the courage of truth manifesting as a virtuous mean-state.

These competing ideas about the ethical basis for truth-telling settle into an uneasy coexistence within the Christian tradition. We see this, for example, when founding members of the Dominican order punningly called themselves *Domini canes*, 'the Lord's dogs', and when Saint Francis likewise described his Franciscan street preachers as 'jesters of God'.[43] In adopting a Cynic-inspired model for evangelising their spiritual truth, members of these orders studiously avoided the impropriety of militant shamelessness – if they acted the part of a dog, it was not by lifting their legs as they urinated

in the marketplace – and yet they still sought to base the efficacy of their truth-telling on an ethics of extremity. At the
time of their order's founding early in the thirteenth century,
Dominican and Franciscan priests pursued the true life in the
same way they understood Christ to have done, by disciplining themselves to a life of extreme poverty and mendicancy.
Here we see the first of two elements at play in the uneasy
coexistence of truth-telling's moderate and immoderate logics: the capacity of those who would realise Cynicism's revolutionary potential to pursue new manifestations of virtuous
extremism when previous ones have been found wanting. The
second, of course, is the capacity of those who grant the inescapability of the golden mean to pathologise each new iteration of Cynic militancy. Hence the debate that erupted within
the Franciscan order shortly after its founding, which centred
on the degree of observance that was required of its members
and that quickly led to numerous secessions from the order.[44]

In the early modern period, debates over the effectiveness
of Cynic truth-telling regain a secular dimension that had
largely fallen out of view during the medieval period. With this
return to the field of politics we see the more zealous would-be
Cynics retrenching yet again, imagining that they can derive
their critical potency from an ethics of extremity uncoupled
not only from diogenical shamelessness, but also from the
rigours of strict asceticism. When Thomas Wilson recounts
being arrested and charged as a heretic in Rome, he makes
good on his previous insistence that 'This worlde wanteth
suche as [Diogenes] was' simply by embodying the courage
of his convictions:[45] 'I tooke such courage, and was so bolde,
that the Iudges then did maruaile at my stoutnesse.'[46] Wilson,
who goes on to become a prominent diplomat and politician
under Queen Elizabeth's Protestant rule, is more than happy
to eat and dress in a manner that befits his station, but despite
his rejection of both shamelessness and asceticism as ethical precepts, he nevertheless understands himself to emulate

Diogenes when he stands firm in his truth. What matters, for Wilson, is the superlative nature of his *ethos* – he 'tooke such courage', he 'was so bolde'. He understands this very excessiveness to endow his manifestation of good character with the quality of stoutness, that is to say, of unyielding rootedness in his principles, a state of absolute firmness that he in turn credits as the source of his veridical force in his moment of defiance. Ultimately, however, this boiled down understanding of revolutionary truth-telling's active ingredients reveals that Cynic *parrhêsia*'s evaluative reversibility stems not from any display of shamelessness but rather from the very extremism a would-be parrhesiast brings to bear on the fashioning of his own character. The stance Francis Bacon takes in a chapter of *The Wisdome of the Ancients* entitled 'Cassandra, siue Parresia' is a case in point. Warning against the 'vnprofitable liberty of vntimely admonitions and counselles', Bacon argues that counsellors who insist upon absolute candour will 'in all their endeauors . . . auail nothing' precisely because they 'are so ouerweened with the sharpnesse and dexteritie of their own wit and capacitie'.[47] Here we see the evaluative flipside of Wilson's bid to derive veridical force from a show of stoutness, which, according to the *Oxford English Dictionary* (OED), also carried negative connotations as a cognate of pridefulness, obstinacy and rebelliousness.[48] For a pragmatist like Bacon, a counsellor's departure from the golden mean spells doom in the manner of Icarus.

It is in the early modern period that the problem of the Cynic truth-teller metastasises quite noticeably. Having unmoored the courage of truth from shamelessness and asceticism, the traditionally Cynic wellsprings of authenticity, sixteenth-century admirers of Diogenes sought to realise parrhesiastic veridiction by exercising virtuous extremism in more than one way; and because each strategy continued to be premised on taking at least one thing to an extreme, each also continued to provoke and perpetuate Cynicism's crisis of character. As we've already seen, what Wilson understands to be a show of excessive stoutness that imbues his truth-telling with untold veridical force is for Bacon a show of obstinacy that makes the overly firm speaker eminently dismissible. Similarly, the posture of Cynic melancholy, which goes all-in on an ethics of contemplation in order to replace personal agency with a sense of communion with larger planes of causality – and which I link to Robert Burton, among others, in Chapter 4 – also suffers from the negative view of melancholia as a humoral and dispositional imbalance that renders the insights of a melancholy intellectual suspect. Both of these critical postures, the one more direct and confrontational, the other more indirect and sublimated, generate a complex admixture of belief and scepticism amongst thinkers in the sixteenth century precisely because they activate two competing logics of moral virtue. To complicate matters further, the diversification of Cynic extremism in this period meant that Cynicism's crisis of character gained an additional multiplying variable, for now one could toggle not only between belief in and repudiation of radically effective truth-telling, one could also toggle between one iteration of Cynic extremism and another. Aspiration for the revolutionary promise of the Cynic critical ideal thus obtains a new degree of irrepressibility in the early modern period, for thinkers who fail on one front in their efforts to emulate Diogenes can always direct their hopes elsewhere. Indeed, the possibility of authorising *parrhêsia*'s veridical force through a different implementation of Cynic extremism can even involve a doubling down on its original attributes. As I show in Chapter 5, this is precisely what Shakespeare illustrates in his depiction of Timon embracing an asceticism even more severe than that maintained by Apemantus, the play's card-carrying Cynic philosopher, in an attempt to speak a truth that exists outside the corrupting influence of money.

It will be the work of later chapters to flesh out my account of Cynicism's unfolding crisis of character in the sixteenth

century and to examine Shakespeare's particular response
to it. For now, it will suffice to demonstrate, if only briefly
and incompletely, that the diversified terms of the problem
of the Cynic truth-teller as they emerge in the sixteenth century continue to operate in later eras. In making this claim,
I both draw upon and depart from Louisa Shea's account of
Diogenes' mixed reception in the eighteenth, nineteenth and
twentieth centuries, an account that tracks just one model of
Cynic truth-telling – the direct approach – as thinkers see-saw
between the competing logics of moderation and extremism,
and hence between Cynicism's rejection and its embrace.[49]
In fact, however, thinkers continue to grapple with multiple
Cynic extremes, and this is exemplified by Denis Diderot,
arguably the most enamoured with Diogenes of all the *philos-
ophes*. Shea ranks Diderot among those thinkers who, after a
failed bid to be the Diogenes of their day, consign themselves
to the pragmatic reality that they must moderate their Cynic
stridency. But it would be more correct to say that Diderot
chafes against this reality and continually looks for a way to
break free of it. This tension between accommodation and
resistance is evident even in the comments Diderot makes following his failed experiment at being overtly diogenical:

> Who today would dare brave ridicule and scorn? In our
> midst Diogenes would live under a roof, not in a barrel; in
> no region of our world would he take on the role he played
> in Athens. He might preserve his independent and firm
> spirit, but he would never say, even to the pettiest of our
> sovereigns, as he did to Alexander; *Get out of my sun.*[50]

Diderot clearly questions whether the conditions of social
life in eighteenth-century France and those of ancient Athens
differ so significantly that Diogenes, were he to have been
born Diderot's contemporary, would himself have failed to
live up to his own standard and would consequently have

lacked the veridical force to speak direct truth to power. And yet, even in articulating his ostensible disillusionment with the Cynic model of truth-telling, Diderot holds to the idea that a time-travelling Diogenes would be able to 'preserve his independent spirit'. In doing so, he clings to the possibility of Cynic *ethos* manifesting in some other form. Indeed, it is worth noting that even Diderot's first, more explicit attempt to embody Cynic extremism assumes that the courage of truth can be demonstrated simply through the discursive work of writing fearless satire, with no need to emulate the asceticism and shamelessness that was so indicative of Diogenes' approach to daily life. It is in the context of this highly modified take on the Cynic critical stance that Diderot's enthusiasm for diogenical truth-telling is put to the test, and, to all outward appearances, entirely snuffed out. Faced with threats of imprisonment for his overbold *Pensées philosophiques* and his salacious novel *Les bijoux indiscrets*, Diderot publicised his renunciation of Diogenes in favour of a more acceptable and generally revered archetype:

> I will not counter your reproaches with the examples of Rabelais, Montaigne, La Mott-le Vayer, Swift, or others I could name who have attacked the fools of their day in the most Cynical manner and yet kept the title of sage. I want the scandal to end, and without losing further time in apologies, I abandon the jester's staff and bells never again to take them up, and I return to Socrates.[51]

Diderot feels genuine social pressure to abandon his 'Cynical manner', and though reluctant to give up this stance, he acknowledges the scandal to which he has exposed himself by assuming the Cynic's aggressively frank posture.

According to Shea, this marks the end of Diderot's project of virtuous extremism, but it does not. Though Diderot abandons abrasive stridency as a model for effective truth-telling, he goes on to pursue an inverted, highly counterintuitive form of Cynic ethical extremity in his work as a co-editor of *L'Encyclopédie, ou dictionnaire raisonné des sciences, des arts et des métiers*, in which he rather ambitiously seeks to house all of the world's knowledge. Ultimately, he wants the *Encyclopédie* to have a critical, world-changing function through its robust cross-referencing apparatus, and while this method of achieving change differs from those he previously deploys as an out-and-out Cynic, it, too, depends on an ethics of excess:

> [The cross references] will counter notions; bring principles into contrast; covertly attack, unsettle, overturn some ridiculous opinions which one would not venture to disparage openly. If the author is impartial, they will always have the double function of confirming and refuting, disrupting and reconciling
>
>   . . .
>
> This means of undeceiving men acts very quickly on good minds, and ineluctibly and without any disagreeable consequences, silently and without scandal, on all minds. It is the art of tacitly deducing the boldest consequences. If such confirming and refuting references are foreseen well in advance, and skillfully prepared, they will give an encyclopedia the character which a good dictionary ought to possess: that of changing the common mode of thinking.[52]

Diderot wants to avoid the 'disagreeable consequences' he faced as a Diogenes-inspired satirist and polemicist, and yet he still wants to bring about a change in 'the common mode of thinking'.

Shea reads Diderot's encyclopedism as part of his return to the Socratic fold, but in fact it is his way of turning from an extremist ethics bent on confrontation toward an equally extreme posture of impartiality. If the author of the cross references is sufficiently impartial, if he links entries together without any favouritism or preferential treatment, then,

Diderot argues, the cross references will create a space of engagement and exchange in which the strengths and weaknesses of various ideas will be exposed by virtue of their new proximity to one another. In order to work – that is, in order to realise Diderot's vision of it working – the cross-referencer must undertake an ethics of critical renunciation, he must give up the ambition of communicating his own views and instead commit to an all-encompassing project of unbiased connection-making, the idea being that this will imbue the encyclopedia itself with the kind of 'character' that will effect large-scale changes in society. Here we have a strategy of sublimated critique akin to the one Hamlet adopts through his posture of Cynic melancholy. Like the philosophers of history who follow in his wake, Hamlet imagines that he can devote himself to an indefinite ethics of intellection in order to perceive the inevitable unfolding of events, ones that will bring about major changes in the world without any direct intervention on his part. This ethereal form of truth-telling – along with the dispassionate breed of virtuous extremism that underwrites it – stands out from other iterations of Cynic critical practice for the lack of pushback that it has received. On this front, at least, proponents of moderation do not see as much of a problem with the Cynic ideal, and, for that reason, Cynicism's indirect approach has become a persistent and largely unchallenged thread in our modern critical tradition.

This is not to say, however, that the aspiration for more overt versions of the Cynic *ethos* go away. As we have already seen, Foucault comes to believe that recommitting to classical Cynicism offers the best and only means of freeing ourselves from a world of instrumentalised reason and (lowercase) cynical malaise – a world whose articulation, Shea teaches us, rests precisely on the failure of strident Cynic truth-telling in the eighteenth century.[53] From Wilson to Bacon to Diderot, from early Foucault to late, we see the pendulum-swing between Cynicism's rejection and embrace as it pertains to one strand of truth-telling's direct approach. But while this particular intellectual history is the most visible manifestation of the problem of the truth-teller in our modern era, it is not the only one. Indeed, in addition to Cynicism's intellectual sublimation as evidenced, among others, by Burton, Diderot and Hegel, modern instances of Cynic anti-capitalism (à la Timon) also continue to crop up. Maurizio Lazzarato, for example, extracts from Foucault's lectures an understanding of Cynic critical practice that eschews the logocentrism of conventional politics in favour of a mute form of communicative action rooted in bodily display. Having linked the system of semantic referentiality upon which political logocentrism depends to the system by which money makes fungible the qualities of the things it commodifies, Lazzarato concludes that '[t]he examination of the Cynics' way of understanding *bios*, existence, and "militant" subjectivation can provide the weapons for resisting the powers of contemporary capitalism'.[54]

Despite its impracticability, the fantasy of embodying Cynic critical agency has endured. Not only that, it has proliferated, splitting into multiple iterations that continue to inform our ideas about the roles and capacities of public intellectuals, philosophers and social critics. I have argued that the sixteenth century is the point of departure for modernity's more diverse, persistent and culturally formative problem of the truth-teller, but it is important to note that the sixteenth century's diversification of the Cynic ideal is not the cause for this change so much as a consequence of it. Something happens in the sixteenth century that brings a new degree of intensity to debates over the powers of veridiction one stands to gain from taking up diogenical figures as practical examples – something that increases the believability of Cynic critical agency in despite of all empirical evidence. It is to this happening, which is specifically literary in nature, that I now turn.

Notes

1. Foucault, *Courage of Truth*, p. 287. Further citations will be in-text.
2. Aristotle, *The Ethics of Aristotle*, 1114b.
3. Foucault, *Fearless Speech*, p. 73.
4. See, for example, Folkers, 'Daring the Truth'; Dyrberg, 'Foucault on *parrhesia*'; Zagan, 'Foucault'; Tamboukou, 'Truth Telling in Foucault and Arendt'; Franek, 'Philosophical Parrhesia as Aesthetics of Existence'; and Scott, 'Games of Truth'.
5. For an example of the former, see Prozorov, 'Foucault's Affirmative Biopolitics'. For examples of the latter, see Lemm, 'The Embodiment of Truth and the Politics of Community'; Tanke, 'Cynical Aesthetics'; and Flynn, 'Foucault as Parrhesiast'.
6. Foucault, *Fearless Speech*, p. 74.
7. Foucault, *The Government of Self and Others*, p. 319.
8. Ibid., p. 6.
9. See ibid., pp. 149–51.
10. For a helpful overview of the reasons for translating Aristotle's use of *eudaimonia* as 'human flourishing', see Rasmussen, 'Human Flourishing and the Appeal to Human Nature'.
11. Foucault, *The Government of Self and Others*, p. 300.
12. Ibid., p. 188.
13. Garver, *Aristotle's Rhetoric*, p. 151.
14. Foucault, *The Government of Self and Others*, p. 313. Foucault first describes the terms of this pact when discussing philosopher-parrhesiasts. However, he goes on to define political *parrhêsia* as an anti-rhetorical ethics that similarly aligns word to deed when, a year later, he rehearses the ground he had covered in the previous lecture series. For this later development, see Foucault, *Courage of Truth*, pp. 13–14.
15. Foucault, *The Government of Self and Others*, p. 305.
16. Ibid., p. 320.
17. See Hadot, *Philosophy as a Way of Life*.
18. For Foucault's reading of the *Laches*, see *Courage of Truth*, pp. 116–53.

19. Aristotle, *Laches and Charmides*, 188C–D.
20. To put the point differently, Laches does not heed Socrates' words on the basis of pre-discursive *ethos*, or prior reputation, which is precisely the kind of proof that rhetoric and discursive *ethos* is meant to replace as a more reliable alternative. Rather, Laches understands Socrates to present him with a show of ongoing and recursive good character – the practice of self on self Foucault calls 'the true life' – that is meant to do discursive *ethos* one better.
21. Foucault, *Courage of Truth*, p. 158.
22. Ibid., p. 165.
23. Ibid., p. 163.
24. Foucault explicitly describes Diogenes as the first to take up 'the militant life' within philosophy, approaching philosophy as a way of life whose purpose is not to gain new philosophical adherents (what he calls 'a closed system') but rather to spread the truth to everyone. See Foucault, *Courage of Truth*, p. 284.
25. See ibid., pp. 218–19.
26. Long, 'The Socratic Tradition', pp. 29–30.
27. See Laertius, *Lives of Eminent Philosophers*, 6.22–3.
28. Foucault, *Courage of Truth*, pp. 258, 227.
29. Ibid., p. 232.
30. Ibid., p. 243.
31. Ibid., p. 244.
32. Ibid., p. 287.
33. Chrysostom, *Fourth Discourse on Kingship*.
34. Foucault, *Courage of Truth*, p. 308.
35. Ibid., p. 208.
36. Ibid., p. 287.
37. At a crucial moment in *The Gay Science*, Nietzsche tells the story of the madman who announces the death of God by wandering the streets with 'a lantern in the bright morning hours', shouting, 'I seek God! I seek God!' Referring to this allusion as well as several others, R. Bracht Branham notes how frequently Nietzsche invokes 'the Cynic *parrhesiast* ("freespeaker") as a model of shameless honesty, a voice of

enlightenment beyond Good and Evil'. See Nietzsche, *The Gay Science*, §125; and Branham, 'Nietzsche's Cynicism, pp. 170–1.

38. Foucault, *Courage of Truth*, pp. 316–17.

39. See ibid., pp. 185–9.

40. For work suggesting that Jesus might himself have taken contemporary itinerant Cynics as a model, see Downing, *Christ and the Cynics*; and Betz, 'Jesus and the Cynics'. For scholarship arguing that Church fathers in the third and fourth centuries worked to cast Jesus in a Cynic light, see Downing, *Cynics, Paul, and the Pauline Churches*; and Krueger, 'Diogenes the Cynic among the Fourth Century Fathers'.

41. Foucault, *Le Courage de la Vérité*, p. 258. My translation. In *The Courage of Truth*, Burchell translates 'roi de misère' as 'king of poverty', a choice that loses the sense of excessiveness that Foucault attributes to Cynic *askēsis*.

42. Augustine, *The City of God against the Pagans*, book XX, p. 369.

43. See Kinney, 'Heirs of the Dog', esp. p. 304.

44. For a history of these debates, their role in early secessions from the order, and the gradual shift in Franciscan orthodoxy from an emphasis on poverty to one on learning, see Şenocak, *The Poor and the Perfect*.

45. Wilson, *Arte of Rhetorique*, sig. Ddii^v.

46. Ibid., sig. A^v.

47. See Bacon, *Wisdome of the Ancients*, sigs. A^v–A$_2$^{v}.

48. See 'stout, A adj.', definitions 1a and 4b, *OED Online* (March 2013, Oxford University Press), http://www.oed.com.ezproxy.princeton.edu/view/Entry/74214?rskey=ovntB5&result=9#eid (last accessed 1 October 2018).

49. See Shea, *The Cynic Enlightenment*.

50. 'Qui est-ce qui oserait aujourd'hui braver le ridicule et le mépris? Diogène parmi nous habiterait sous un toit, mais non dans un tonneau; il ne ferait dans aucune contrée le rôle qu'il fit dans Athènes. L'âme indépendante et ferme qu'il avait reçue, peut-être l'eût-il convervée, mais il n'aurait point dit à un de nos petits souverains comme à Alexandre le Grand: *Retire-toi*

de mon soleil.' Diderot, 'Essai sur les règnes de Claude et de Néron', 13:295, quoted in Shea, *The Cynic Enlightenment,* p. 43. Shea's translation.

51. Diderot, 'Mémoires sur différents sujets mathématique', 2:232, quoted in Shea, *The Cynic Enlightenment,* p. 41. Shea's translation.

52. Diderot, 'Encyclopedia', quoted in Shea, *The Cynic Enlightenment,* p. 34.

53. See Shea, *The Cynic Enlightenment,* esp. pp. 47–65.

54. Lazzarato, *Signs and Machines.*

CHAPTER 2

THE REALIST TURN: *PARRHÊSIA*, CHARACTER AND THE LIMITS OF DIDACTICISM

In Chapter 1, I rehearsed Foucault's genealogy of philosophical *parrhêsia* in order to show how classical responses to the problem of the truth-teller bend inexorably toward a logic of ethical extremism, one that imagines a truth-teller's veridical force to increase exponentially (and with no apparent limit) the more absolutely he matches word and deed, principle and practice, in every aspect of his daily life. Having drawn out Foucault's insight that the Western critical tradition is founded on the idea that a truth-teller's constitutive virtue – the courage of truth – is a virtuous extreme, I then showed how later thinkers struggled to reconcile this logic of extremism with the competing logic of virtuous moderation upon which the real-world pragmatics of argument and debate are, by sheer practical necessity, based. If there is one take-away from the intellectual history of truth-telling I have laid out (albeit briefly and in highly selective form), it is that this struggle translates into a series of pendulum swings between extremism and moderation as favoured strategies for delivering effective critique, a back-and-forth that has been proceeding in cyclical fashion from late antiquity through to the present day. But while the tension between truth-telling's competing moral frameworks has always posed a problem for the world's aspiring revolutionaries, that problem has not always been felt to the same degree. Indeed, it is a central premise of this book that debates over the efficacy of extreme truth-telling rise to the level of a crisis – and thus become a central driver of our modern cultural formation – only in the sixteenth century, the period in which discussion of, and agitation over, Diogenes increases by many orders of magnitude. In this chapter, I explain why this second crisis of character – which coheres specifically around the figure of the Cynic truth-teller and not, as in the Athenian instance, around the figure of the truth-teller more generally – comes to be felt so acutely in Shakespeare's day.

Disagreement over the practical value of Cynic critical activity intensifies in the sixteenth century because the ethical questions provoked by the figure of the inveterate truth-teller become newly problematised in the wake of a paradigm-changing development in the representational techniques of literary didacticism. In contrast with the didacticism of medieval drama, which principally calls on allegory and symbolism as vehicles for the delivery of prescriptive instruction, early modern dramatists increasingly deploy a new representational mode – what I call characterological realism – that can serve as a vehicle for the delivery of practical instruction. I argue that literary realism first emerges at the level of character (with sixteenth-century drama, and not the eighteenth-century novel, as its incubator) and I further contend that this turn to realist characterisation serves to instruct viewers and readers in the ethics of self-care by offering up to judgment the actions and outcomes of characters fashioned to be verisimilar to people.[1] Narratives wedded to characterological realism provide a virtual arena in which to exercise and refine a reader's prudential judgments about the ethical means and political ends of action, and it is precisely because of this practical value that literary realism (which finds its beginnings in the dramatic form and eventually extends beyond it) becomes fictionality's dominant representational mode in the late sixteenth century onward.

Producing a full account of characterological realism's emergence would require a monograph of its own, but I tell, in brief, the history of realism's didactic success as prelude to my true goal: making visible the concomitant history of its nagging failure. To the extent that literature of the sixteenth century and beyond succeeds as a vehicle for practical instruction, it does so because the protocols for this kind of didacticism hew to an Aristotelean ethics of moderation. In other words, the practical instruction to be gleaned from increasingly verisimilar characters and plot-outcomes tends to involve negative lessons about characters that fail to achieve an appropriate mean-state and therefore meet undesirable ends. Alternatively, it involves positive examples of characters that make the right prudential judgments given the circumstances and consequently meet happier ends. This is the context in which the figure of the Cynic becomes the site of interpretive crisis in early modernity, for the representation of a virtuous extreme confounds the hermeneutics of practical didacticism that readers bring to bear on realist literature, leading them to lose their sense of distinction between the real and the ideal. Read under the rubric of dramatic realism, Diogenes is taken up by some as a practical example of radically effective truth-telling even though Cynic critical activity is understood to be achieved through a project of (anti-Aristotelean) ethical extremism. At the same time, the logic of probable causality upon which dramatic realism depends leads others to assert the sheer impossibility of a Cynic truth-teller having outsized veridical force and to insist instead on the much greater likelihood that such a person would be especially easy to discount. Realism acts as a vehicle both for a new level of belief in the efficacy of Cynic critical activity and to that belief's undoing.

The Rise of Dramatic Realism, or, the Art
of Learning Prudence

Professional scholarship of early modern drama – and of Shakespeare's plays, most especially – has tended to take as a given that playwrights of the period strove for a higher degree of realism than their medieval forebears. The Romantics set this assumption on its lasting path with their appreciation of Shakespeare's genius for evoking passionate character, thereby inaugurating a tradition of character criticism that holds up verisimilitude as an aesthetic ideal – a tradition for which medieval drama's flatter, more allegorical characters could never be a suitable object. To be sure, critics like A. C. Bradley are frequently held to account for indulging in the kind of character criticism that speculates well beyond a given play's evidentiary bounds.[2] Nevertheless, it remains widely accepted that the characters populating early modern plays are, arguably for the first time, written in a way that invites this kind of speculation. Early modern playwrights imbue their characters with more markers of class, race and gender, more particulars of a character's past history and present agenda. And through the aggregated interactions between such characters, early modern playwrights invest more realism in their depiction of the social field these fictional people must navigate.

The formal innovations of early modern drama reflect this change. For example, as James Hirsch astutely notes, the device of the aside undergoes a transformation from its medieval implementation as a form of direct address between character and audience to a form of self-directed address that makes visible to the audience a character's inward deliberation.[3] Whereas the former draws attention to the artificiality of performance, the latter uses artifice to create a naturalistic impression of a given character's thought process. As a result of this and other innovations in early modern drama, nearly all literary critics of the period, even those who agree with L. C. Knights that it would be ridiculous to wonder precisely how many children Lady Macbeth may have had, indulge to one extent or another in character criticism premised on this period's realist turn. This is precisely the point Lorna Hutson makes in the context of her argument that early modern playwrights repurpose forensic rhetoric's topics of circumstance (time, opportunity, means, motive, etc.) in order to make their fictional worlds more inferentially replete:

> Critics of all kinds, from liberal humanist to poststructuralist, from text-based to performance-based, tend to offer readings which assume the validity of inferring both a coherent fictional 'outer' world – including the existence of times and places other than those that are staged – as well as the fictional 'inner' world of *dramatis personae* construed as characters into whose motives it makes sense to enquire.[4]

Underwriting this shared interpretive practice is an assumption – a faulty one, I would argue – that early modern playwrights strove for realistic characterisation primarily as a means of exploring individual psychology, broadly conceived. This assumption marks the point of intersection between the Romantic tradition of character criticism, which does not inquire into the reasons for early modern drama's realist turn, and historicising efforts to tie this development to the period's emerging preoccupations with individualism and inwardness.[5]

But while richer psychologisation is certainly an effect of early modern drama's newfound realism, achieving this effect is not its founding objective. Rather, the more immediate and driving goal of early realism was to teach people how to act prudently under the circumstances of various situations. In this respect, we would do well to take seriously

Hamlet's advice to the Players just before they perform *The Mousetrap*. When Hamlet urges the Players to act their parts realistically, he does so because he understands dramatic naturalism to be the enabling basis for theatre's didactic function as a training manual in virtue ethics:

> Suit the action to the word, the word to the action, with this special observance: that you o'erstep not the modesty of nature. For anything so overdone is from the purpose of playing, whose end, both at the first and now, was and is to hold as 'twere the mirror up to nature, to show virtue her own feature, scorn her own image, and the very age and body of the time his form and pressure.[6]

Hamlet's personification of 'nature' obscures the true object of drama's mirror-function, which is to present playgoers with a reflection of their own nature – not, of course, the nature of individual onlookers, but rather the nature of people as a whole, what we might call the laws of human nature governing social interaction. For Hamlet, this mirroring is not directed at the personifications of 'virtue' and 'scorn' – as a literal reading of his line would suggest – but rather at the play's audience, who are thereby made to confront the relative virtuousness and viciousness of actions strategically undertaken by virtual people. Hence Hamlet's supposition that 'the judicious' would grieve at having to watch an overacted play, for they would then be denied the opportunity to exercise their prudential judgment on ethical scenarios that are true to nature (III, ii, 24).

Needless to say, there is no record of Shakespeare or any other early modern playwright describing characters as virtual people, nor is there evidence of playwrights calling the fictional worlds these characters populate virtual realities. But there is a way in which this distinctly modern understanding of virtuality is precisely what's on display in early modern drama, albeit intertwined with a now-lost sense of 'virtual' that denotes the quality of '[p]roducing, or [being] capable of producing, a particular result; effective'.[7] When it comes to this particular denotation, 'virtual' and 'virtuous' are not simply cognates of one another; they are synonyms. Early modern drama is virtual in the sense that it is concerned with virtuous (i.e. effective) action, and at the same time it is virtual in the sense that it mirrors nature. This latter sense marks the hypothetical side of virtuality, which the *OED* dates back to the mid-eighteenth century: 'Designating a notional property, dimension, etc., of a thing which would produce an observed effect if counteracting factors such as friction are not allowed for.'[8] Following this definition, that which is virtual deviates from at least some of the rules governing reality (i.e. the inescapability of friction), meaning that propositions tied to virtual conditions cannot apply to real ones. However, the virtual does not always separate so cleanly from the real, and this is especially true when it comes to human action and the counterfactual possibilities that attend to it. As Stuart Hampshire points out, the work of evaluating both one's own actions and the actions of others involves comparing real history to counterfactual alternatives. What path would a person's life have taken if a given pivotal moment had been comprised of slightly different circumstances? What would have happened if the person in question had responded to the circumstances of that moment in a different way?[9] Because human beings are caught in the movement of time, the propositions we develop in answer to these questions cannot apply to the real conditions of those past moments into which we retrospectively inquire; however, they absolutely can apply to the real conditions of future moments that have yet to arise. Hampshire calls this kind of speculative retrospection 'optative', and Andrew Miller, drawing on Hampshire's work, argues that the realism on display in the nineteenth-century British novel is premised on literature's capacity to explore the optative mode, its capacity to depict a social field with enough circumstantial detail and causal verisimilitude to allow characters, narrators and readers alike to speculate on how things might have played out differently.[10]

Understanding that virtuality underwrites the category of literary realism allows us to extend our sense of how and why we read realist fictions optatively. Without a robust conception of the virtual, we might make the mistake of thinking that the optative deliberation is chiefly deployed in the arena of counterfactual fictions like Michael Chabon's *The Yiddish Policemen's Union*, in which the counterfactual death of a single US Senator leads to a large settlement of refugee Jews being formed in Sitka, Alaska (reducing the Holocaust's death toll from 6 million to 2 million). These are the kinds of fictions that Catherine Gallagher has recently considered in isolation, ones that take up the optative strategy common among historians of speculating about the alternative timelines we might have inhabited had a decisive moment in history worked out differently from how it did.[11] However, to the degree that a work of counterfactual literature achieves realism, it does so by producing a fictional world that is virtual with respect to our own. This is to suggest that virtuality figures as the organising principle upon which the construction of plausible alternative worlds – where we are able to bring to bear the same deliberative logics as we would on the actual happenings of the real world – depends. Counterfactual fictions thus belong to the broader category of literary realism not because they are optative vis-à-vis history but because they aim to be virtual vis-à-vis the conditions of human sociality. All realist fiction, not just the subset we deem to be counterfactual, is so because it is virtual, and it is precisely because of such fiction's virtuality – that is to say, its degree of probable causality in the effects of characters acting upon one another – that it can serve as the object of readers' optative reflections as they vicariously exercise their practical wisdom. The principle of virtuality enables us to expand the scope of those optative speculations through which we train our practical wisdom, applying them not only to real lives but also to purely fictional ones. It is through this understanding of the virtual that fictional realism acquires its capaciousness, its ability to depict verisimilar action that is not limited to slight alterations of real historical events, and it is important to understand that the first flourishing of literature's virtual mode takes place not in the context of the nineteenth-century novel but rather in the context of sixteenth-century drama.

Although the *OED* dates the hypothetical dimension of virtuality only to the mid-eighteenth century, I would argue that Hamlet's defence of dramatic naturalism draws on the same conceptual architecture as Miller's association of nineteenth-century novelistic realism and the optative mode. This is evident in Hamlet's assertion that theatre at its best strives never to 'o'erstep the modesty of nature', a statement that holds nested within it two interrelated claims: (1) that a law of moderation is essential to the natural order of things, and (2) that dramatic representation can and should mirror this order. With respect to the first, Hamlet simply gives voice to the Aristotelean view that, in the context of effective action, moderation amounts to a universal law of nature, one that brings rational order to the causes and effects of interpersonal endeavour and that consequently allows us to inquire into past actions for the sake of better outcomes in the future. With respect to the second, he invokes the logic of practical didacticism that underwrites virtuality's emergence, arguing that drama should hew as closely as possible to the modesty of nature so that its represented action can become an object of inquiry for 'the judicious'.

Hamlet is entirely right to understand the 'purpose of playing' in terms of realism's practical value, but only if we qualify his transhistorical assertion that this purpose attaches

to drama 'both at the first and now'. In fact, the late sixteenth century is arguably the first time that Hamlet's
normative claims about dramatic naturalism and its purpose
would have made any kind of sense, for it is only in the last
few decades of this century that this kind of realism starts to
cohere and becomes ubiquitous as a representational standard. That being said, the shift toward characterological
realism and the attendant emphasis on practical over prescriptive instruction, while most obviously emergent in the
sixteenth century, is itself the consequence of a problem that
began to preoccupy moralists and theologians several centuries earlier upon the rediscovery of Aristotle's *Nichomachean Ethics*: the problem posed by *phronesis* – the practical
wisdom to determine what actions will, in a given situation,
result in a good and virtuous outcome – and the uncertain
means of teaching people how to increase their measure of
it. It is principally in the context of this problem that early
modern playwrights turn to the topics of circumstance not,
pace Hutson, as an enabling basis for viewers to infer (and
even invent) more than has been staged about a character,
but rather as a means of turning literary representation into
a medium through which viewers can learn how to act prudently in various situations.

In the mid-thirteenth century, Robert Grosseteste translated Aristotle's *Ethics* into Latin. In doing so, he facilitated
a new era in the study of moral philosophy throughout the
Latin-speaking world, and medieval commentators soon
began to grapple with Aristotle's prioritisation of *phronesis*.
Though Aristotle insists that the life of the mind is superior
to the political life, meaning theoretical wisdom (*theoria*) is
superior to practical wisdom, he nevertheless grants the latter functional priority over the former. *Phronesis* is lower, but
foundational. It is impossible for a human being to engage
in continuous contemplation, and so, while contemplative
activity is necessary for the fullest realisation of happiness,

only a person with robust practical wisdom can strike the ideal balance between engaging in philosophical contemplation and living in a way that contributes to a just and good society. The fact that the life of the mind must be reconciled with the demands of political life is, for Aristotle, precisely what makes *phronesis* the most essential component of virtue ethics. Medieval commentators, who equated Aristotle's account of happiness (*eudaimonia*) with beatitude, the living soul's fullest communion with the divine, immediately latched onto the *Ethics*. Just as quickly, however, efforts to construct a Christian moral philosophy out of Aristotle's ethical system were complicated by his functional emphasis on practical wisdom over intellectual wisdom.[12] Commentators who placed prudential judgment on the path to beatitude had to take up the difficult question of how, exactly, one is supposed to know what choices to make in a given situation.

The *Ethics* imposed this question on medieval theologians without supplying a corresponding answer. In a chapter devoted to the active application of his ethical system, Aristotle outlines the scope of the problem:

> It is hard to be good; for surely hard it is in each instance to find the mean, just as to find the mean point or center of a circle is not easy for any man to do, but only he who knows how; just so to be angry, to give money, and be expensive is what any man can do; but to do these to the right person, in due proportion, at the right time, with the right object, and in the right manner, this is not as before what any man can do, nor is it easy; and for this cause goodness is rare, and praiseworthy, and noble.[13]

Aristotle understands *phronesis* to be necessary because virtuous mean-states are moving targets. Giving someone a car, for example, would be an act of liberality under one set of circumstances and an act of stinginess (or prodigality) under another. To make matters worse, a person needs practical wisdom in order to determine which moral virtue to prioritise in a given situation, and if more than one virtue is called for, to know how best to balance those competing imperatives. Faced with the innumerable contingencies inherent to every situational judgment, Aristotle has no way to offer the case-by-case guidance that would be needed for someone to put their principles reliably into practice, and so he limits his advice to the observation that using one's common sense can at least help one to avoid the worst deviations from the good. For medieval commentators, Aristotle could provide an account of what practical wisdom is and why it is necessary, but he could do little to instruct them in its cultivation beyond describing broad principles of application.

The problem Aristotle confronts – and that his commentators necessarily confront in turn – is one of genre. The philosophical treatise is a textual form that simply cannot accommodate the demands for circumstantial specificity that offering case-by-case instruction in practical wisdom would require. Were a treatise to attempt such instruction, it would have to take an anatomised approach to the topics of circumstance, laboriously constructing a scenario and describing the probable outcomes of acting on those circumstances in a particular way. In order to hold instructional value for a person seeking to improve their prudential judgment, this exercise would have to be repeated ad nauseum, with differently fixed variables each time. By contrast, narrative forms – both dramatic and otherwise – provide an iterative field better suited to the demands of ethical particularity. Of course, this becomes the case only as literary fiction comes to be more particular, only as characters acquire more attributes and personal history and as plot comes to be viewed as the consequence of realistic interactions between various characters in a shared social arena. When these conditions are met, literature propagates itself with any number of highly defined ethical scenarios, and it therefore provides people with a uniquely robust means of exercising their prudential judgment without having to hazard themselves in the process. Literature that is imbued with characterological realism offers readers a way to sharpen their prudential judgment to an exponentially greater degree than people who cultivate their practical wisdom only by reflecting on personal experience and general advice.

Characterological realism emerges in its more mature and pervasive form quite suddenly near the end of the sixteenth century, but the earliest seeds of its development can be traced back to the late-medieval reception of Aristotle's *Ethics* and that reception's impact on early English drama. This is particularly true of the fourteenth-century invention of the morality play. Earlier dramatic forms like liturgical drama and the mystery play, which instruct viewers in biblical history, were ill-suited to the didactic task of teaching viewers how to make good choices in their own lives. By contrast, the morality play dramatises the interactions between a protagonist and a range of personified virtues and vices to present viewers with lessons about good conduct and the choices that lead to heaven or hell. Of course, the allegorical nature of a morality play means that its moral instruction is almost entirely prescriptive, but there is a way in which this genre's central didactic ambition – to teach right action in the context of ending up either in heaven or hell – puts pressure on this dramatic form to become something that it is not: a representational mode capable of exercising its viewers' practical wisdom.

We see clear signs of this metamorphosis when writers try to repurpose the morality genre, applying this established didactic form not to the moral maintenance of the soul but rather to the courtly politics of the day. John Skelton's *Magnificence* (originally published in 1519) claims first position in this genealogy. Following its titular character's struggle to achieve the quality of magnificence – generosity combined with good sense and grandeur, the ideal virtue for a king – the play depicts the character of Magnificence being tempted by political vices (Cloaked Collusion, Courtly Abusion) and restrained by political virtues (Measure, Perseverance). Notably, the designation of these particular virtues and vices breaks from the psychomachic allegorisation of earlier morality plays in order to instead represent the broad outlines a socio-political field – without which there can be no practical instruction in the dos and don'ts of political action. In contrast with previous stock vices like the seven deadly sins, Cloaked Collusion and Courtly Abusion are not aspects of Magnificence himself; instead they allegorise the activities of agenda-bearing members of his court.[14]

The play is decidedly allegorical, its didacticism inescapably prescriptive, yet Skelton forges a new kind of link to the real world by building details into dialogue and plot that induce contemporary viewers to recognise Magnificence as a proxy for Henry VII, and the principle vice, Folly, as a stand-in for Cardinal Thomas Wolsey. This pointed topicality is significant because it calls for a more tailored form of literary didacticism, one that offers advice to one person in particular, Henry VII, rather than all people in general. Even taken more broadly, we must say that it directs advice to the category of person hailed by the particularising subject-position of a monarch. Either way, the play strives to have didactic value for a target audience defined by its circumstantial specificity, and it tries to fulfil this instructional mandate by gesturing toward the optative mode. First, it does so by presenting Henry VII with alternate paths that his own life could take, one in which he overindulges in kingly license and consequently loses everything (as happens to Magnificence partway through the play), and another in which he moderates his sovereign liberality to the great benefit of both himself and the commonweal (as happens by play's end). Second, the play gestures toward the virtual mode in the sense that its fictional universe, however allegorised it may be, still holds its main character to the same law governing ethical action that holds true in the real world. As Measure explains quite early in the play:

> With every condition measure must be sought
> Wealth without measure would bear himself too bold;
> Liberty without measure prove a thing of nought.
> . . .
> Where measure is master, plenty doth none offence;
> Where measure lacketh, all thing disordered is;
> Where measure is absent, riot keepeth residence;
> Where measure is ruler there is nothing amiss.[15]

Here we have the rule of moderation, a law of human nature that Skelton, drawing on Aristotle's *Ethics* and its medieval commentaries, seeks to mirror in dramatic form, thereby instructing Henry VII in its inescapability: when Magnificence forgets Measure's lesson, he begins to fail as a king; when he remembers it again, he begins to succeed. But while Skelton's fictional world resembles our own in its predication on the golden mean, it largely fails to reflect the kind of circumstantial texture that Henry VII inevitably has to navigate in his own bid to embody the virtue of magnificence. Although the play teaches a lesson about virtue, the fictional construct through which it routes this lesson does not manage to be virtual in the modern sense of the term. It does not, in other words, produce an optative mirror-image of our own world, a fictive realm that simulates real conditions of political existence in order to experiment in various what-if and if-only scenarios.

Published twenty years after Skelton's *Magnificence*, John Bale's *King Johan* comes much closer to doing just that. The play is not, of course, realistic in its fidelity to the historical King John. It is notoriously a work of Protestant propaganda, one that recasts a thirteenth-century dispute between John and the Pope over who should be raised to the Archbishopric of Canterbury as a vanguard event in the Protestant Reformation. Yet this fictionalising of history doesn't detract from the play's realism so much as contribute to it, for the play engages with historical example in the virtual register. It may never have been the case that King John opposed the Catholic Church on theological grounds, but in order to explore this counterfactual premise – or, more precisely, in order to present its relation of events as plausible history – the play moves in the direction of portraying characters that make calculated actions vis-à-vis the specific circumstances they encounter, thereby generating a realistic socio-political field that the characters successfully and unsuccessfully navigate in realistic ways. Crucially, *King Johan*'s characterological realism extends beyond its convention-breaking depiction of real historical people like King John, Cardinal Stephen Langton and Pope Innocent III to include its portrayal of allegorical figures like Clergy, Nobility and Sedition, who are themselves imbued with sufficient individuating markers of class, profession, ideology and temperament to aid in the production of a fictive social sphere that mirrors the one real courtiers and kings in the mid-sixteenth century had to navigate. As we have already seen, Skelton's *Magnificence* lays the groundwork for this with its presentation of characters like Cloaked Collusion and Courtly Abusion, but whereas *Magnificence* uses its allegorical characters to denote categories of action, *King Johan* uses them to denote categories of people (i.e. Nobility, Clergy and Civil Order, a character that stands for all lawyers), thereby naming distinct constituencies that can all collude against the king, but for different reasons and to different ends. Ultimately, then, the play's increased degree of realism is produced by each character's alignment with the kind of agenda-bearing subject-position that adheres to a specific type of person: the noble who must balance loyalty to liege-lord with religious duty and the advancement of his own position, the Catholic clergy member who (from a Protestant prospective, at least) self-indulgently contributes to ecclesiastical bloat. Indeed, even a character like Sedition, whose name continues to denote a category of action, is portrayed in the dialogue as a specific type of person: the ambitious up-and-comer who conspires against one authority figure (the king) in order to ingratiate himself with another (the Pope). These characters lack the granular detail to stand for individual people, but their main positions and attributes allow them to be read as 'social persons', Elizabeth Fowler's term for 'familiar concepts of social being that attain currency through common use'.[16] They are not individuals so much as types, and as such they convey just enough about each character's goals and disposition to collectively generate a virtual field of sociality, albeit a rough-hewn one.

The play begins with King Johan encountering Ynglond, a widow who tells him about the injustices heaped upon her by the Catholic Church. This information leads Johan to secure the agreement of Nobility, Civil Order and Clergy (the first two quite willingly, the last, with reluctance) to break from the Pope. These preliminary scenes are not particularly realistic, but they pave the way for the play's second movement, in which Clergy, Usurped Power, Sedition, Dissimulation, Stephen Langton and the Pope plan and enact their opposition. This is where we see the play's political virtuality emerge in a more robust way, beginning with a series of scenes devoted to strategic thinking. First, lesser characters speculatively game out the various power plays in which the Pope and King Johan might engage (a dramaturgic technique that will become widespread in realist drama of the late sixteenth century). Then, the Pope devises a three-pronged strategy that includes excommunicating King Johan, reasserting authority over the English bishops, and pressuring other monarchs to abjure the English king. These scenes of prudential deliberation are then followed by scenes of calculated action.

Sedition administers the rite of confession to Nobility, using the occasion to convince Nobility that the fate of his soul lies in allegiance to the Pope's cause, and Stephen Langton and Clergy pair up to approach Civil Order and draw out his more worldly investment in the status quo:

> For yf the church thryve than do we lawers thryve,
> And yf they decay ower welth ys not alyve.
> Therfor we must helpe yowr state, masters, to uphold,
> Or elles owr profyttes wyll cache a wynter colde.[17]

Instead of depicting the implementation of the Pope's three-part plan, which viewers understand to be carried out off-stage, Bale dramatises the opportunity and means by which agents of the Pope subvert King Johan's political support-ers, those to whom Johan turns for aid when fending off the Pope's pressure campaign and whose betrayal finally breaks Johan and leads to his capitulation. Taken together, Bale's realistic staging of (1) the Catholic opposition's strategic planning, (2) the subversion of Nobility and Civil Order, and (3) King Johan's subsequent collapse under pressure creates the dramatic conditions for a multiplicity of practical lessons. Viewers can engage in optative evaluation of King Johan, noting his overconfidence in the loyalty of his subjects and speculating on what he'd need to have done differently to secure a better outcome. Alternatively, they can attend to the Catholic contingent's more effective navigation of political circumstance, reflecting on this successful example of practi-cal wisdom in action (regardless of the negatively valenced ends to which this *phronesis* is put). Finally, in the play's denouement, viewers can join Nobility, Civil Order and Clergy in their regretful reconsideration of their own com-plicity in King Johan's fall, parsing their past actions (and the moral calculations that prompted them) to see where they went wrong.

Compared to earlier, more conventional morality plays, *King Johan* innovates in its effort to engage viewers' capacity for prudential judgment, shifting the play's didactic balance away from prescriptive instruction and toward practical instruction by depicting a field of socially placed agents striving to exert their wills upon one another. Yet the representational techniques Bale uses to achieve these effects – dependent as they are on characters figured primarily as 'social persons' – result in only a rudimentary sort of realism, one that does not capture the degree of circumstantial specificity (of a given situation, but also of the dispositional and experiential attributes characters bring to that situation) to serve as a nuanced and flexible training ground for viewers' practical wisdom. Indeed, we do not see this more mature form of characterological realism for another forty or so years, and when we do, we begin to see it everywhere. What can explain this sudden change? As we will see, dramatists in the late sixteenth century develop new and significantly better ways to make drama serve as a vehicle for practical didacticism by modelling themselves on the historians of their day.

Learning from History: Realism's Maturation in Early Modern Drama

From its beginnings in late fourteenth-century Italy, humanist historiography has looked to historical events for moral, ethical and political lessons that can be applied to the present day. Early Italian humanists like Leonardo Bruni and Poggio Bracciolini were politicians with an abiding interest in mastering precisely the kind of practical wisdom that Aristotle addresses in his *Ethics*.[18] Consequently, they approached history as an archive of situationally specific examples from which to infer practical insights that could be put to use in future political manoeuvres. To view historical particularity in this way is in one sense to depart from Aristotle, for whom historical events are too causally chaotic and unpredictable to be an object of philosophical inquiry, but this reversal in history's philosophical standing is driven by a competing element of Aristotle's legacy: the impulse to solve the didactic problem posed by *phronesis*.[19] Indeed, Isaac Casaubon, one of the great French humanists of the sixteenth century, describes the discipline of history as 'nothing else but a kind of philosophy using examples', a definition that positions historical inquiry as a means of conducting the project of moral and political philosophy with an object of analysis that affords greater circumstantial nuance, thereby generating insights that have targeted applicability in the real world.[20]

The fact that humanist historians rely on books for their knowledge of past events might be taken to indicate an engagement with history that relies on an Aristotelian conception of probability, but this assumption is contradicted by the revisionism often on display in humanist historiography.[21] Machiavelli, for example, portrays Castruccio Castracani not as a petty tyrant of Lucca but as a great statesman able to unify and defend Italy, a transformation that, as Irving Ribner notes, he accomplishes by larding his description of Castracani with events drawn from the life of Agathocles, the tyrant of Syracuse, as reported by Diodorus Sicilus.[22] Set against 'historical truth', Machiavelli's Frankenstein-like amalgamation might more appropriately be called a fiction, but if that is the case, it is a fiction he assembles out of probabilistic building blocks, ones that are the product of applying an intuitive form of statistical likeliness to the complex causality encountered in real life. This is to suggest that Machiavelli takes up the idea of history's reproducibility – the idea that a given set of circumstances leveraged in a given way is likely to result in a given outcome – and applies it to the construction of a hypothetical progression of circumstances, actions and consequences upon which readers can exercise their practical wisdom.

I would argue that all humanist historians, both those who work hard to separate myth from historical truth and those who, like Machiavelli, purposefully take creative licence, hold to a notion of probable causality in their construction of history. But I highlight the heuristic value to be found in the kind of prudential analysis Machiavelli undertakes because it rests on examples that are fictional as much as they are historical. In the case of Castracani, Machiavelli bases his optative speculations not on the circumstances of a real happening but rather on a virtual (and therefore realistic) sequence of his own devising, one ideally suited to the lesson he seeks to impart. In doing so, he anticipates fiction's capacity to overtake history as a more flexible and far-reaching 'kind of philosophy using examples'. As we have already seen, playwrights like Skelton and Bale set a precedent early in the sixteenth century for drama with the didactic ambition to address the concerns of political philosophy, and in Bale we even see clear gestures toward virtuality as the representational means of accommodating this ambition. Yet characterological realism undergoes its most notable uptick both in degree and ubiquity only in the late sixteenth century onward, and the influence of humanist historiography – most especially that of Machiavelli – plays a large role in the period's growing expectation for practical didacticism in the dramatisation of social life.

Most obviously, the line of influence between early modern historiography and the rise of dramatic realism can be seen in the development of the English history play, especially with the emergence of its mature form as instantiated by Christopher Marlowe's *Edward II* (1594). The difference lies in the fact that Marlowe looks to contemporary works of history not only for raw source material but also, and much more importantly, for lessons in historiography's general mode of inquiry – that of examining the causality of events in order to produce optative judgments about the ethics of

effective action. In this latter respect, Marlowe takes his cue
not from Raphael Holinshed, whose *Chronicles of England,
Scotland, and Ireland* provides much of the source material
for the play, but rather from Machiavelli, whose approach to
historical example better intuits that fidelity to probable causality offers a more flexible and nuanced basis for prudential
instruction than fidelity to real happenings. In *Edward II*,
Marlowe reduces Holinshed's long and winding account of
Edward's twenty-year reign to a plot that is much narrower
in scope, both in terms of time frame and the number of
active participants represented in the socio-political field.
In doing so, he departs from Holinshed's didactic emphasis on Edward's wanton overindulgences and rash approach
to decision-making in order to instead focus on the political
consequence of his immoderate favouritism of Gaviston.[23] In
his pared down rendering of events, Marlowe weaves into the
dialogue those details of circumstance and personal disposition that enable viewers to understand the threat Gaviston's
preferential treatment poses to members of England's peer-
age. What's more, in the action that follows from this point
of contention, Marlowe adheres to a principle of probable
causality that allows viewers to evaluate Edward's failure to
act upon the circumstances of his nobles' unrest in a way
that would have saved his throne. As an occasion for vicarious prudential training, the accurate historicity of a play like
Edward II is essentially beside the point, and this becomes
especially clear in light of another history play that moralises
on a young king's approach to managing friendships: Shakespeare's 2 *Henry IV*. Shakespeare inserts Falstaff and the rest
of Hal's rabble-rousing crew into the play's action as entirely
fictional characters, and one obvious reason for his doing
so is to establish the realistic terms under which Hal must
distance himself from the obligations of friendship in order
to secure the allegiance of his noble vassals upon elevation

to the throne. Here, we have an instance of dramatic realism teaching practical wisdom by way of a positive example.

In these and other history plays, dramatic realism underwrites the commensurability between the historical and the fictional, both of which can be the basis for practical instruction so long as a character's actions produce realistic outcomes given the circumstances in which they occur. Yet it is important to understand that playwrights in this period arrive at this working understanding of dramatic realism precisely by taking their cue from contemporary historians, whose prudential analysis of historical example calls on a different way to think about, and make use of, the topics of circumstance so essential to forensic rhetoric and arguments of proof. Forensic rhetoric, as conceived in Aristotle's *Art of Rhetoric*, pertains to the discussion of past actions. It chiefly serves as a means of substantiating truth-claims about consequential events when, as is often the case, there is incomplete evidential and testimonial knowledge of what happened and of the precise role a given person played in its happening. To this end, the forensic rhetorician attends to the topics of circumstance (time, place, opportunity, means, motive, etc.) because they offer a way to infer beyond what is strictly known about a past deed, especially when it comes to the element least available to direct verification: an actant's internal causes. In the legal context from which forensic rhetoric largely springs, proving an alleged criminal's guilt without recourse to smoking-gun evidence requires more than establishing opportunity, means and a possible motive; one must also establish that the proposed motivating factors would plausibly move the specific person in question to commit the alleged act. Evidence that a man had discovered signs of his wife's infidelity prior to her untimely demise does not, in itself, mean that he killed her, for cuckoldry does not drive every man to murder. However, if the man in question is a military hero with both a history of upholding his masculine honour and considerable experience in ending people's lives, then it becomes more plausible that marital infidelity would cause him to enact his wife's death. Crucially, what makes the husband's guilt believable – or, let us say, realistic – in this instance, is our trust that personal circumstances (blooded soldier, honour-bound masculinity) index the probability that someone will react to situational circumstances (unfaithful wife) in a certain way.

When it comes to legal arguments that deal in matters of guilt and innocence – wherein the aim is to know exactly what a person did in a given time and place and to determine precisely what he or she meant by it – realism figures as a necessary but uneasy stand-in for reality. But for someone like Machiavelli, who invokes the past both to exemplify and to particularise his political philosophy, realism, not reality, serves as the benchmark for accurate argumentation. We see this subordination of the real when, in a dedicatory letter appended to his *Discourses*, Machiavelli acknowledges that he 'may have erred in many circumstances herein', a deployment of the humility topos that is at once earnest and wholly unconcerned.[24] Acknowledging errors in the facticity of historical detail comes at no particular cost to his vicarious exercise of *phronesis*, a procedure requiring only that his examples connect the internal and external elements of a causal chain of events on a probabilistic basis. For dramatists in the late sixteenth century, Machiavelli's insight into the value of virtuality offered a way forward for a dramatic tradition that, despite being ill-equipped to do so, had already taken up the didactic challenge of improving viewers' practical wisdom. With this lesson in hand, it quickly becomes possible to produce the kind of mature realism that we see in a play like Shakespeare's *Othello*, in which a rich tapestry of circumstantial detail serves not only to make believable Othello's decision to murder

Desdemona (the goal of forensic rhetoric), but also to create the conditions under which viewers and readers can parse Othello's errors of judgment and to speculate on the means by which he might have avoided his tragic fate (the goal of prudential analysis, both in history and in fiction).

In history plays like *Edward II* and *2 Henry IV*, characterological realism bears the most obvious family resemblance to Machiavelli's objects of ethico-political analysis, for they, too, dress virtual fictionality in the guise of real historical event, like a cuckoo putting its eggs in another bird's nest. And yet, as my reference to *Othello* demonstrates, playwrights of the period clearly saw the potential to deploy realism without the protective veneer of reality. Across a number of genres, Shakespeare and his contemporaries developed a new dramaturgy defined by its sensitivity to the protocols of practical didacticism, and this is perhaps nowhere more evident than in their modernisation of tragic form. We know from Aristotle that, in classical theatre, tragedy follows from the mimesis of an action that involves *hamartia*, an error that is entirely beyond the protagonist's control (as is the case when Oedipus unknowingly kills his father and sleeps with his mother).[25] But as François Rigolot reminds us, early modern thinkers interpreted *hamartia* in two different ways, distinguishing between 'normal' errors (what we might call accidents of fate), and 'abnormal' errors (in which an individual's ethical failings result in incompetent and imprudent actions).[26] In classical Greek tragedy, the audience is provoked to feelings of pity and fear because they are made to reflect on the unavoidability of certain disasters. In early modern tragedy, by contrast, the audience bears witness to a form of tragic action understood to hinge on the protagonist's ethical shortcomings, a state of affairs that in turn leads theatregoers to reflect on the best means of actively avoiding the protagonist's tragic end. We might think, here, of the unforced error Hamlet is understood to commit when he indulges his melancholy disposition at the expense of avenging his father, or of the mistake Bussy D'Ambois makes when he gives free rein to his 'cannibal valour', thereby exposing himself as an ungovernable threat to the ambitious nobles at the court of France's Henri III.[27]

The handful of early modern plays that I've highlighted are, I argue, indicative of a widespread shift toward characterological realism. Of course, decisively proving the ubiquity of this period's realist turn would take more space than I can afford to give, for such a task calls for close analysis of a great many plays spanning a wide sweep of generic terrain, and I must move more quickly if I am to arrive at this chapter's ultimate aim of attending not to realism's didactic success but rather to a key site of its failure. That being said, it will help to ground my claims about characterological realism in at least one sustained close reading of a play that speaks to the larger trend. Thomas Kyd's *The Spanish Tragedy*, however sensational its plot may seem to be, does just that, for it sets a lasting precedent in its ambition to distribute virtuality across an entire social field, enabling practical didacticism to operate in a more decentralised way.

Characterological Realism: A Case Study

Kyd alerts viewers to the omnivorousness of his play's practical didacticism though a subplot that centres on a cast of otherwise marginal characters. Comprising two disparate scenes spanning only 203 lines, this subplot concerns one Portuguese nobleman's ploy to gain political advantage while simultaneously doing away with a competing peer. Act I, scene iii begins with the Viceroy of Portugal lamenting his decision to squander his treasure, his people's blood, and, most damningly, his own son in a failed bid to conquer Spanish lands. Alexandro, a Portuguese nobleman, interrupts his lord's mournful complaint about actions gone awry to offer a ray of hope: Prince Balthazaar must still live, albeit as a prisoner of war. The Viceroy doubts that Spain will have spared Balthazaar's life, and Villuppo, another nobleman, turns the Viceroy's fears into an opportunity for personal advancement. Villuppo attests to witnessing Alexandro cooperate in a Spanish ploy to unseat Balthazaar from his horse and to seeing the Spanish drag Balthazaar's lifeless corpse back to their tents. An enraged Viceroy then sentences Alexandro to a slow and painful death. In Act III, scene i, the Portuguese ambassador returns from his mission to Spain, bringing news that Balthazaar is not only alive but is a candidate for royal marriage to Bel-Imperia, the Spanish king's niece, leading the Viceroy to free a vindicated Alexandro and sentence Villuppo to death instead.

Notably, this subplot's characterological realism springs from Villuppo's delivery and the Viceroy's receipt of a forensic argument of proof. When Villuppo accuses Alexandro of traitorously colluding with the Spanish, he paints a picture that strategically invokes circumstantial details about Alexandro's opportunity (he was standing close behind Balthazaar) and his means (he loudly shot his pistol, thus surprising and unhorsing the prince). Alexandro protests this 'wicked forgery', but the Viceroy is so taken with the plausibility of Villuppo's forensic theory that he adds to it:

> Thou false, unkind, unthankful, traitorous beast,
> Wherein had Balthazaar offended thee,
> Was't Spanish gold that bleared so thine eyes
> That thou couldst see no part of our deserts?
> Perchance, because thou art Terceira's lord,
> Thou hadst some hope to wear this diadem,
> If first my son and then myself were slain;
> But thy ambitious thought shall break thy neck.
> Aye, this was it that made thee spill his blood. (I, iii, 77–86)

First entertaining the prospect that Spain has bribed Alexandro with money, then settling on the more grounded possibility that Alexandro, a powerful landed noble, is making a play for the Portuguese crown, the Viceroy does exactly what forensic rhetoric and the evaluation of circumstantial evidence requires: he turns to probability as a way to construct truth-claims about actions and events about which he possesses incomplete knowledge. As many philosophers have liked to note, it is illogical for fictional characters to make truth-claims about a non-real world, yet the Viceroy's realism rests not on the technical validity of his truth-claims but on the probabilistic approach he takes to making them. More specifically, the Viceroy's characterological realism rests on Kyd's having crafted a fictional world whose probabilities more-or-less map onto our own, meaning that viewers are able to follow and evaluate the Viceroy's circumstantial judgments. Like the Viceroy, we can understand that Alexandro, as a landed noble, is plausibly motivated by the prospect of becoming king; and we can also discern the Viceroy's hastiness in rushing to judgment, armed as we are with retrospective knowledge of Alexandro's innocence. A philosopher might rightly insist that nothing in this scene is real, but this scene's dramatic action can be deemed realistic to the degree that viewers and readers are put in a position to judge a character's circumstantial judgments.

Of course, this subplot's overt practical didacticism focuses not on the Viceroy but on Villuppo. While the Viceroy makes a circumstantial judgment that viewers can in turn evaluate, his forensic analysis of a past event does not involve *phronesis*. In other words, he does not engage in a forward-looking determination of the actions that will result in a particular outcome under a given set of circumstances. By contrast, Villuppo presents his argument of proof to the Viceroy with a specific political objective in mind, a guiding motive that viewers learn about when, at the end of the first scene, he indulges in a moment of private self-address:

> Thus have I with envious, forgèd tale
> Deceived the king, betrayed mine enemy,
> And hope for guerdon of my villainy. (I, iv, 93–5)

The disclosure of this political motive makes legible Villupo's prudential bid to advance his position at court, his seizing on the opportunity presented by Balthazaar's capture (along with the Viceroy's doomsday imagination) and his constructing an argument of proof as the means of achieving his objective. In doing so, it also makes legible the lesson of Villuppo's poor judgment in claiming to have seen Balthazaar's corpse, thereby building his argument of proof on the edifice of an easily disproven falsehood.

Taken on its own, this subplot's didacticism might be mistaken for Christian moralising on the penalties and rewards meted out by divine providence, but Kyd's investment in a more secular and amoral form of practical didacticism becomes apparent in the broader context of the play's consistent representational levelling of its villains and revengers – a levelling instantiated most clearly in the utilisation of soliloquys and asides. In *The Spanish Tragedy*, only villains and revengers publicly divulge their innermost thoughts, moments of disclosure in which these characters deliberate on the means they should apply toward achieving their particular ends. In the scene following Villuppo's private confession of villainy, Bel-Imperia wrestles with her newfound attraction to Horatio – a courtship she is reluctant to indulge before she has 'revenge[d] the death' of her first love, Andrea – and she resolves this conflict by instrumentalising her new romance:

> Yes, second love shall further my revenge.
> I'll love Horatio, my Andrea's friend,
> The more to spite the prince that wrought his end.
> (I, iv, 65–8)

Shortly thereafter, Bel-Imperia's brother, Lorenzo, discusses his plan to cement his friendship with Balthazaar by killing Horatio, who they identify as the obstacle to Balthazaar's romantic success; subsequent scenes are peppered with soliloquys in which Lorenzo reflects on the best means by which to commit the series of murders that become necessary to the maintenance of his interests. Like Villuppo's moment of self-address, Bel-Imperia's and Lorenzo's soliloquys provide viewers with an understanding of their objectives along with at least some of their practical calculations for bringing them about, information that enables viewers to test each character's practical wisdom against the unfolding plot and the knowable circumstances of the play-world depicted therein. For a theatregoer interested in the vicarious exercise of his or her own prudential judgment, it does not matter whether the goal belongs to a revenger or a villain. Viewers judge Bel-Imperia's prudence in instrumentalising her romantic attachment to Horatio – a decision that leads to his murder – for the same reason they judge the efficacy of Lorenzo's efforts to cover up his role in Horatio's death: to submit their own powers of judgment to trial.

Kyd's deployment of soliloquys and asides suggests that the construction of interiority – often thought to be a defining feature of the late sixteenth-century's bourgeoning modernity – is something of a side effect, a secondary, almost accidental feature of a literary realism primarily geared toward the edifying dramatisation of lifelike characters exercising their prudential judgment. This is especially true when it comes to Hieronimo, the play's principle revenger. To be sure, key moments of Hieronimo's self-address – like his initial lamentation at discovering Horatio's body or his brief bout of weighing the satisfaction of revenge against the release of suicide – are introspective rather than action-oriented, but the majority of his soliloquys are devoted to prudential strategising, and these moments provide the foundation for the revenge plot's characterological realism. Take, for example, the dramatisation of Hieronimo's thought-process when he discovers Bel-Imperia's letter communicating the facts of his son's murder:

> My son slain by Lorenzo and the prince!
> What cause had they Horatio to malign?
> Or what might move thee, Bel-imperia,
> To accuse thy brother had he been the mean?
> Hieronimo, beware; thou art betrayed,
> And to entrap thy life this train is laid.
> Advise thee therefore; be not credulous.
> This is devisèd to endanger thee,
> That thou, by this, Lorenzo should draw
> Thy life in question and thy name in hate.
> Dear was the life of my belovèd son,
> And his death behoves me be revenged;
> Then hazard not thine own, Hieronimo,
> But live t'effect thy resolution.
> I therefore will by circumstances try
> What I can gather to confirm this writ. (III, ii, 33–49)

In this passage, both Hieronimo's characterological realism and the psychological depth that attends it are tied to his scepticism. I do not say this simply because Hieronimo's unwillingness to be credulous about the content of Bel-Imperia's letter marks him out as worldly (as opposed to being unrealistically naïve), but also, and more importantly, because the logic underwriting his scepticism can only be legible to viewers and readers if the terms of his fictional worldliness more-or-less mirror the terms of real worldliness. If we find realism in Hieronimo's sceptical reaction to the letter, it is because we understand his experience-based calculation regarding the improbability of Bel-Imperia wanting to betray her own brother to correspond to the improbability of a sister wanting to betray her own brother in the real world. In other words, we understand Hieronimo to be operating in a probabilistic universe that nominally replicates the probabilities of our own.

Of course, viewers know that Hieronimo is wrong to base his calculations on the most probable relationship between a generic brother and sister, and this knowledge – which likewise springs from the play's reproduction of real-world probabilities – is the very thing that renders Hieronimo's subjectivity legible to us. Unbeknownst to Hieronimo, Bel-Imperia has been kidnapped by her brother after seeing him murder Horatio in cold blood. From the perspective of viewers and readers, who are privy to this additional information, Bel-Imperia has a perfectly valid motive for betraying her brother, and we can recognise that motive's validity precisely because the average real-world sister would feel less than loyal to her brother under the same set of circumstances. As viewers, we have an advantage over Hieronimo that makes us aware of the epistemological asymmetry between ourselves and him. We possess a set of facts about Bel-Imperia that we know to be unavailable to Hieronimo, and our knowledge of this asymmetry forces us to recognise his other-mindedness, his lifelike possession of a subject-position that differs from our own. By having Hieronimo soliloquise over the reliability of Bel-Imperia's letter, Kyd depicts Hieronimo's interiority with a degree of realism that has little precedent in medieval drama, and we can see, in this instance, that Kyd's representation of interiority does not function as an aesthetic goal in and of itself. Instead, Kyd's portrayal of subjectivity emerges as a secondary effect of his concerted effort to depict a character engaging in circumstantial analysis.

For Kyd, the guiding purpose of conducting such an analysis – both in life and in fiction – is prudential rather than forensic. To be sure, Hieronimo most obviously weighs circumstances in a forensic register; he sifts through evidence of a past event to infer more knowledge about it and its agents, and his subjectivity comes into dramatic relief as a result of this deliberative activity. But Hieronimo's concern for understanding past actions stems from his ongoing need to determine what he should do in the future and how he should go about doing it. This prudential orientation is encoded in his resolution to 'by circumstances try / What [he] can gather to confirm this writ.' Precisely because his forensic analysis of Bel-Imperia's letter remains inconclusive – the details he knows of her do not fit together in a way that can make the letter and its information plausible in his eyes – Hieronimo commits himself to discovering the particulars behind Bel-Imperia's writing of the letter so he can better determine what to believe about its contents. In this context, Hieronimo's chosen method to achieve his goal (trial 'by . . . circumstances') does not name an argument of proof, the forensic act of inferring additional likely particulars behind Bel-Imperia's letter writing from the more knowable circumstances to be deduced from the evidence of the letter itself. Rather, it names the prudential act of determining when the particulars of a new situation, if leveraged in the right way, will result in his uncovering the information he seeks. In this sense, to try by circumstances is to set one's practical wisdom to the task of determining when, in the midst of unfolding events, serviceable conditions arise for achieving one's goal.

Kyd uses this soliloquy to draw viewers' attention to Hieronimo's heightened need of *phronesis*, a need that extends – quite pointedly – to the actual commission of his vengeance. When Hieronimo later confirms Lorenzo's hand in the murder of his son, he renews his determination to avenge Horatio's death, a soliloquy in which Kyd once again has his protagonist reflect on the practical wisdom he must exercise in order to bring about his objective:

> I will revenge his death!
> But how? Not as the vulgar wits of men,
> With open, but inevitable ills,
> As by a secret, yet a certain mean,
> Which under kindship will be cloakèd best.
> Wise men will take their opportunity,
> Closely and safely fitting things to time.
> But in extremes advantage hath no time,
> And therefore all times fit not for revenge.
> Thus, therefore, will I rest me in unrest,
> Dissembling quiet in unquietness,
> Not seeming that I know their villainies. (III, xiii, 20–31)

By having Hieronimo describe, in general terms, the practical wisdom he must employ in the undertaking of his revenge, Kyd primes viewers to evaluate his protagonist's application of prudential judgment in the action that follows. Does Hieronimo succeed at being wise? Does he fit things to time in a manner that effects the maximum amount of vengeance? The answers to these questions are, of course, open to debate, but viewers and readers have a strong impulse to engage in such a debate precisely because the play's characterological realism invites interpretations motivated by a hermeneutics of practical didacticism. Viewers can disagree over the precise lesson to be drawn from Hieronimo's vengeful appropriation of dramatic spectacle, debating not only the broader question of whether his utilisation of available circumstances is exemplary or cautionary, but also the more nuanced question of whether his responses to particular conditions might be altered to better effect. In bringing the play to a close, Kyd avoids heavy-handed moralising, instead leaving viewers to judge matters for themselves, and in doing so he proves to be especially canny about the source of characterological realism's practical value.

In laying out the broad strokes of what characterological realism is and why it was valued by early modern producers and consumers of drama, I have neglected a necessary proviso: it should go without saying that no work of literature is perfectly realistic – far from it. First, just as a digital photograph is made of a finite number of pixilated colours and thus falls short of visible reality, so too does the mimesis of action carry within it fewer circumstantial particulars than cohere around a real event. In such matters, one can strive for completeness, but one can never achieve it. Second, it is impossible for any author to consistently join actions to consequences through links of the very most probable causality, not least because such a superlative judgment of the probable is itself an impossibility. Third, authors who are aiming in many respects for realism continue to draw on narrative and symbolic logics that are not realistic at all. For these reasons, no instance of characterological realism is ever truly real. Nevertheless, the very fact that this representational mode becomes so widespread as to be normative – first with respect to drama, then, in the eighteenth century and beyond, with respect to the novel – suggests that viewers and readers seeking to exercise their prudential judgment found characterological realism to be real enough.

When Hamlet asserts that the purpose of playing is 'to hold as 'twere the mirror up to nature', thereby showing 'virtue her own feature' and 'scorn her own image', his qualifying 'as 'twere' announces the non-identity of the so-called mirroring function he understands realism to accomplish, a non-identity that nevertheless reflects enough of ourselves back to us to be a viable means for ethical self-inspection (III, ii, 20–1). Hamlet's 'as 'twere' is especially significant, in this context, because it invokes the means by which drama achieves its proxy reflective status. Dictionaries and style guides tell us that 'were' is a conjugation of the verb 'to be' set in the subjunctive past tense, the mood used to discuss various states of nonreality, including expressions of possibility and judgment. In claiming for drama the capacity to serve as a kind of subjunctive mirror through which we can inspect our virtues and vices, and in attributing that edifying function only to dramatisations that 'o'erstep not the modesty of nature', Hamlet implies that realism assembles its image of reality out of judgments of the possible and the probable – especially when it comes to the field of human action to which the moral virtues pertain. Moreover, in acknowledging that the failure to achieve dramatic naturalism 'make[s] the judicious grieve', Hamlet also attributes to the more discerning of viewers a capacity to judge when a dramatisation is sufficiently realistic to be the object of prudential analysis (III, ii, 24). Here, Hamlet appeals to something like the common-sense judgments that Aristotle, having confronted his inability to exercise readers' practical wisdom in anything but a general way, recommends for people who do not already possess an above-average degree of *phronesis*. In the case of literary realism – which exists precisely to provide the sort of iterative field for circumstantial particularity that, compared to the treatise form, can better exercise and strengthen an ordinary person's *phronesis* – common sense instead takes on a sorting function: it becomes the means by which viewers and readers discriminate between moments of fictional representation that pass a certain bar of virtuality and those that do not. This common-sense sorting function is essential to the rise of literary realism, for it is only through this more-or-less intuitive faculty of discrimination that realist literature of the early modern period onward has been able to serve with sufficient reliability as a source of practical instruction.

Belief in the Cynic Ideal, or, Practical Didacticism
Gone Wrong

Our ability to use characterological realism as an effective training ground for real-world *phronesis* is premised on our capacity to judge when verisimilitude is being achieved, and our capacity to separate realistic emplotment from the other literary logics that may at times guide an otherwise lifelike narrative. But while this faculty of common-sense judgment tends to perform its sorting function with approximate reliability, representations of the Cynic ideal seem perpetually to confound it. In part, this happens because a logic of ethical extremism subtends the courage of truth, the virtue understood to be the authorising basis for a truth-teller's effective critical practice and that Foucault shows to be at the heart of the critical tradition in the West. While a principle of moderation serves as the default rubric for judging the realism of action in a fictive social field, the history of associating truth-telling with a virtuous extreme introduces a different standard for depictions of the uncompromising truth-teller at work. And because literature is not in fact bound to the practical realities of life, it can represent action in ways that validate the Cynic ideal under the ostensible sign of realism. Just as in the *agora*, Diogenes let loose in the grounds of realist convention finds a way of challenging norms and defying standards.

This is precisely what happens in John Lyly's *Campaspe* (originally published in 1584). Set during the peaceful interlude separating the Theban and Persian wars, the play's primary plot revolves around the love triangle between Alexander, Campaspe (a captured handmaiden of mean parentage) and Appelles (an artist Alexander hires to paint Campaspe's portrait). The scenes that advance this plot fall into two categories, both of which possess a notable realism: the first focusing on Alexander and his efforts to position himself as a peacetime ruler, the second following Campaspe and Appelles as they navigate the constrained circumstances of their illicit romance. By contrast, the scenes that centre on Diogenes – which Lyly intersperses throughout the play, almost at the rate of one-to-one alternation – are a great deal flatter, offering almost nothing in the way of circumstantial detail and character development and instead presenting for viewer enjoyment a sort of 'best-of' montage of diogenical exchanges and ripostes. Nevertheless, Lyly's portrayal of Diogenes is essential to the didacticism he ultimately attaches to the play's central plot, for he makes it clear that Diogenes is the one and only person who can get Alexander to accept that he cannot command his way to Campaspe's love. Hence Diogenes' promotion (and Appelles' concomitant demotion) in the play's original title, *A moste excellent Comedie of Alexander, Campaspe, and Diogenes*. Depicting Diogenes as an effective truth-teller, Lyly rewards his radicality by giving him an honorary place in the play's love triangle.

Critics have tended to overlook Lyly's interest in the possibility of radically effective truth-telling, instead locating his didactic intent in what they understand to be Alexander's display of sovereign magnanimity, a lesson they expect a courtier like Lyly to advance for Elizabeth I's benefit in a play first performed at her court.[28] However, Lyly pointedly fends off this interpretation. Early in the play, Alexander resolves to make his court a place of genuine learning and enlightenment: 'My court shall be a school wherein I will have used as great doctrine in peace as I did in war discipline.'[29] To this end, Alexander invites a number of prominent philosophers to join his court, a sovereign request to which all but Diogenes graciously comply. These philosophers, headed by Aristotle, expect to counsel Alexander on matters pertaining to his rule, thus bringing him 'as near to the gods in wisdom' as he already is 'in dignity'. Yet Alexander quickly disabuses Aristotle and the others of this notion by withholding from them full freedom of speech: 'in kings' causes I will not stand to scholars' arguments' (I, iii, 89–90). By depicting Alexander and his obedient coterie of philosophers as they negotiate the rhetorical terms of their free speech – what they can and cannot discuss as if equals – Lyly lays the groundwork for his understanding of Diogenes' quite different freedom of speech.

In stark contrast with Aristotle and the others, Lyly's Diogenes does not depend upon Alexander's sanction and the precariousness of a merely rhetorical equality. Instead he speaks with the authority of a person whose way of life authenticates a new standard of sovereign autonomy, a person whose singular, self-authenticating *ethos* enables him to challenge Alexander so thoroughly on the subject of 'king's causes' that the philosopher brazenly refutes a premise the others take for granted: that Alexander stands above other men and is 'near to the gods . . . in dignity':

> *Alexander*: If Alexander have anything that may pleasure
> Diogenes, let me know, and take it.
> *Diogenes*: Then take not from me that you cannot give me,
> the light of the world.
> *Alexander*: What does thou want?
> *Diogenes*: Nothing that you have.
> *Alexander*: I have the world at command.
> *Diogenes*: And I in contempt.
> *Alexander*: Thou shalt live no longer than I will.
> *Diogenes*: But I shall die whether you will or
> no. (II, ii, 155–64)

Notably, the scene in which this first encounter takes place begins with an exchange between Alexander and his general, Hephastion, who tries to temper his lord's ardour for Campaspe by reminding him that 'affection commeth not by appointment or by birth; and then as good hated as enforced', to which Alexander testily responds, 'I am a king and will command' (II, ii, 114–17). Thus, it is only after Alexander asserts that his sovereignty extends to the commandment of love that Lyly stages the first of several encounters in which Diogenes refutes the supposed powers of Alexander's kingship – powers that, we have been made to understand, neither his soldiers nor his sages are allowed to question. In the last of these exchanges, Lyly's Alexander openly admits to the exceptionality of Diogenes' truth-telling: 'It skilleth not; I cannot be angry with him' (V, iv, 62). Almost immediately after making this admission, Alexander discovers the affair between Appelles and Campaspe and promptly grants them his blessing. The implication is clear: for Lyly, Diogenes shows that it is possible to successfully transact criticism without a sovereign interlocutor's willing participation. By this view, Diogenes acquires full freedom of speech through the practice of a particularly robust way of life – the only way of life understood to bring its practitioner into a state of true sovereignty, and therefore the only way of life to invest its practitioner with the power of sovereign truth. The play seems to suggest that when Diogenes critiques Alexander, he speaks with the force of an incontrovertible assertion.

Such a power of speech simply does not exist, but viewers and readers of the play can nevertheless conclude that it does because the logic of narrative emplotment equates sequence with causality. Diogenes confronts Alexander with the fact that his sovereignty has limits; shortly thereafter, Alexander renounces his claim to Campaspe and blesses her union with Appelles. This is not to suggest that sequence alone can convince discerning viewers that a given representation of causality is realistic, but viewers can find this particular instance of implied causation to be convincing for two reasons. First, the play achieves more realistic causality elsewhere and therefore establishes itself as a more-or-less credible object of practical analysis. Second, and most importantly, the history

of associating radically effective truth-telling with a virtuous extreme invites viewers to see the Cynic critical ideal as
being practicable, even though it isn't. Taken together, these
factors make it possible for the representation of effective
Cynic truth-telling to operate under the sign of realism and
hence to be read through a hermeneutics of practical didacticism, thereby enabling it to be taken more seriously than
ever before.

This, at least, is one consequence of applying the protocols of characterological realism to the representation of
Cynic truth-telling. But there is also another, opposing effect
in which the judgments that produce realism deny Cynic *parrhêsia*'s revolutionary potential, leading to depictions that
insist on the inevitable failure of any parrhesiast who resorts
to an ethics of extremity. Indeed, Lyly, despite his pointed
endorsement of diogenical truth-telling in the context of confronting Alexander, is guided by the pressures of realism to
stage this latter outcome when Diogenes deploys the same
frank acerbity against the coterie of obedient philosophers
who answered Alexander's call. Immediately after Alexander
makes clear that he will heed no scholar's advice when it
comes to 'king's causes', Alexander departs, leaving his par-
rhesiastically circumscribed philosophers to indulge in a brief
walk-and-talk that results in their coming across Diogenes:

> *Plato*: Let us question a little with Diogenes, why he went
> not with us to Alexander.
>> [*Exeunt* CLEANTHES and CHRYSIPPUS.]
>> [DIOGENES *is discovered in his tub*.]
> Diogenes, thou didst forget thy duty, that thou wentst not
> with us to the king.
> *Diogenes*: And you your profession, that you went to the
> king.
> *Plato*: Thou takest as great pride to be peevish, as others do
> glory to be virtuous. (I, iii, 127–33)

This is the first time playgoers get to see Diogenes in action, and what they witness is the Cynic chastising Plato for not performing his philosophical duties correctly, the implication being that Plato abandoned his parrhesiastic responsibilities the moment he made himself subservient to Alexander's will. What's more, viewers witness the relationship between Diogenes' extreme way of life and his blunt truth-telling – figured here by his inhabitation of a tub, on the one hand, and his bracingly informal second-person address of Plato, on the other – that presumably underwrites his unparalleled veridictive powers later in the play. In this instance, however, Plato is not bowled over by Diogenes' criticism. Quite to the contrary, he interprets Diogenes' candid denunciation of him as incontrovertible evidence of the Cynic's faulty disposition, his peevish pride. Here, realism asserts itself over Cynic idealism rather than the other way around.

I do not see Lyly's intention and self-reflexivity in the juxtaposition of these two assessments of Cynic *parrhêsia* (as if evidence of Diogenes' critical failures were intended to signal Lyly's scepticism toward the Cynic philosopher's one spectacular success). Rather, it seems to me that Lyly's overt didactic aim is to celebrate Cynic truth-telling's revolutionary potential and that the protocols of characterological realism simultaneously facilitate and thwart that aim. This, above all, is why the rise of dramatic realism raises Cynicism's crisis of character to an entirely new pitch, for it creates the conditions under which a person can mistake the Cynic ideal for something real, on the one hand, while also establishing the prudential framework under which a person will deny the possibility of ever acquiring unmitigated powers of veridiction, on the other. In Lyly's play, we encounter the two antithetical assessments of Cynic truth-telling that operate under the sign of realism, and we therefore see, in miniature, the conditions that produce Cynicism's crisis of character from the sixteenth century through to the present day.

Notes

1. The *locus classicus* for tying the rise of realism to the eighteenth-century novel is Watt's *The Rise of the Novel*.
2. For an early instance of the anti-Bradleyan critique, see Knights, *How Many Children Had Lady Macbeth?*
3. For scholarship on the early modern invention of self-addressed soliloquys and asides, see Hirsh, 'The Origin of the Late Renaissance Dramatic Convention of Self-Addressed Speech'.
4. Hutson, *Circumstantial Shakespeare*, p. 13. For an earlier iteration of Hutson's argument that is both more sustained and less focused on the dramatic deployment of topics of circumstance, see *The Invention of Suspicion*.
5. Jacob Burckhardt set the precedent for defining the Renaissance in terms of its emerging culture of individualism in 1860. See Burckhardt, *The Civilization of the Renaissance in Italy*. For examples of scholars advancing the Burckhardtian individualism thesis, see Cassirer, *The Individual and the Cosmos in Renaissance Philosophy*; Martin, *Myths of Renaissance Individualism*; and Strier, *The Unrepentant Renaissance*. As Strier puts it, 'Obviously there have always been individuals, but there has not always been individualism – an ideology that placed value on distinctiveness and personality' (p. 4). For examples of scholars who extend the individualism thesis to include the period's increased preoccupation with inwardness, see Maus, *Inwardness and Theater in the English Renaissance*; and Skura, *Tudor Autobiography*.
6. Shakespeare, *The Tragedy of Hamlet, Prince of Denmark* in *The Norton Shakespeare*, III, ii, 16–22.
7. 'Virtual', adj. *OED* 2a.
8. 'Virtual', *OED*, 2b.
9. Hampshire, *Innocence and Experience*.
10. Miller, *The Burdens of Perfection*, esp. pp. 191–218. Rooted in her theorisation of the indicative mood, Sarkar makes a similar point about 'speculative *poeisis*' in '*The Tempest*'s Other Plots'.
11. See Gallagher, *Telling It Like It Wasn't*.

12. For an account of the various ways medieval commentators dealt with Aristotelean *phronesis*, see Cerano, 'The Relation between Prudence and *Synderesis* to Happiness in Medieval Commentaries on Aristotle's *Ethics*'.

13. Aristotle, *The Ethics of Aristotle*, 1109a.

14. Though I point to Skelton's *Magnificence* as the first play of note in the shift from psychomachic to social allegorisation, this is not to say that there are not earlier, even less developed iterations of this change. For example, the characters New Guise and Nowadays in *Mankind* (Anon. *c.*1470) index a contemporary worldliness – a prioritisation of the fashionable here-and-now over any real concern for the afterlife – that taps into ideas about broad societal trends in a particular time and place. Thus, while New Guise names a mentality that a central dramatic character like Mankind can either possess or be tempted by, there is no psychomachic understanding of New Guise without a prior, nested understanding of the broader social matrix from which new fashions spring.

15. Skelton, *Magnificence*, pp. 115–24.

16. Fowler, *Literary Character*, p. 2.

17. Bale, *King Johan*, pp. 1263–6.

18. For an account of the specifically political didacticism that humanist historians brought to bear on history, see Ribner, *The English History Play in the Age of Shakespeare*, esp. pp. 12–24.

19. For an account of Aristotle's view that 'the actual world of the particular (the world of history) was imperfect and often incomprehensible because subject to the causation of mere accident', see Newsom, *A Likely Story*, p. 72.

20. Quoted in Ribner, *The English History Play in the Age of Shakespeare*, p. 16.

21. Aristotle defines probability as a way to speak about things that lack complete certainty as if they are universals. In the *Prior Analytics*, he explains that a probability is 'a generally approved proposition: what men know to happen or not to happen, to be or not to be, for the most part thus and thus, ... e.g. "the envious hate," "the beloved show affection"'.

In the *Art of Rhetoric*, he adds that '[t]he Probable is that which usually happens; (with the limitation, however, which is sometimes forgotten – namely that the thing may happen otherwise:) the Probable being related to that in respect of which it is probable as Universal to Particular'. Aristotle uses probability to name a relationship between things that is more understandable than the particularised world of real things. Not every envious person is hateful, but most are, and Aristotle understands fictional narratives to be probable to the extent that they fulfil this universalising gesture, meaning that all envious characters will also be hateful characters. Aristotle's account of literary probability thus inhibits realism to the extent that its deployment leads to representations that cannot capture the causative reasons why, under a particular set of circumstances, a person would be envious but not hateful. See Aristotle, *Prior Analytics*, 70a; and Aristotle, *Art of Rhetoric*, 1357a–b.

22. Ribner, *The English History Play in the Age of Shakespeare*, p. 17.

23. It is important to note that while Holinshed's history-telling aims for comprehensiveness (as compared with Machiavelli's emphasis on edifying examples) his relationship to history remains a didactic one. As Joan Parks notes, even Holinshed's *Chronicles*, which tends to be viewed as a hands-off compilation of competing historical accounts, frequently evaluates the effect an important figure's command of virtue ethics has on unfolding events. Hence Holinshed's remark that Edward II took 'small heed unto the good government of the commonwealth' because he 'gave himselfe to wantonness, passing his time in voluptuous pleasure, and riotous excesse'. Quoted in Parks, 'History, Tragedie, and Truth in Christopher Marlowe's *Edward II*', p. 281. See Holinshed, *The Chronicles of England, Scotland, and Ireland*, p. 847.

24. Machiavelli, *Machivael's [sic] discourses upon the first decade of T. Livius*, p. 498.

25. For an account of the scholarly consensus that understands Aristotelian *hamartia* to mean 'mistake of fact', and hence

an error that falls outside the protagonist's moral control, see Stinton, '*Hamartia* in Aristotle and Greek Tragedy'.

26. Rigolot, 'The Renaissance Fascination with Error', esp. pp. 1222–3.
27. Chapman, *Bussy D'Ambois*.
28. For an example of criticism that credits Alexander with magnanimity and faults Diogenes for being 'obstinate and self-centered', see Westlund, 'The Theme of Tact in *Campaspe*'.
29. Lyly, *Campaspe*, I, iii, 72–4. Further citations will be to this edition and in-text.

PART II

SHAKESPEARE'S CYNICS

CHAPTER 3

SHAKESPEARE'S BITTER FOOL:
THE POLITICS AND AESTHETICS
OF FREE SPEECH

Being asked what was the most beautiful thing in the world,
[Diogenes] replied, 'Freedom of speech [*parrhêsia*].'

Diogenes Laertius[1]

Shakespeare poses the problem of the frank truth-teller in the
test of love that famously opens *King Lear*. When Cordelia
refuses to participate in a rhetorical game that structurally
favours flattery over truth, she pegs her critique of the love-
test – and hence Lear's demand for it – on the assumption
that absolute candour will invest her statements with the
force of self-evidence. Yet this strategy quickly backfires, and
it is precisely Cordelia's principled inflexibility that allows
an offended Lear to discredit her:[2] 'Let pride, which she
calls plainness, marry her' (Q i, 118).[3] Coming to Cordelia's
defence, yet eager to avoid a similar fate, Kent endeavours
to moderate his firm admonishment of Lear by combining
his honesty with a healthy measure of praise.[4] But despite his
concession to pragmatism, Kent's more courtly strategy of
curbing his free speech does nothing to advance the goal of
curbing Lear's poor judgment:[5]

Kent: Royal Lear,
Whom I have ever honoured as my king,
Loved as my father, as my master followed,
As my great patron thought in my prayers –
Lear: The bow is bent and drawn, make from the shaft.
   (Q i, 28–32)

Now faced with decorum's insufficiency, its failure as a means
of communicating truth to an unwilling king, Kent returns to
the rigid stance initially held by Cordelia:

Be Kent unmannerly
When Lear is mad. . . . To plainness honour's bound
When majesty stoops to folly. (Q i, 134–8)

As we can now predict, this return to the strategy of speaking
freely and fearlessly does not go according to plan; instead
of persuading Lear to 'revoke [his] doom', Kent's 'unmannerly' conduct prompts Lear to denounce him as an unruly
subordinate who, like Cordelia before him, has displayed the
degenerate fault of 'strayed pride' (Q i, 152, 156).[6]

   In Cordelia's and Kent's sequential efforts to be honest with Lear, Shakespeare captures in miniature the cycle
of aspiration and failure that leads admirers of Diogenes
throughout the centuries to toggle between extremism and
moderation when acting the part of the Cynic truth-teller.
But while Shakespeare thematises the problem posed by
Cynic *parrhêsia* in this play's opening scene, this fact is only
apparent retrospectively. Shakespeare makes no allusion
whatsoever to Cynicism in these introductory pages, and
so there is no particular reason critics would think to read
Cordelia's and Kent's alternately blunt and decorous modes
of address in the context of Cynicism's vexed critical legacy.
However, this play features a third truth-teller – indeed,
much more centrally so – in the character of Lear's Fool, a

character that Shakespeare explicitly aligns with the figure of Diogenes in order to comment on the interpretive error that observers commit when evaluating representations of Cynic critique. Shakespeare, as we will see, understands that competing reactions to Cynic critical activity are the by-product of a practical imperative – to maximise one's communicative efficacy – that cannot come to grips with a specifically formal and aesthetic problem. I am referring to the problem of an aggressively free-speaking stance that can be viewed as either the most or the least tenable position from which to speak truth to power. Drawing our attention to both the beauty and the beastliness of the rigidly Cynic stance, Shakespeare invites us to get stuck, to pause at the very cusp of this reversibility, to dwell at the impossible juncture between antithetical perspectives; he invites us to see both sides of the Cynic coin in one instant, and, in so doing, to understand that the joke of its shifting value is on us. In order to achieve this effect, Shakespeare undertakes the characterisation of a composite Cynic stance, and, as I will show, it is precisely this undertaking that gives form to the Shakespearean fool.

In his depiction of wise fools, Shakespeare isolates the formal problem that lies at the heart of Cordelia and Kent's practical dilemma, the problem, that is to say, of a single socio-ethical stance that can be viewed as the basis for achieving either maximal or minimal critical agency. To support my claim that Shakespeare demonstrates a sustained interest in addressing the conflicting literary and practical dimensions of Cynic truth-telling through his characterisation of wise fools, I begin with a section on Shakespeare's appropriation of diogeneana in *Timon of Athens*, *Twelfth Night* and *King Lear*. In the first two plays, Shakespeare directly links the figure of the fool to the composite Cynic stance, and in *King Lear*, he uses this established affiliation to mark the mistake that Lear makes when identifying Tom o'Bedlam as a Cynic instead of the Fool. I then turn to the scene in which Lear's Fool first makes his entrance, a scene that epitomises Shakespeare's characterisation of a composite Cynic stance. This evaluative harlequinism is rendered most vividly in a passage, unique to the Quarto edition of *King Lear*, wherein the Fool offers his response to Lear's accusation of bitterness.

Characterising the Composite Cynic

Shakespeare most obviously reflects upon Cynicism through the figure of Apemantus, a character in *Timon of Athens* who is described in the dramatis personae as 'a churlish philosopher'.[7] Though never explicitly identified as a Cynic, Apemantus discloses his philosophical commitments through an antagonistic stance toward others and an insistence on 'plain dealing' (I, i, 221). Moreover, the rejoinders of his stung interlocutors point to Cynicism's etymology, which stems from the Greek adjective for dog-like, *kynikos*: 'You're a dog'; 'Away, unpeaceable dog, or I'll spurn thee hence!' (I, i, 203, 270). Though Apemantus plays an important role as a foil for Timon (the play's misanthropic protagonist), our more immediate concern is the conspicuous trouble to which Shakespeare goes in order to forge a connection between Apemantus and the play's professional fool, whose stage presence extends for a brief 78 lines in Act II, scene ii. Apemantus and the Fool enter and exit together, and they share the duty of disparaging the three servants who wait to collect money from Timon on behalf of their masters. This tag-teamed volley of criticism ends with the kind of dialogue that unapologetically explains its own agenda:

> *Varro's Servant*: Thou art not altogether a fool.
> *Fool*: Nor thou altogether a wise man. As much foolery as
>   I have, so much wit thou lack'st.
> *Apemantus*: That answer might have become Apemantus.
>   (II, ii, 118–22)

In reciprocal fashion, the Fool likens himself to Apemantus when the departing Cynic instructs his associate to withdraw: 'I do not always follow lover, elder brother, and woman; sometime the philosopher' (II, ii, 125–6). As their brief collaboration comes to an end, each currish figure reflects on the overlapping of their offices, thereby establishing a Shakespearean equation between the Cynic and the wise fool as types. And yet, even as Apemantus and the Fool turn toward one another and acknowledge that their modes of conduct reflect a shared critical mission, they also turn against one another and engage in mirror-like gestures of characterological diminishment. Apemantus's ironic 'might have' in his observation of likeness implies that the correspondence between the Fool's jesting and his own is merely accidental. And the Fool, besides suggesting that he is guided by philosophical wisdom, mocks Apemantus by equating him to accepted figures of folly, like the elder brother who precedes the younger (and wiser) sibling in many parables. Pointedly, each character sees in himself a valorised picture of Cynic truth-telling and in the other its debasement.

Chronologically, *Timon of Athens* is the last of the plays in which Shakespeare links Cynicism to his depiction of wise fools. I begin at the end, so to speak, because Shakespeare presents his agenda most explicitly in his pairing of Apemantus and the Fool, a character that flits in and out of existence for no discernible purpose other than to serve as Shakespeare's chosen tool for reflecting upon the composite Cynic type. In *Twelfth Night* and *King Lear*, Shakespeare achieves a similar effect through his targeted citation of diogeneana, which he links to his wise fools in such a way as to align them with a composite Cynic stance.

In *Twelfth Night*, Shakespeare's citation of diogeneana tellingly coincides with Feste's act of defining the nature and the purpose of his foolery. At the beginning of Act III, scene i, Viola comes across Feste playing a musical instrument and enters into conversation with him on the topic of his profession: 'Save thee, friend, and thy music. Dost thou live by thy tabor?'[8] Initially at a disadvantage, Viola quickly learns from Feste how to 'dally nicely with words' (III, i, 13), and, armed with this skill, she eventually succeeds at identifying Feste's vocation, or so she thinks:

> *Viola*: Art not thou Lady Olivia's fool?
> *Feste*: No indeed, sir, the Lady Olivia has no folly, she will keep no fool, sir, till she be married, and fools are as like husbands as pilchards are to herrings – the husband's the bigger. I am indeed not her fool, but her corrupter of words. (III, i, 27–31)

Because Feste has been instructing Viola in the art of word-play, we are invited to read his self-definition as yet another playful formulation, as a formal non-equivalence that happens to equate. In this sense, to be a fool is to be a 'corrupter of words', it is to play an active role in loosening semantic 'bonds' such that words become 'rascals' (III, i, 18–19). By calling himself a 'corrupter of words', then, Feste in effect presents himself as the rascal of all rascals. He defines the artificial fool as someone whose verbal activity constitutively evades interpretive clarity, a type of person whom others either should not or cannot take seriously.

Given Feste's trivialising self-definition, it is especially noteworthy that his preference of the title 'corrupter of words' references an anecdote in which Diogenes defines the nature and purpose of Cynic critical activity, an activity, moreover, in which Diogenes corrupts a word in order to protect its meaning from abuse:

> The scholastical exercitacion and conferryng of *Plato* called in greeke διατριβή [*diatribê*], *Diogenes* by deprauyng and corruptyng the woorde called κατατριβή [*katatribê*], y[t]

is, myspendyng of muche good labour & tyme, because
that *Plato* beeyng sequestred & exempted from the prac-
tike liuyng emong menne abrode in yᵉ worlde, did spend
all his dayes & tyme in disputacions of woordes, wher as
Diogenes liuyng emonges yᵉ thickest of the worlde abrode,
had more mynde and affection to liue philosophically, that
is, accordyng to perfecte vertue, then onely in woordes to
dispute & reason therof.⁹

In this story, Diogenes mounts a critique of Plato's philosophical enterprise by corrupting the term used to describe
Plato's school: *diatribê*, a place for 'scholastical exercita-
cion and conferryng'. Deriving the word's meaning from
the verb τρίβειν (*tribein*), which literally means 'to rub', and
the prefix *dia*, which indicates duration, Plato uses *diatribê*
to name his school as a place where one goes to spend time
'rubbing away' at ideas, concepts and philosophical quan-
daries. By contrast, *katatribein* modifies the verb 'to rub'
with a prefix that means 'down', and Diogenes calls Plato's
school a *katatribê* in order to suggest that these men do
not 'rub continuously' at the object of their attention so
much as they 'rub it down', much in the way that a piece of
wood forever burnished by sandpaper will eventually cease
to exist.¹⁰

Though Diogenes' pun is a deft play on words, it serves
to maintain rather than undo the meaning of *diatribê*.
According to Diogenes, Plato's approach to philosophy has
always been a *katatribê* (what Udall loosely translates as a
'myspendyng of muche good labour & tyme'), whereas Diogenes demonstrates his commitment 'to liue philosophically'
by practicing a way of life that fashions his very person into
a *diatribê*, an abrasive object that continuously rubs away at
society's false values. Diogenes therefore counters the empty
activity undertaken by the members of Plato's school, who

philosophise 'onely in woordes', by insisting that true *dia-tribê* – now synonymous with the practice of Cynicism – affects the world not through words but deeds. Diogenes presents Cynic *diatribê* as a socio-ethical stance that enables him to translate his lived philosophy into concrete worldly effects, to challenge more forcefully the falsely held values of individuals and of society-at-large.[11]

Restored to our view, Shakespeare's reference to this particular anecdote can once again do the work of locating Feste at the point of intersection between two contradictory assessments of Diogenes' critical activity, a mode of critical practice that can be heralded as extraordinarily effective, on the one hand, and lambasted for being utterly inconsequential, the mere antics of a parasite-jester who has renounced all claims to seriousness, on the other. By having Feste define his foolery both in terms of its maximal and of its minimal critical efficacy, Shakespeare achieves a composite Cynic stance that resists assimilation to one or the other of these categorical judgments.

To be clear, the structural fact of Feste's composite Cynicism does not prevent an observer from deeming Feste a highly skilled pragmatist, an interpretation of his craft that must undoubtedly strike readers as being more obvious than my reading of composite Cynicism can ever hope to be. Nevertheless, it seems to me that the obviousness of viewing Feste as a tactful provocateur need not invalidate my claims, and indeed, may go some way toward proving them. As Richard Strier would remind us, there are 'structures of and in particular texts that produce "bafflement", that surprise or puzzle the reader . . . and that in some sense resist assimilation to totalizing interpretive strategies'.[12] Strier calls these 'resistant structures'. One must attend with great care to structures of this kind in order to feel their resistance; and in the absence of such care, one feels no resistance at all.

I take Shakespeare to be making precisely this point when he shows how easy it is for Viola to understand Feste's foolery as a modified version of courtliness:

This fellow is wise enough to play the fool,
And to do that well craves a kind of wit.
He must observe their mood on whom he jests,
The quality of persons, and the time,
And, like the haggard, check at every feather
That comes before the eye. (III, i, 53–7)

Viola's assessment of Feste – which we might be tempted to discuss as if it were the play's assessment as well – will only seem obvious if we share her assumption that Feste subscribes to the pragmatist's ideal, that precarious and presumably universal goal of maximising one's freedom and agency within a world of practical constraints. However, Shakespeare does not present Feste as a pragmatic social actor in this moment of diogenical citation. Instead, he composes Feste out of the two evaluations of Cynic critical activity on which courtiers of his period were beginning to cathect as visions of an antipragmatic heaven and hell. By combining the otherworldly prospects of an unrestrainable critical agency and of an oppositional posture that provokes its own dismissal, Shakespeare works to characterise the composite Cynic stance. In other words, Shakespeare turns to composite Cynicism in order to fashion an 'impossible' character, one that presses viewers to recognise the purely formal operations of character as such, while at the same time signalling its status as the place-holder for an embodied social agent. This act of characterisation results in a resistant structure that the audience should notice, even if Viola does not.

Shakespeare stages a more elaborate lesson on the reading and the misreading of the composite Cynic stance when he makes reference to Diogenes in *King Lear*. The chief citational moment takes place out on the heath, where the sight of Edgar (disguised as the pitiful beggar Tom o'Bedlam) prompts Lear to reflect on the idea of a human being stripped of all comforts and accessories: 'Thou art the thing itself. Unaccommodated man is no more but such a poor, bare, forked animal as thou art' (Q xi, 90–2). Lear's Cynic identification with Tom, rather than the Fool, corresponds to Lear's misreading of the anecdote from which he quotes, an anecdote in which Diogenes once again defines the nature of his Cynic practice by defending the accuracy of a word's meaning:

> *Plato* had thus deffined a manne: A manne is a liuethyng with twoo feete, hauyng no fethers. And when the scholares of *Plato* had made signes and tokens of well allowyng thesame diffinicion, Diogenes brought foorth into the schole, a cocke pulled naked out of all his fethers both great & smal, saying: loe, here is Plato his manne. Wherupon it was added to the diffinicion, hauyng brode nailles, for that no byrdes haue any suche.[13]

In offering up a de-feathered chicken as an adequate example of 'Plato his manne', Diogenes mounts a parodic assault upon the very notion that Platonic dialogue brings its practitioners into contact with worldly truths. The suggestion is that Plato and his disciples are no closer to being real men than is the chicken that they have reasoned to be their equal. By contrast, Diogenes lives up to the title of 'manne' by embodying Cynic *diatribê*, an authentic and therefore abrasive way of life that exposes the fraudulence of Plato and his school (that place where lesser beings collectively delude themselves through 'disputacions of woordes').[14]

Shakespeare cites this particular anecdote because it already contains the resistant structure that he is working to locate in his characterisation of wise fools. In addition to depicting the vitality and robustness of Cynic critical activity, this anecdote also demonstrates the practical inefficacy of Diogenes' blunt critique. Though Diogenes offers a challenge to Plato's entire philosophical enterprise, Plato and his circle quite effortlessly assimilate Diogenes' Cynic *diatribê* into the discursive field of their Platonic *diatribê*. In other words, they interpret Diogenes' global critique as merely a rude and inelegant observation that their definition requires more specificity: 'Wherupon it was added to the diffinicion, hauyng brode nailles, for that no byrdes haue any suche.' Taken as a whole, then, this anecdote asks readers to attend to a form of critical activity that is as aggressive and far-reaching as it is ineffectual; it presents Diogenes as the practitioner of a uniquely incongruous way of life, one that figures as both a continuously abrasive mode of social critique and also a complete waste of time.

Associating Cynicism with 'Poor Tom', Lear arrives at an understanding of Cynic practice that does not correspond to the anecdote he cites. For Lear, the 'poor, bare, forked animal' does not refer to Plato's chicken–man but rather to Lear's new ethical ideal of an 'unaccommodated man', a practitioner of Cynic asceticism who achieves virtue through the active embrace of poverty. This is a noble ideal, and Shakespeare treats it as such, but he also builds irony into Lear's interpretation by having the landless king draw his Cynic inspiration from the language of Plato's flawed definition of man. Taking Lear at his word, the few critics who note Shakespeare's reference to Diogenes have endorsed Lear's admiration of Cynic asceticism because it corroborates a redemptive reading of the play's tragic king.[15] E. M. M. Taylor, for example, understands Lear's moment of Cynic identification in the context of the play's overarching moral 'that a man who grossly overvalues material things and the outward trappings of state, virtue, and affection must be schooled by disaster and suffering into truer, more adequate, and more charitable assessments'.[16] In a similar vein, Jane Donawerth asserts that Tom-as-Cynic suits Lear best as a schoolmaster in the lesson of renunciation: 'Lear's madness in calling Poor Tom "philosopher" is a wise one: he is looking for someone to teach him to bear suffering.'[17] By this view, Lear's attempt to disrobe at the sight of Tom o'Bedlam – 'Off, off, you lendings!' (Q xi, 92) – stems from a newly kindled desire to follow the example of the scantily clad Diogenes, who once discarded his wooden bowl as 'a thyng superfluous' upon seeing a boy eat food out of a hollow round of bread.[18] Whereas Lear previously sought to maintain his retinue of personal attendants by claiming that the human condition is one of necessary excess – 'O, reason not the need! Our basest beggars / Are in the poorest thing superfluous' – he now follows an example that prompts him to voluntarily 'shake the superflux' (Q vii, 417–18, xi, 32).

By having Lear invoke the story of Plato's Man, Shakespeare manages to juxtapose a composite Cynic stance with a version of Cynic practice that is more politically actionable, one that foregoes Diogenes' critical mission and that instead focuses entirely upon an ethics of material renunciation. As if to make room for both avenues of interpretation, Shakespeare signals the availability of two Cynic figures – one ascetic, the other (impotently) critical – by way of Lear's confused address of Tom as a potential counsellor of variously Greek origin: 'Let me talk with this philosopher', 'I'll talk a word with this most learnèd Theban', 'Noble philosopher, your company', 'Come, good Athenian' (Q xi, 131, 134, 152, 157). As F. G. Butler has argued, Lear's designation of Tom as a 'learned Theban' refers to Crates of Thebes, a pupil of Diogenes who in turn mentored Zeno, the founder of Stoicism.[19] Whereas Diogenes would take every opportunity to criticise those around him, Crates practiced a less antagonistic brand of Cynicism that focused more exclusively on acquiring peace of mind through the embrace of poverty, a proto-Stoic attitude to which we can see Lear attempting to conform. By contrast, Lear's later designation of Tom as a 'good Athenian' – which R. A. Foakes identifies as a reference to Diogenes – alerts us to something like an interpretive road not taken. It points our attention (though not Lear's) to a more critically oriented (and also more paradoxical) brand of Cynicism that Shakespeare principally deploys in his characterisation of Lear's Fool.[20]

In making this claim, I am first of all suggesting that Shakespeare subordinates Lear's Fool to the same logic of expediency that he employs in his brief depiction of the Fool in *Timon of Athens*, a character that enables Shakespeare to reflect upon, and thus to characterise, the composite Cynic stance. By this view, it is no coincidence that Lear's Fool drops out of the play shortly after Shakespeare makes reference to the story of Plato's Man, for this anecdote's resistant figuration of Diogenes marks the reflective end of the Fool's Cynic beginning.

The Bitter Fool

By citing the story of Plato's Man, Shakespeare pointedly tropes upon the basic circumstances of his play's tragic *dénouement*. Like the love-test, this anecdote stages an encounter between a figure of authority (Plato), his flatterers (Plato's followers, who make 'signes and tokens of well allowyng' their master's definition) and an indecorously frank critic (Diogenes). Yet the story of Plato's Man does not entirely echo the events and consequences that surround Lear's test of love, for Diogenes' blunt criticism – though it proves to be just as ineffective as Cordelia and Kent's freedom of speech – does not result in his banishment from the

Platonic community. In this respect, Shakespeare's allusion to Diogenes most properly corresponds to his characterisation of Lear's Fool, a figure that Shakespeare first calls into being in order to stage a diogenical revision of the play's inaugural scene:

> *Fool*: How now, nuncle? Would I had two coxcombs and
>   two daughters.
> *Lear*: Why, my boy?
> *Fool*: If I gave them my living I'd keep the coxcombs myself.
>   There's mine; beg another off thy daughters.
> *Lear*: Take heed, sirrah – the whip. (Q iv, 91–6)

Just before Kent embarks upon his banishment, he asserts that Regan and Goneril's 'large speeches' must still be confirmed by their 'deeds', and here we see the Fool make a similar point from his vantage of retrospection (Q i, 171); he suggests that Lear has made himself doubly foolish by exchanging his kingdom for a matching set of hollow proclamations. By having the Fool mount precisely this critique, Shakespeare identifies this encounter as a rewriting of the previous confrontation between Kent and his king. Accordingly, Shakespeare has an offended Lear threaten the Fool with punishment, just as Lear once threatened to punish Kent for his forthright defence of Cordelia: 'The bow is bent and drawn; make from the shaft' (Q i.132). In this context, it is noteworthy that Shakespeare does not entirely reproduce the play's foundational tragic event, for the Fool's refusal to heed Lear's whip does not result in a lashing. And yet, one would be hard put to say whether the Fool's exercise of free speech falls into the category of failure or success.

Furthering this characterisation of a composite Cynic stance, Shakespeare has the Fool counter Lear's warning with a diogenical rejoinder. Whereas Kent responds to

Lear's threats by insisting upon the political necessity of his plainspoken resistance – 'To plainness honour's bound / When majesty stoops to folly' – the Fool turns aside the prospect of punishment by observing that all acts of candid admonishment, including his own, inevitably result in communicative failure: 'Truth is a dog to kennel. He must be whipped out when Lady the brach may stand by the fire and stink' (Q i.137–8). Here, Shakespeare aligns the Fool with certain anecdotes in which Diogenes enacts a global critique of his society by publicly dramatising his condition of perpetual critical inefficacy. In one such story, Diogenes walks the streets of Athens with a lit candle in broad daylight, explaining when questioned by passers-by that he is searching for a man.[21] This anecdote registers Diogenes' radical critique of his society – he suggests that no one he has ever encountered lives up to the title of 'man' – but it also presents readers with the challenge of reconciling the obvious ambitiousness of Diogenes' critique with what must inevitably be seen as his practical inconsequentiality: who, after all, will heed a man using a candle in broad daylight, or one conversing with statues (as he does in another anecdote) in order to dramatise the limits of his discourse with men?[22] These anecdotes offer a template for the Fool's composite Cynic gesture, wherein he mounts a trenchant critique of Lear precisely by admitting that he can do no such thing. In light of Cordelia and Kent's earlier banishment, the Fool is of course right to assert that free speakers will always be 'whipped out' while flatterers are allowed to 'stand by the fire and stink', and it is an irony inherent to the Fool's truthfulness that his observation of this fact loses all critical potency upon the instant of its frank utterance. Shakespeare thus locates the Fool's critical activity within the enactment of a logical paradox, and in doing so, he works to frustrate his viewers' ability to resolve the Fool's composite Cynicism into the aspect of a critical practice that is either singularly effective or constitutively ineffective.

One might understandably view this reading with a degree of scepticism. Why, for example, might it not be the case that the Fool speaks with knowing irony, announcing his critical impotence at precisely the moment when he is being the most incisive and critically forceful? This is a valid question insofar as it conforms to Viola's understanding of the courtier-like means by which Feste negotiates his critical agency. However, Shakespeare works to counter this line of thought by setting the Fool in direct contrast with Kent, who re-enters Lear's service (only moments before the Fool's appearance) under the assumed identity of Caius, a man who 'can keep counsel' and 'deliver plain messages bluntly' (Q iv, 28–9). Kent's assertion of plain-spokenness calls to mind his earlier act of transgressive honesty, but he now claims as his chief characteristic the ability to exercise tact (to always 'keep counsel'). Though Kent will deliver blunt missives to the interlocutor of Lear's choosing, he promises never again to breach all bounds of decorum when addressing Lear himself. The larger implication of Kent's return is clear: in order to rejoin his king, Kent agrees to loosen his commitment to absolute Truth so as to inhabit a more liveable socio-ethical stance, one that affords him the greatest realisable degree of critical agency, given the many practical limits that the world imposes upon his free speech.

Lear's Fool represents an impracticable alternative to Kent's virtuous pragmatism, and Shakespeare flags this for his viewers by having the Fool materialise just as Lear agrees to employ the disguised and newly discreet Kent. More precisely, the Fool gives a form to both of the alternatives to the pragmatics of free speech. He is at once the brave and unassailably correct counsellor and also a typologised humours-character, the sort of person whose spleen speaks for him, and who therefore has nothing legitimate to say. Shakespeare works to disclose the formal coincidence of these divided Cynic types when he once more has the Fool recall Lear to the scene of sovereign renunciation, an encounter that similarly positions the Fool within a modified re-enactment of Kent's communicative failure:

> *Fool*: Can you make no use of nothing, uncle?
> *Lear*: Nothing can be made out of nothing.
> *Fool* [*to* Kent]: Prithee, tell him so much the rent of his land comes to. He will not believe a fool.
> *Lear*: A bitter fool. (Q iv, 115–19)

By way of an opening riddle, the Fool draws Lear into a refrain of his earlier answer to a non-compliant Cordelia: 'Nothing can come of nothing' (Q i, 79). Seizing upon this verbal recurrence, the Fool connects Lear's past rejection of frank speech to his present lack of material support, a lack that Lear has brought upon himself by exchanging his kingdom for Regan's and Goneril's glitteringly empty words. Once again, Shakespeare puts the Fool in the position of delivering an undeliverable critique, of disclosing to Lear that he rejects honest censure while embracing silver-tongued praise, and the Fool accomplishes this task by engaging in yet another Diogenes-like dramatisation of his own critical inefficacy. With an ironic flourish, Shakespeare has the Fool entreat a disguised Kent to serve as his frank middleman, insisting that he cannot deliver his critique personally because Lear 'will not believe a fool'. Without doubt, the Fool's comment stings Lear deeply. But while viewers may be tempted to interpret this composite Cynic gesture as a sign of the Fool's robust critical agency, Shakespeare frustrates this simplifying impulse by way of Lear's delegitimising assessment of the Fool. Just as Lear denounces Cordelia and Kent for being proud, he now accuses the Fool of being bitter.

Shakespeare achieves his most resistant figuration of the composite Cynic stance in a passage that only appears in the Quarto edition of *King Lear*. As Robert Hornback notes, in both the Quarto and the Folio texts the Fool takes mention of his bitterness as an opportunity to further engage with Lear: 'Dost know the difference, my boy, between a bitter fool and a sweet fool?' (Q iv, 120; F I, iv, 122).[23] But whereas the Folio Fool responds to Lear's 'No, lad, teach me', by oddly shifting to another riddle entirely – 'Nuncle, give me an egg and I'll give thee two crowns' – the Quarto Fool goes on to position himself as the bitter alternative to sweet counsel.[24] Thus we once again find ourselves with a version of the play's original opposition between persuasive flattery and ineffective frankness:

> *Fool* [*sings*]:   That lord that counselled thee
>   To give away thy land,
>   Come, place him here by me;
>   Do thou for him stand.
>   The sweet and bitter fool
>   Will presently appear,
>   The one in motley here,
>   The other found out there.
> *Lear*: Dost thou call me fool, boy?
> *Fool*: All thy other titles thou hast given away. That thou
>   wast born with.
> *Kent* [*to* Lear]: This is not altogether fool, my lord.
> *Fool*: No, faith; lords and great men will not let me. If I had
>   a monopoly out, they would have part on't, and ladies
>   too, they will not let me have all the fool to myself –
>   they'll be snatching. Give me an egg, nuncle, and I'll give
>   thee two crowns. (Q iv, 123–38)

As an act of frank critique, the riddle makes explicit Lear's double duty as both the recipient and the supplier of counsel, standing both for himself – the king – and for 'That lord that counselled' him. The Fool's odd construction leaves it unclear whether the sweet fool names the person who gives fawning advice or a person who readily takes it, an ambiguity that draws attention to Lear's closed economy of counsel, that is, to the fact that Lear has counselled himself into destitution. The Fool renders visible, in retrospect, the fact that Lear decides to 'shake all cares and business off our state' prior to Goneril and Regan's flattery or Cordelia's jarringly frank speech; and although Lear promises his 'largest bounty' to the daughter who professes to love him most, he demonstrates the persuasive limits of Goneril and Regan's obsequiousness by only giving them their predetermined thirds. This is not to suggest that flattery plays no part in Lear's conduct but rather to emphasise his request for adulation over his elder daughters' production of it, an orchestration of the ensuing exchange that substantiates the Fool's conflation of Lear with those who validate his intentions. If Lear meets the requirements of the sweet fool, it is because he displays a lack of self-knowledge: he does not recognise that the advice he likes best is always of the sort that corroborates his self-image.

Though Lear understands the Fool's jest enough to identify himself as its target – 'Dost thou call me fool, boy?' – the distinction being drawn between the sweet and the bitter fool entirely escapes him. It is therefore a matter of profound irony that the Fool wholly substantiates his critique of Lear by failing to convey that critique to Lear. Whereas Lear demonstrates his sweetness most conclusively when he fails to see that which the Fool bitterly endeavours to show him, the Fool manifests his bitterness most decisively when he identifies Lear's pathologising dismissal of him as the definitive feature of his critical activity. If the Fool persists in the failure to prove his point, it is because an unconditional and indefinite demonstration of his failure serves as the best and only means of proving his point.

Here, Shakespeare achieves his most resistant characterisation of the composite Cynic stance, for the Fool's critical activity takes the ethical form of a means to an end even as it marks the absence of any means and the lack of any end. Here, too, the Cynic ideal of an anti-rhetorical counsellor and the debased Cynic archetypes of the misanthrope and the zany are shown to coexist in an irresolvable formation. The result is an especially ambivalent configuration of Shakespeare's 'bitter fool'.

Immediately after the Fool's bitter self-definition – which I have read as Shakespeare's most resistant characterisation of the composite Cynic stance – Shakespeare continues to toy with his audience by having the Fool single out King James as the true target of his bitter critique, a move that reopens the possibility that the Fool models a politically viable socio-ethical stance. As Gary Taylor has established, the Fool's assertion that he does not hold a monopoly over foolishness must be understood in the context of James's controversial granting of monopolies to his favourites, a practice to which many objected on the grounds that it contributed to the decadence of the Jacobean court and to the culture of self-interested flattery among the lords that counselled James.[25] With James as the Fool's new target, Shakespeare renews his viewers' sense that the Fool may still model a mode of conduct that lends authority and persuasive force to incendiary acts of free speech. Tellingly, the Fool's critical intervention does not persuade James to alter his ways, and if Taylor is correct, then this passage does not appear in the Folio text precisely because the Fool's topical reference led to its censorship.

Immediately following his reference to monopolies, the Fool engages Lear with his most direct critique of the king's sovereign error, and, like Diogenes in the story of Plato's Man, he uses poultry to make his point:

Fool: Give me an egg, nuncle, and I'll give thee two crowns.
Lear: What two crowns shall they be?
Fool: Why, after I have cut the egg in the middle and eat up
   the meat, the two crowns of the egg. When thou clovest
   thy crown i'th'middle and gavest away both parts, thou
   borest thy ass o'th back o'er the dirt. Thou hads't little
   wit in thy bald crown when thou gavest thy golden one
   away. (Q iv, 138–44)

The Fool ultimately makes a point about Lear's fatal error –
the division of his kingdom between Regan and Goneril –
but this riddle first concerns the Fool's act of splitting rather
than that of his king. We are therefore invited to understand
this riddle in the context of the Fool's ability to divide his
critical activity between two sovereign audiences, the one on
stage and the other at Whitehall. But if Shakespeare tempts
his audience to admire bitter foolery as a mode of critique
with remarkably broad reach, he also reminds viewers
that the characterisation of a composite Cynic stance only
achieves this effect by 'cut[ting] out the middle and eat[ing]
up the meat'; it delivers critique by representing the form of
a critical practice that has evacuated itself of all practical
substance.

In the end, Shakespeare does not, indeed cannot, overcome our cognitive limits. No matter how resistant its structure, composite Cynicism will always be filtered through that
mechanism of our apprehension that ensures we perceive only
one of its faces at a time. Nevertheless, Shakespeare seems to
understand that – when it comes to the politics and aesthetics of free speech – we must at least attempt to resist the
irresistible, to think beyond the interpretive procedures that
bring one of Cynicism's two aspects into view only by being
unmindful, in that moment, of the other. Shakespeare's bitter
fools serve to destabilise our attachment to a single perception of free and fearless speech, to lure us into a heightened

experience of our own evaluative instability. By encapsulating a composite Cynic stance in a single figure, the wise fool, Shakespeare poses this problem of perspective so inexorably that attentive viewers will be moved to wrestle with it to the point of exhaustion. Thus wearied, careful readers of Shakespeare will be wary of Cynicism's two faces, lest the push and pull of their anti-rhetorical aspirations and fears forever lead them on a not-so-merry chase.

Notes

1. Laertius, *Lives of Eminent Philosophers*, 6.69.
2. Francis Bacon makes precisely this point in a chapter of *The Wisdome of the Ancients* entitled 'Cassandra, siue Parresia'. Warning against the 'vnprofitable liberty of vntimely admonitions and counselles', Bacon argues that counsellors who insist upon absolute candour will 'in all their endeauors . . . auail nothing' precisely because they 'are so ouerweened with the sharpnesse and dexteritie of their own wit and capacitie'. See Bacon, *Wisdome of the Ancients*, sigs. A^v–A$_2^v$, quoted in Colclough, *Freedom of Speech in Early Stuart England*, p. 61.
3. Shakespeare, *The History of King Lear* in *The Norton Shakespeare*, II, i, 118. In a key instance, my analysis requires me to work with the Quarto edition of *King Lear*. For the sake of uniformity, all further citations will be to the same edition and in-text.
4. The widely read and anonymously authored *Rhetorica ad Herennium* (at the time attributed to Cicero) recommends that an advisor moderate his candour in order to benefit from its forcefulness without losing all authority with his interlocutor. See Anon. *Ad C. Herennium, de ratione dicendi*, IV.xxxvii.49, pp. 350–3. 'If Frank Speech [*licentia*] of this sort seems too pungent, there will be many means of palliation, for one may immediately thereafter add something of this sort: "I here appeal to your virtue, I call on your wisdom, I bespeak your old habit", so that praise may quiet the feelings aroused by the frankness. As a result, the praise frees the

hearer from wrath and annoyance, and the frankness deters him from error.'

5. Richard Strier is especially alert to Kent's initial courtliness in his analysis of 'impossible radicalism' in *King Lear*. See Strier, *Resistant Structures*, esp. pp. 182–3.

6. For Kenneth Graham, these two failures of free speech, combined with Kent's return to a moderated stance when later disguised as Caius, serve as Shakespeare's way of drawing out the moral that 'to make its resistance matter, plainness must therefore cease to insist that it is absolutely powerful and absolutely true; and it must instead find new ways to perform'. But whereas Graham attributes to Shakespeare a sense of conclusiveness on this matter, I think it more precise to say that Shakespeare diagnoses the problem of the truth-teller as being one of eternal return. See Graham, *The Performance of Conviction*, p. 193.

7. Shakespeare, *The Life of Timon of Athens* in *The Norton Shakespeare*, p. 2252. Further citations will be to this edition and in-text.

8. Shakespeare, *Twelfth Night* in *The Norton Shakespeare*, III, ii, 1.

9. Erasmus, *Apophthegmes*, sig. I.vi^r. Daniel Kinney off-handedly observes Shakespeare's citation of Diogeneana in a footnote. See Kinney, 'Heirs of the Dog', p. 300 note 16.

10. I am indebted to Chris Geekie for his help in translating and interpreting the Greek in this passage.

11. This conception of Cynic diatribê thus forms a pair with Lyly and Wilson's interpretation of Cynic parrhêsia. For an account of *diatribê* as a specifically Cynic mode of democratic critical engagement (speaking to the masses rather that addressing only select philosophical community), see Foucault, *Fearless Speech*, pp. 219–20.

12. Strier, *Resistant Structures*, p. 1.

13. Erasmus, *Apophthegmes*, sig. Nii^r (#65 in 'Diogenes', book I). In 'An Apologie of Raymond Sebonde', Michel de Montaigne also refers to the story of Plato's Man. See Montaigne, *The Essayes or Morall, Politike and Millitarie Discourses*, pp. 315–16.

14. Erasmus, *Apophthegmes*, sig. I.vi[r].
15. E. M. M. Taylor, Jane Donawerth, F. G. Butler and Steven Doloff have all noticed the topical references to Cynicism in Lear's address to, and reflection upon, Tom o'Bedlam. See Taylor, 'Lear's Philosopher'; Donawerth, 'Diogenes the Cynic and Lear's Definition of Man'; Butler, 'Who Are King Lear's Philosophers?'; and Doloff, 'Let me talk with this philosopher'. In a recent article, Laurie Shannon acknowledges the play's reference to Cynicism, though she goes on to discuss Lear's definition of unaccommodated man in broader terms as the basis for investigating the play's anti-exceptionalist vision of humankind. See Shannon, 'Poor, Bare, Forked'.
16. Taylor, 'Lear's Philosopher', p. 365.
17. Donawerth, 'Diogenes the Cynic and Lear's Definition of Man', p. 14.
18. Erasmus, *Apophthegmes*, sig. Mii–Miii. In a similar anecdote, Diogenes sees a boy drink water with cupped hands, and realising that 'this lad is in frugalitee a degree aboue me, y[t] dooe carry about me superfluous furniture', he immediately throws his cup away (sig. Mii).
19. Butler, 'Who Are King Lear's Philosophers?', esp. pp. 511–13. For a useful primer on Crates, see Dudley, *A History of Cynicism*, esp. pp. 42–53; as well as Navia, *Classical Cynicism*, esp. pp. 119–44.
20. Foakes, *King Lear*, III, iv, 153 note.
21. Erasmus, *Apophthegmes*, sig. Niii[r]. '*Diogenes* on a tyme, bearyng in his hande a lighted candle, walked vp and downe the mercate stede, in a veraye bright and clere daye, like one that sought a thyng loste. And diuerse persones askyng, what he did: Mary I seeke a man, quod he.'
22. Erasmus, *Apophthegmes*, sig. Six[r]. 'He vsed now and then to resorte to ymages of stone or brasse, or other metalle, sette vp in the honour of this or that Godde, and to aske one or other boune of theim. And to such persones as made great woondreyng, wherfore he so did, y[t] I maye enure myself, quod he, not to bee moued, ne to take in eiuill parte, if at any tyme, I dooe not obtein my requestes & peticions that I aske of menne.'

23. For a thorough account of the differences between the Quarto and Folio that cumulatively effect a recharacterisation of the Fool, see Hornback, 'The Fool in Quarto and Folio *King Lear*'. For an entry into the debate concerning the relation of the Quarto to the Folio editions of *King Lear*, which some view as differentiated texts with distinctive dramatic visions, and others view as less and more revised versions of a single dramatic ideal, see Urkowitz, *Shakespeare's Revision of King Lear*; and Taylor and Warren, *The Division of the Kingdoms*.

24. In his editorial footnote, Bevington suggests that the 'Fool identifies himself as the sweet fool, Lear as the bitter fool who counseled himself to give away his kingdom'. The Riverside and Arden editions contain similar glosses. However, I follow Hornback's contention that the Quarto edition of *King Lear* consistently depicts the Fool as a figure that engages in 'bitter truth-telling', making the Fool the proper target of the riddle's bitter designation. See Bevington, *King Lear*, p. 1216, I, iv, 144 note; Blakemore Evans et al., *The Tragedy of King Lear*, p. 1310, I, iv, 147 note; Muir, *King Lear*; Hornback, 'The Fool in Quarto and Folio *King Lear*', esp. pp. 318–22.

25. Taylor, 'Monopolies, Show Trials, Disaster, and Invasion', p. 103.

CHAPTER 4

CYNICISM, MELANCHOLY AND HAMLET'S
MEMENTO MORIAE

Every select man strives instinctively for a citadel and a
privacy,
where he is *free* from the crowd, the many, the majority.
                                                    Friedrich Nietzsche[1]

In the character of Hamlet, Shakespeare takes up an unlikely
iteration of the Cynic truth-teller that first begins to circu-
late in the sixteenth century and that continues to hold currency today: that of the intellectual who foregoes any effort
to change the world directly and who instead seeks to comprehend the forces of historical process through which fundamental changes in the world order will be brought about
in due time. As we will see, the figuration of this sublimated
approach to Cynic truth-telling takes shape through lines
of affiliation between the Cynic-inspired fantasy of unstoppable critical agency and early modernity's romanticised
portrait of intellectual melancholy. The result is a posture
of Cynic melancholy that foregoes Jaques's fruitless critical
ambition to 'Cleanse the foul body of th'infected world'
in the Diogenes-like manner of a licensed fool in favour of
pursuing an ethics of melancholy rumination. Thus, as we

will see, Hamlet adopts a posture of Cynic melancholy in
order to comprehend the manifold rationality of the cosmos – to find solace, we might say, in knowing that the
world in which he unhappily finds himself continues to
undergo a process of historical unfolding, meaning that a
time will eventually come when the world will have man-
aged to cleanse itself.

My aim, in offering this account of Hamlet's Cynic melancholy, is to cast in a new light the tradition of reading
Hamlet as modernity's first 'man of thought', a tradition
that finds its origins in the German reception of Shakespeare in the late eighteenth and early nineteenth centuries.
According to Margreta de Grazia, this reading of Hamlet –
which understands him to be trapped in the state of existential crisis that attends to the modern human condition
– does not properly originate from Shakespeare's play and
instead emerges, right on cue, out of the existential vac-
uum that is modernity itself.[2] In this chapter, I push back
against de Grazia's account of this modern philosophical
tradition and its alleged dissociation from Shakespeare's
seventeenth-century Hamlet. First, I argue that the modern way of reading Hamlet is not as detached from the
play's governing concerns as de Grazia claims it is; as I will
show, Shakespeare's depiction of Cynic melancholy largely
anticipates the philosophical reception of Hamlet that only
emerges and flourishes some 200 years later, at a time when
thinkers were just beginning to grapple with the fact of the
Enlightenment's failure. Second, I argue that G. W. F. Hegel,
among others, is right to locate modernity's nascence in the
figure of Hamlet, yet I contend that he, like many of his
contemporaries and later disciples, is right for the wrong
reasons. This is to suggest that Hamlet's modernity does
not lie in his experience of existential impasse so much as
in his experience of thinking beyond that impasse. Hamlet,

I argue, is at bottom satisfied by his ceaseless thinking, which he feels cannot (but also need not) be translated into actions that materially right a world of perceived wrongs. In this respect, Hamlet's posture of Cynic melancholy inaugurates a modern subjective position that Hegel himself, and later, Karl Marx, adopt as well, and this is especially true when it comes to the privileged role that their intellectual activity is understood to play in the production of their philosophies of history and their understandings of the historical dialectic.

This is an admittedly counterintuitive claim, and I defend it by emphasising the link between Hamlet's posture of Cynic melancholy and his tendency to engage in speculative philosophy, to imagine, for example, that 'a king may go a progress through the guts of a beggar' or that 'the noble dust of Alexander the Great' might eventually be found 'stopping [the] bung-hole' of a beer barrel.³ These speculations – both of which point back to the story of a beggarly Diogenes fearlessly critiquing Alexander the Great – do nothing to further Hamlet's action-oriented agenda against Claudius. Instead, they allow Hamlet to imagine a broader historical process by which the politics of kingship (for which he is not fit) will eventually be supplanted by a new, more ideal formation of the political.⁴

My goal in this chapter is to show that Shakespeare concerns himself with both the attractions and the dangers of adopting Cynic melancholy as a critical orientation. Indeed, Shakespeare seems to understand quite well that both the appeal and the risk of Cynic melancholy stem from the way in which a person's identification with this critical stance makes it difficult for him or her to experience what Richard Strier would call its resistant structure.⁵ In the figure of Hamlet, Shakespeare pursues a characterisation of the melancholy Cynic that is designed to lure his viewers into recognising (with bafflement and discomfiture) the unthinking ease with which they align themselves with Hamlet's intellectual posture. Of course, Shakespeare's impact on the intellectual history of Cynic melancholy has more to do with his intervention's failure than its success, and I therefore attend to the influential role that Hamlet's Cynic melancholy plays in the emergence of nineteenth-century German speculative philosophy, and, in particular, the development of Hegel's and Marx's philosophies of history. However, having established the Cynic contours of Hamlet's ruminative stance, and having shown how Hegel and Marx variously adopt this brand of Cynicism for themselves, I conclude this chapter by rehearsing Shakespeare's effort to expose the essential fraudulence of Hamlet's posture of Cynic melancholy. But first, allow me to establish the larger context for Shakespeare's engagement with the figure of the melancholy Cynic, a figure that Shakespeare does not invent so much as discover in the diogeneana of his day.

The Melancholy Cynic

Just as the figure of the Cynic was the subject of highly divergent assessments in early modern England, so too was the figure of the melancholy man. On the one hand, early modern thinkers remained indebted to the medieval tradition of Galenic medicine, which viewed melancholy in purely pathological terms. But, on the other hand, many of these same thinkers had begun to self-identify with a valorised conception of intellectual melancholy; like Jaques, scholars of the sixteenth and seventeenth centuries often viewed a disposition towards sadness as the defining characteristic of a person with superior powers of reflection.[6]

We should therefore not be surprised to find Renaissance thinkers associating these two character types with one another, as Thomas Walkington does in his description of the melancholy man in *The optick glasse of humours* (1607):

> The melancholick man is said of the wise to be *aut Deus aut Daemon,* either angel of heauen or a fiend of hell: for in whomsoeuer this humour hath dominion, the soule is either wrapt vp into an *Elysium* and paradise of blisse by a heauenly contemplation, or into a direfull hellish purgatory by a cynicall meditation.[7]

Here, Walkington associates the debased view of Cynicism with the kind of melancholy that is 'hellish' and purely pathological. His description would therefore seem to support David Mazella's claim that the discourses of Cynicism and of melancholy were linked to one another only with respect to the negative evaluations of each.[8] In fact, however, at least some thinkers of the period envisioned a quite different conjunction of Cynicism and melancholy, one in which the extreme Cynic stance valorised by Thomas Wilson and John Lyly finds an unlikely bedfellow in the idealised interpretation of immoderate melancholy.

Walkington does not invoke this particular conjunction of melancholic and Cynic figures. Nevertheless, he participates in one of the key developments that made such a confluence possible, for his conception of 'heauenly' melancholy – set, as it is, in stark opposition to a 'hellish' counterpart – mirrors Lyly and Wilson's Cynic ideal in its rejection of the Aristotelian mean. The very idea of there being a genial form of melancholy finds its origins in the pseudo-Aristotelian *Problemata* XXX.1, which tries to make sense of the fact that many of the most eminent philosophers, politicians, poets and artists clearly suffered from an excess of black bile. The answer lies in the existence of a second golden mean, a state of equilibrium achieved not through the balancing of the humours, but rather through the counterbalancing of

innate disposition, on the one hand, and habituated practice, on the other:

> For as men differ in appearance not because they possess
> a face but because they possess such and such a face, some
> handsome, others ugly, others with nothing extraordinary
> about it (*hoi de methen echontes peritton*) (i.e. those whose
> looks are ordinary (*hoitoi de mesoi ten phusin*)); so those
> who have a little of [the melancholy] temperament are ordi-
> nary (*mesoi eisin*), but those who have much of it are unlike
> the majority of people (*tois pollois*). For if their melancholy
> habitus is quite undiluted they are too melancholy; but if it
> is somewhat tempered they are outstanding (*perittoi*).[9]

According to the author of the *Problemata*, the philosopher
and the madman do not differ in terms of their bilious excess,
for both are of an equally melancholic disposition. But
whereas the madman does nothing to offset his unhealthy
temperament, the philosopher achieves greatness by exercising self-control. Marsilio Ficino, early modernity's first influential commentator on intellectual melancholy, follows the
Problemata in endorsing habitual moderation. At the same
time, however, Ficino also lays the groundwork for Walkington's later radicalisation of 'heauenly' melancholy, and
he does this by introducing a new rationale for exhorting
'learned people' to temper their melancholy habits. Ficino,
concerned that philosophers expose themselves to mortal
danger when they try to get too much of a good thing, warns
that 'the soul contemplating divine things assiduously and
intently grows up so much on food of this kind and becomes
so powerful, that it overreaches its body above what the cor-
poreal nature can endure'.[10] Ficino speaks of the quite practical limitation that a scholar's body must stay alive in order
for his mind to continue thinking, and so he urges scholars
to moderate their devotion to philosophical contemplation

lest their mind become so powerful that it leaves their body behind to die. But despite Ficino's pragmatic note of caution, an aspirational value nevertheless adheres to the notion that one's interior philosophical landscape acquires divine power through the contemplation of 'divine things'. I would like to suggest that Walkington extends this premise to its radical limit, positing that the condition of melancholy wraps a philosopher up in 'heauenly contemplation' only when he does nothing whatsoever to dilute melancholy's influence upon him.

There is, of course, a problem with Walkington's formulation, and it is the same problem that plagues Lyly's valorised conception of Cynic critical practice: though Walkington vigorously segregates 'heauenly' melancholy from its debased, 'hellish' counterpart, this very opposition binds the two together in a relation of formal equivalence. In other words, Walkington's effort to differentiate between the good and the bad kinds of melancholy, 'said of the wise to be *aut Deus aut Daemon*', in fact figures his attempt to reify the two antithetical assessments of a single untempered disposition.

Though Walkington does not seem particularly troubled by this formal dilemma, we can find other thinkers in the period who grappled quite self-consciously with the question of whether their melancholia amounted to a blessing or a curse. Robert Burton, for example, admits to feeling especially torn between the advantages and disadvantages of his lugubrious disposition in his preface to *The Anatomy of Melancholy*. On the one hand, Burton acknowledges that his melancholy is the catalyst for his social and intellectual peripheralisation. But on the other hand, he considers his propensity for sadness to be the undeniable source of his most invaluable insights. Indeed, as Douglas Trevor has persuasively argued, Burton understands his melancholy to grant him a privileged critical insight into the very social and institutional problems that have led to his undeserved marginalisation.[11] Ultimately, Burton justifies his embrace of intellectual melancholy by settling upon a unique solution to this dilemma: he simultaneously invokes the valorised accounts of melancholy and of Cynicism, thereby allowing the one to corroborate the value of the other.

This is encapsulated in Burton's move from lamenting his walled-off disposition to celebrating it – 'I have nothing, I want nothing' – a reversal in which Burton articulates a particularly Cynic attitude of ascetic self-sufficiency in order to posit an ethics of private rumination as the very foundation of his critical insight:

> All my Treasure is in *Mineruas* Tower. Preferment I could neuer get, although my friendes prouidence care, alacritie and bounty was neuer wanting to doe me good, yet either through mine owne default, infelicity, want or neglect of opportunity, or iniquitie of times, preposterous proceeding, mine hopes were still frustrate, and I left behind, as a Dolphin on shore, confined to my Colledge, as *Diogenes* to his tubbe.[12]

Burton acknowledges that his personal disposition has made it impossible for him to succeed as a public figure, and he therefore writes from the self-pitying perspective of an underappreciated intellectual. But he also defends his scholarly isolation as being necessary to the production of his most valuable insights: 'All my Treasure is in *Mineruas* Tower.' Though Burton admits to having once nurtured 'hopes' in the direction of exercising a vigorous presence in the public sphere, he now announces a commitment to the alternative strategy of encasing himself in a world of contemplation. Thus he adopts a language of enclosure that proceeds from 'Mineruas Tower' to the confines of his 'Colledge' and that finally terminates in the analogous residence figured by Diogenes' tub.

Burton plays up the pathos of his political failure by likening himself to a lonely dolphin that has driven itself ashore and has subsequently been abandoned by its fellows, and this note of poignancy persists into his account of his ensuing devotion to scholarly pursuits, an arena in which Burton imagines himself to be similarly marginalised by his peers. It is in the context of his self-pity that Burton first invokes Diogenes, whose inhabitation of a tub serves to index the extremity of Burton's melancholy withdrawal. Whereas a college offers shelter to a whole community of scholars, Diogenes' tub registers its occupant's estrangement from all men, including the other philosophers of his day. The suggestion is that Burton so thoroughly wraps himself up in his sadness that he is marginalised even in the eyes of his fellow scholars and intellectuals, and he acknowledges as much when apologising for the topic of his current scholarly pursuit:

> There bee many other subiects I doe easily grant, both in humanity and diuinity fit to be treated of, and of which had I written *ad ostentationem* only, to shew my selfe I should haue rather chosen, and in which I could haue more willingly luxuriated, and better satisfied my selfe and others; but that at this time I was fatally driuen vpon this rocke of Melancholy.[13]

When Burton compares himself to Diogenes, he does so in order to sound his sharpest note of self-pity. And yet, it is also by way of his analogy to Cynicism that Burton restores value to his posture of extreme melancholy withdrawal. As with every aspect of Diogenes' way of life, his inhabitation of a tub serves to publicise his rejection of society and its many false values; it evokes Diogenes' Cynic commitment to an outward-looking, action-oriented mode of social critique. Taken together, the image of Diogenes confined to his tub therefore figures as a chiasmus of opposing socio-ethical stances; it functions as the vehicle for Diogenes' retreat from the world of men, and, at the same time, it instantiates itself as a vigorous, open challenge to society at large. It is my contention that Burton seeks to align himself with both of these stances, despite the fact that they logically run counter to one another. By likening himself to Diogenes, Burton tries, however improbably, to locate a valorised conception of Cynic critical practice at the very core of his inward-looking, highly self-recursive life of the mind. In this way, he lays claim to a specifically Cynic form of melancholy, one that posits contemplative self-enclosure as public activism's final frontier.

This first invocation of Diogenes contributes significantly to Burton's formulation of, and identification with, the posture of Cynic melancholy. However, the precise nature of Burton's Cynic affiliation only becomes clear when he alters the terms of his analogy. Though he initially aligns himself with diogenical hermeticism – thus blurring the distinction between Cynic extroversion and melancholy introversion – the true target of Burton's comparison lies in the notion of Diogenes freely and fearlessly speaking his mind:

> I [was] left behind, as a Dolphin on shore, confined to my Colledge, as *Diogenes* to his tubbe. Sauing that sometimes as *Diogenes* went into the citty, . . . I did for my recreation now and then walke abroad, and looke into the world, & could not choose but make some little obseruation.[14]

Burton places himself in a position analogous to that of Diogenes, a truth-teller who takes everyone's measure and who immediately delivers his observations in the form of withering, first-hand critiques. The implied comparison is therefore quite striking, for this is exactly what Burton does not do. To begin with, Burton's word choice strategically aligns his activity not with the work of criticism, but rather with the work of impersonal, thoroughly disinterested scientific empiricism. Moreover, readers familiar with the humility topos understand the general implication of Burton's proviso: he is presenting *The Anatomy of Melancholy* as the sum total of his 'little obseruation[s]', meaning that Burton's scholarly activity figures as an evasion of direct critical encounter.

According to the *OED*, 'to observe' – within the emergent scientific community of mid- to late sixteenth-century England – was 'to take note of or detect scientifically; to watch or examine methodically, esp. without experimental or therapeutic intervention; to perceive or learn by scientific inspection or measurement'.[15] To observe but not to intervene – that is the melancholy Cynic's motto. But whereas Jaques follows this precept only by abandoning his earlier commitment to a world-cleansing ideal, Burton does so in a way that continues to invest his empiricism with Cynic potentialities. These potentialities are most obviously at play in Burton's claim that he 'could not choose but make some little obseruation', the phrasing of which draws a parallel to Diogenes' compulsive truth-telling while also reminding readers of the rhetorical freight that the act of observing can be made to carry. I am not interested, here, in catching Burton out for merely feigning impartiality; rather, I wish to take seriously the interplay between scientific observation and the common-sense usage by which 'to observe' means something like 'to say by way of comment; to remark or mention in speech or writing'.[16]

Burton's 'little obseruation[s]' insistently straddle these two senses of the word; they are at once self-directed and other-directed, subjective and objective, and, in this respect, they closely resemble the ambiguity of address coded into Hamlet's opening line: 'A little more than kin, and less than kind' (I, ii, 66). This is a line that Hamlet may or may not deliver as an aside (editors can never agree on this point), and, as we will see, it is also a line that Shakespeare shows to be Hamlet's melancholy refashioning of a diogenical retort.

Diogenes, Alexander, and Hamlet's 'Melancholy Aside'

Though Shakespeare could not have been influenced by Burton's *Anatomy*, his depiction of Hamlet shows him to possess a similar understanding of Cynic melancholy. In this respect, Shakespeare's portrayal of the melancholy Dane is the consequence of his further reflecting upon both the failure of, and the desire for, direct diogenical critique, which together inform Shakespeare's Cynic characterisation of Lear's Fool, Feste, and the Fool in *Timon of Athens*. In *Hamlet*, this desire finds new expression in the posture of Cynic melancholy, and Shakespeare alerts viewers to this repurposing of Cynicism by placing Hamlet's first line – a distinctly melancholic aside – in the context of the Diogenes/ Alexander paradigm.

As I established in this book's introduction, the story of Alexander's making a personal visit to Diogenes, whereupon a sunbathing Diogenes asks Alexander to get out of his light, held a particularly iconic status in early modern England. In Nicholas Udall's translation of this anecdote, Alexander offers to grant the Cynic any favour of his choosing, to which Diogenes responds with a request that Alexander 'not make shadoe betwene the sonne and me'.[17] The suggestion is that Alexander is not the god-like sovereign that he thinks he is; his patronage only amounts to an interposing shadow, something that deprives Diogenes of his access to true sunlight (which is to say, personal freedom and self-sovereignty). More than anything else, this is the anecdote that informs Wilson's and Lyly's interpretations of Cynic critical practice, and, we should not be surprised to learn, this is the anecdote that Shakespeare invokes when introducing Hamlet to his audience.[18]

We will recall that Hamlet first speaks only when provoked into a verbal sparring match with his uncle, who has recently been crowned as King. Claudius, in the midst of solidifying his kingship through an exercise in political theatre, turns his attention to his broody nephew, whom he addresses in a manner that signals his intention to name Hamlet heir to the throne:

> *King*: But now, my cousin Hamlet, and my son –
> *Hamlet*: A little more than kin, and less than kind.
> *King*: How is it that the clouds still hang on you?
> *Hamlet*: Not so my lord. I am too much in the sun.
>   (I, ii, 65–8)

Where Alexander offers Diogenes any favour of his choosing, Claudius offers Hamlet the title of 'son' and the status of heir-apparent, and, in keeping with Diogenes' response, Hamlet turns down the proposed act of munificence. In this brief exchange, which contains Hamlet's first lines of the play, we see an inversion of Diogenes' wish that Alexander 'not make shadoe betwene the sonne and me' to Hamlet's riddling insistence that he finds himself 'too much in the sun'. This reversal is, for Shakespeare, a pointed one, but only in the context of Hamlet's larger resemblance to Diogenes; Hamlet does not want to bathe in the sunshine of Claudius's favour, and so his contradiction of Claudius – 'Not so my lord. I am too much in the sun' – amounts to a Cynic rejection of a false king's beneficence.

Reading this encounter through the lens of the Diogenes/ Alexander paradigm, we might further note the degree to which Hamlet figures as a truth-teller who says exactly what he thinks. In the context of Claudius's statesmanlike accounting of his marriage to Gertrude, 'our sometime sister, now our queen, / Th'imperial jointress to this warlike state' (I, ii, 9), Hamlet's qualification that he is, to Claudius, 'A little more than kin, and less than kind' is unambiguous in its scornful implications. First, 'A little more than kin' names the incestuous link now doubling Hamlet's relation to Claudius, thereby countering the logic of imperial jointure upon which Claudius has hung his legitimacy as king. Second, Hamlet's assertion that he and his uncle are 'less than kind' mounts an evaluative contrast between himself and Claudius. It serves to assert Hamlet's superiority over Claudius on the basis of his cultivated Cynic stance, his more kingly relation to self and other. Whereas Claudius must be stately and cautious, and is therefore of a kind with Alexander, Hamlet presents himself as being fearlessly free-speaking, and thus of a kind with Diogenes.

By pausing on Hamlet's first line, I have tried to demonstrate the degree to which it functions as a diogenical zinger, a devastating critique of an interlocutor's essential flaws as a person. Hamlet's observation, as at the climax of most diogenical anecdotes, takes the form of a withering punchline. But this is as far as I can take the parallel without acknowledging the obvious: it is not at all clear that Hamlet ever delivers this critique. From the start, Hamlet folds in upon himself at the very moment when Diogenes would face the world head-on, and it is precisely this difference in overall conduct that distinguishes the rigidly Cynic stance from the posture of Cynic melancholy. Whereas Diogenes turns Alexander's offer down, Hamlet turns Claudius's offer aside. Hamlet thus engages in a form of critical activity that does not aim to be the passive, inward-looking inversion of diogenical critique so much as to be an (impossible) third way, a critical alternative that splits the difference between outward-facing and inward-facing orientations. 'A little more than kin, and less than kind' straddles ambiguously between public and private address, a circumstance that has prompted about half of the play's modern editions to mark the line as an 'aside', a dramatic convention that allows Hamlet to speak as if to himself, despite being in the presence of others.[19] In my own analysis, I call Hamlet's first line an aside not to take sides in this editorial debate, but rather to name the quality inherent to Hamlet's first utterance that makes its orientation so hard to decipher.

Understood as an aside, Hamlet's first line registers his inward turn toward an ethics of melancholy rumination; it suggests that he would endorse Jaques's claim that it is 'good to be sad and say nothing' (*As You Like It* IV, i, 8). And yet, insofar as the aside functions as a publicly constituted dramatic device, its depiction of interiority formally corresponds with the dramatisation of an outward, critique-oriented mode of address (Hamlet speaks out loud and in front of potential interlocutors). As theatregoers, we are accustomed to ignore the aside's cognitive dissonance, but Shakespeare reactivates our sense of this moment's critical potential by tying Hamlet to Diogenes, a figure who would, in exactly this circumstance, 'speake boldely, & without feare, euen to the proudest of them'.[20] In consequence, Hamlet's aside figures as a discursive space in which the transcendent view of Cynicism (as a practice that furnishes critique with the force of an incontrovertible assertion) continues to operate within the framework of a melancholy retreat into private interiority.

Ultimately, Shakespeare presses his viewers to see that his characterisation of Cynic melancholy is itself a resistant structure, to see, in other words, that this posture's formal and aesthetic attributes cannot be squared with the philosophico-political work to which Hamlet would have it put. Yet Shakespeare begins his engagement with Cynic melancholy in such a way as to allow his viewers to encounter this contemplative stance without any sense of its structural resistance, and thus to embrace Cynic melancholy as an unproblematic, indeed, an appealing, critical orientation. In making this claim, I draw upon Drew Daniel's account of Hamlet's 'melancholic aside', in which he argues that Hamlet's first line – much like Burton's professed affiliation with Diogenes – 'showily announces the very anti-social withdrawal that it also violates'.[21] According to Daniel, melancholy should be understood 'not as a private trait but as a kind of dynamic relationship of assemblage which solicits interpretation, ascription and diagnosis in exchange for the teasing revelation of a rhetorically staged interior'. Manifesting itself as 'a relational network rather than an isolated condition', melancholy connects one person's performance of sadness to a community of witnesses who, in an act of 'interpretive charity', 'complete and ratify its gestures and announcements'. Hamlet's aside actively prompts viewers to 'cultivat[e] a certain kind of attentiveness' – to put themselves in Hamlet's shoes – and it therefore enfolds a wider audience into Hamlet's palimpsest of a critical orientation, his inward turn that remains invested in the project of outward critique.

For Daniel, all displays of melancholy should be understood to function as socially constituted assemblages, and, in this respect, Hamlet's aside is remarkable chiefly for its exemplarity. However, I would argue that Hamlet's aside, along with Burton's 'little obseruation[s]', are crucially different from generic instances of melancholy in that they enfold a specifically Cynic priority into their assembled networks of 'spectatorship and shared experience'. From the start, we are taken in by Hamlet, made part of his melancholy assemblage, and, in this way, we become willing accomplices in Hamlet's posture of Cynic melancholy. It therefore behoves us to think carefully about the critical orientation that we 'approve' and 'ratify' as a result of participating in Hamlet's aside.

Born to Think It Right

After swearing to avenge the ghost of his murdered father at the conclusion of the play's first act, Hamlet utters a famously despairing couplet: 'The time is out of joint. Oh, cursèd spite / That ever I was born to set it right!' (I, v, 189–90). From this moment on, Hamlet finds himself caught in a quite debilitating double bind, for even as he accepts the role of revenger, he also acknowledges that he is utterly unfit to carry out the requisite tasks. In the scenes that follow, Hamlet puts off the culminating act of his revenge in order to think, and, as we all know, many of his thoughts dwell on the very fact that he seems better equipped for thinking than for acting. It is clear that Hamlet experiences distress over his failure to act, and critics have understandably concentrated on this failure in their readings of the play. But while Hamlet never quite abandons the idea that he could and should carry out his revenge (evidenced by his accidentally killing Polonius and his nearly killing Claudius while he is at prayer), I would argue that he does not view his inward turn solely as a failure of action. Embracing the very melancholy that makes him unfit to act, Hamlet often foregoes an effort to set time back into joint through individual action. In these moments, he turns to an ethics of melancholy rumination in order to further disjoin himself from time; he compensates for the pain of his personal failure to act by speculatively aligning himself with the impersonal agency of the cosmos.

This is particularly true on those occasions when Hamlet imagines a sequence of plausibly interrelated events, thereby contemplating his way out of time in order to view worldly happenings from an incorporeal vantage, a perspective from which he can claim to see the inevitability of things as they have been, are and are going to be. For example, we can trace this line of thought in Hamlet's riddling comment when pressed by Claudius to disclose the location of Polonius's body. Here, Hamlet imagines a food-chain involving a dead king, a worm, a fish and a fisherman, in order to assert that 'a king may go a progress through the guts of a beggar' (IV, iii, 31–2). That Hamlet replaces a dead counsellor

(Polonius) with a dead king might indicate that this comment operates as a veiled threat, in which case Hamlet remains conventionally action-oriented, if only in the future tense. Yet Hamlet does not articulate a threat against Claudius so much as he engages in the contemplation of natural history, a turn to the theoretical by which Hamlet aligns himself with cosmic, rather than individual, action.[22] In a manner quite similar to that of his opening line, Hamlet uses his riddling non-threat to turn aside from committing an act. Here, and elsewhere, Hamlet employs his rational powers of distance in order to bear witness to the larger cosmic forces that will enact his revenge for him.

This aspect of Hamlet's Cynic melancholy is especially evident in the graveyard scene, wherein the sight of Yorick's skull prompts Hamlet to descend into a state of melancholy contemplation. Hamlet's meditation over the ossified remains of a free-speaking fool – a figure that Jaques, in *As You Like It*, aligns with the emancipatory powers of Cynic free speech – at first implies that an ethics of rumination has entirely replaced an ethics of combative social critique (imagined here to be dead and devoid of agency). However, it quickly becomes clear that Shakespeare presents the latter as enjoying new life within the ethereal domain of the former. Having already unfurled a series of well-worn and impersonal memento mori tropes – imagining a politician, a courtier and a lawyer each meeting the same ignoble end despite all of their worldly achievements – Hamlet allows his musings to gain a new edge after identifying Yorick's remains. In addition to being a memento mori (a reminder of death), Yorick's skull serves as a *memento moriae* (a reminder of the fool).[23] It reminds Hamlet not only of death's final embrace, but also of the critical activity that can be delivered through passing of time itself.[24] Now Hamlet deploys the memento mori trope with a particular target in mind. 'Get you to my lady's chamber', he instructs the skull, 'and tell her, let her paint an inch thick, to this favour she must come' (V, i, 178–9). The skull will of course tell Gertrude no such thing, an incongruity often understood in terms of its comic effect. Yet Hamlet does not look to the Fool's mute remains in search of communicative agency. Rather, Hamlet satisfies himself with the knowledge that Gertrude will come to this favour whether she's told or not, and, in this way, he subsumes a sense of critical agency under the operations of his thought.

Turning his attention to Claudius, the implicit target of his next flight of fancy, Hamlet further enfolds the model of an outwardly critical Diogenes into the ethereal substance of his inward reflection: 'Why may not imagination trace the noble dust of Alexander till a find it stopping a bunghole?' (V, i, 187–9). Against Horatio's objection that ''Twere to consider too curiously to consider so' (V, i, 190), Hamlet defends the plausibility of this event by further reasoning upon his imagined scenario: 'Alexander died, Alexander was buried, Alexander returneth into dust, the dust is earth, of earth we make loam, and why of that loam whereto he was converted might they not stop a beer barrel?' (V, i, 192–5). Lodging Alexander's dust in the bunghole of a barrel – an iconographically loaded fantasy, given that Diogenes was said to live in a tub – Hamlet imaginatively demonstrates Diogenes' superiority over Alexander, a superiority that pertains to the difference in each figure's 'kind'. As Michel Foucault puts it, Diogenes is the 'king of misery': his self-mortifying way of life allows him to find strength in abjection, and death therefore consolidates his kingliness rather than taking it away.[25] The same cannot be said of Alexander, whose tenuous hold on kingship crumbles to dust along with his body.

By imagining Alexander's bodily dissolution and his eventual incorporation into the structure of Diogenes' tub, Hamlet engages in a speculative philosophy with far-reaching implications. He conceives not simply of a time when Alexander will fall from power, but, more ambitiously, of a time when the very model of sovereign power to which Alexander subscribes will have dissolved and been replaced by a Cynic form of sovereignty (one that stands for the negation of political sovereignty). In other words, Hamlet imagines that history holds – imminent to itself – the unfolding of an altogether new state of affairs, one in which the Cynic mode of sovereignty is the only one to stand the test of time.

Tellingly, the plot of *Hamlet* invites us to compare this conception of historical imminence to the repetitive model of dynastic time figured in Hamlet's two foils: Laertes and Fortinbras. No matter which of these young men succeeds in claiming the throne, one dynasty will have ended and another will have begun in its place. This new dynasty will bear a fresh name, but in formal terms will be no different from the one that came before it, or from the one that will eventually come after.[26] As Margreta de Grazia has keenly noted, Shakespeare's *Hamlet* is thematically preoccupied with the rise and fall of dynasties: 'Its action blocks out the major event punctuating one of the earliest schema for organizing world history: the fall of empire.'[27] But whereas de Grazia understands Hamlet to be chiefly motivated by the desire to assert his rightful claim as King of Denmark – this being her interpretive counterweight to modernity's thought-bound Hamlet – I understand Hamlet to be taking a stance that sets him apart from the interchangeable ambitions of the play's many kings and kingly aspirants.

To be sure, de Grazia is on solid ground when she claims that the plot of Shakespeare's play corroborates the repetitive model of dynastic history, a model that, in early seventeenth-century England, was just beginning to make its rounds.[28] Yet Hamlet, in resisting this dynastic model of history, hews more closely to the biblical schema that served both as this model's historiographic precedent and as its eschatological counterpart. In the Book of Daniel, the prophet Daniel interprets King Nebuchadnezzar's dream as signifying that there will be a succession of four worldly kingdoms, all of which will eventually be subsumed under a fifth and final kingdom, the kingdom of heaven on earth. The four monarchies schema offered a view of history in which worldly forms of power and domination would eventually be supplanted by an entirely new state of affairs, but whereas this biblical template for a 'revolutionary eschatology' looks forward to the second coming of Jesus Christ, Hamlet looks forward to the second coming of Diogenes the Cynic.[29]

My claim that Hamlet replaces Jesus with Diogenes might seem specious, but it in fact draws upon a clear set of precedents. As F. Gerald Downing and others have taken care to demonstrate, early Christians explicitly modelled their asceticism, principled outspokenness and mendicant itinerancy upon the established social protocols of Cynics in the first and second centuries CE.[30] Moreover, many of these same scholars have argued that this line of influence between Cynicism and Christianity began with the historical Jesus himself, a connection that may have been further augmented by Christians of the second and third centuries, who deployed Cynic iconography in their efforts to memorialise the sayings and doings of their Christ and saviour.[31] Shakespeare aligns Hamlet with Christianity's Cynic underpinnings in order to shift away from an eschatology in which the revolutionary moment must proceed from divine intervention and toward an eschatology in which the potential for radical change inheres in earthly processes alone.

Grounded in his posture of Cynic melancholy, Hamlet's conception of the revolutionary moment is keyed to a secular register that both predates and subtends the messianic. It is in this context that Hamlet presents himself as the second coming of Diogenes, a 'king of misery' who seeks out endless suffering not of the body but of the spirit. Through the practice of melancholy Cynicism, Hamlet exposes himself to the painful knowledge that individual critical agency is insufficient to the task of enacting a radical change in the way that society is structured. But rather than falling into a state of existential crisis, Hamlet instead finds strength in his mental abjection; his contemplation of cosmic process gains him access to a view of world history that is rational and developmental, one in which an out-of-joint present must evolve, with logical inexorability, into an ideal future.

Shakespeare's valorised depiction of Cynic melancholy reaches its zenith in the graveyard scene, and it is therefore quite jarring when, in moving from the play's penultimate to its ultimate scene, he allows a Christian, providential vision of history to suddenly snap back into place. This is first made clear when Hamlet – praising the rashness that leads him to snoop on Rosencrantz and Guildenstern and thus to discover the plot against his life – concludes that the unreasoned actions of individuals are in fact guided by the overarching rationality of divine intent: '[t]here's a divinity that shapes our ends, / Rough-hew them how we will' (V, ii, 10–11). A short while later, Shakespeare puts an even brighter spotlight on Hamlet's theological turn by having him appeal to divine providence immediately prior to the climactic fencing match. Hamlet, who has no idea of the fatal events about to take place, nevertheless experiences sudden misgivings over the wager. But when Horatio suggests that Hamlet mould his actions to his thoughts and call the whole thing off, he refuses, insisting that he finds solace in the inevitability of all things:

> *Horatio*: If your mind dislike anything, obey it. I will fore-
> stall their repair hither, and say you are not fit.
> *Hamlet*: Not a whit. We defy augury. There's a special
> providence in the fall of a sparrow. If it be now, 'tis not
> to come. If it be not to come, it will be now. If it be not
> now, yet it will come. The readiness is all. Since no man
> has aught of what he leaves, what is't to leave betimes?
> (5.2.155–61)

For Shakespeare, the irony of Hamlet's apparently sharp reversal lies in his continued dependence upon Christian eschatology's pre-messianic subtext, its specifically Cynic, and therefore secular, remainder. This is first of all true with respect to Hamlet's culminating rhetorical question, whose theme of Christian asceticism holds the faint echo of its Cynic antecedents. But more importantly, a vestige of Hamlet's earlier speculative philosophy remains hidden within the tautological rationale that he now applies to the work of theological moralising. The Hamlet of Act V, scene ii insists that 'a divinity . . . shapes our ends', yet the logic with which he props up his providential reasoning can easily be viewed as a secular tautology, one that ascribes reason to history's unfolding sequences of cause and effect simply by observing that things happen the way they do because that is the way they happen. (This, after all, is precisely how Hegel secularises the rationality of historical process, perhaps most famously in his claim that '[w]hat is rational is actual and what is actual is rational'.[32]) Taking these Cynic remainders into account, it becomes easier for us to see that Hamlet is not disavowing his earlier posture of Cynic melancholy so much as he is trying to supplement for its insufficiencies.

I understand Hamlet's need for this supplement to be symptomatic of the two distinct problems with Cynic melancholy that Shakespeare seeks to diagnose. First, the fact that Hamlet must add providence to his picture of history goes to show that something crucial had been missing all along from his Cynic eschatology, something that could have explained, without recourse to providence, the means by which a fundamental change in society might actually come into being. In his earlier effort to do just that, Hamlet posits that humanity undergoes change through its mediating contact with inhuman natural forces. However, the ecological and geological processes to which Hamlet appeals only grant humans revolution in the cyclical sense, for to be human is always to begin and end as dust, it is always to eat and then to be eaten.[33] Ultimately, it is not at all clear that Hamlet has thought his way through to a revolutionary event, for the come-uppance Alexander receives in becoming part of a beer barrel does nothing to ensure that the barkeep who owns it will live in a world free of kings. To put the point differently, Hamlet's account of historical development does not locate the mediating agency of change within humanity itself, and so, faced with nature's failure to do the work of mankind, Hamlet turns his mind's eye toward providence.

Second, Hamlet's defiance of augury as a means of foretelling the future is a way for Shakespeare to signal the inherent insufficiency of Cynic melancholy as a ruminative stance that is imagined to gain its practitioner privileged access to the cosmic plane of existence. This latter reversal, on Hamlet's part, is especially important for us to consider, for it calls into question the very notion that an individual's ethics of contemplation can deliver to its practitioner a superior view of world-historical truth. It is my contention that this second problem is, for Shakespeare, the more central one, and I say this because it is here that Shakespeare figures Cynic melancholy as a problem of character, a problem of the hermeneutic irreducibility of literary form and practical ethics when attending to character as such.

I will say more about Shakespeare's strategies for disclosing this second problem in this chapter's conclusion, but I identify now the core dilemma that Shakespeare seeks to diagnose because it is one that continues to subtend the modern philosophical tradition that claims Hamlet's intellectual stance for itself. This is particularly true, I argue, with respect to the German philosophy of history that emerges in the context of that country's growing devotion to Shakespeare, in general, and to the character of Hamlet, in particular. As we will see, Hegel and Marx both do better than Hamlet in answering the first problem posed by Shakespeare, for each thinker finds a way to identify humanity as the driving medium of its own historical development. But while Hegel and Marx bring about advancements in the kind of intellection that is understood to grant the fullest possible access to world-historical truth, each thinker manages these achievements while adopting Hamlet's posture of Cynic melancholy, thereby incorporating into their own stance the very problem of character that Shakespeare would have us recognise in Hamlet. In order for us to feel the full import of Shakespeare's diagnosis, we must therefore consider the philosophical tradition that looks to Hamlet for its own point of origin, and, in so doing, learns precisely the wrong lessons from Hamlet's Cynic life of the mind.

'Deutschland ist Hamlet': Germany's Shakespeare and the Philosophy of History

As many critics have noted, Hamlet's modern philosophical reception finds its origins in the intellectual climate of late eighteenth-century Germany, where an emerging interest in the works of Shakespeare played a central role in the articulation of German Romanticism. During the 1770s and 1780s, thinkers in the proto-Romantic *Sturm und Drang* movement began to champion Shakespeare as their preferred model of artistic genius, a model that they adopted in order to escape the aesthetic rigidity of French neoclassicism.[34] Writers such as Johann Herder, Freidrich Schiller and Johann von Goethe, among others, vehemently countered the neoclassical view that Shakespeare's plays were wild and dramaturgically undisciplined, arguing instead that Shakespeare's genius lay in his ability to excite the passions, that is, to access human truths that neoclassical aesthetics and Enlightenment rationality could never hope to grasp. These intellectuals lauded Shakespeare for his wide-ranging talent at evoking passionate character, and, at least early on, they paid no more attention to Hamlet than they did to Shakespeare's other great tragic figures (Othello, Macbeth and Lear) or to the star-crossed Romeo and Juliet.[35] However, as the *Sturm und Drang* movement gave way to a more fully developed Romanticism, Hamlet increasingly came to figure as Germany's representative man, a character whose passionate agitation held particular resonance for those thinkers who had borne witness to Napoleon's co-option of the French revolution and his subsequent ascent into empery. These events were felt by many to announce the general failure of the Enlightenment, and it is in the context of this failure that Adam Müller draws an explicit parallel between Hamlet and a 'new generation' of young Germans that, Hamlet-like, 'arises out of the corruption'.[36] Indeed, Germany's post-Napoleonic identification with Hamlet and his plight proved to be a persistent one, so much so that Ferdinand Freiligrath, writing in 1844, defined his country's national character with the equation 'Deutschland ist Hamlet'.[37] Reading Hamlet as a proxy for their own disappointment over the Enlightenment's failure, German Romantics understood Hamlet's exemplarity to lie in his being a 'rational' character forced to confront the limitations of rationality itself, a character whose elevated passions stem from his terrible awareness of the disjunction between his capacity for reason, on the one hand, and his incapacity for action, on the other.[38]

It is easy enough to see that Hegel's Hamlet – a 'noble soul' who is not 'fit' for the task set before him; a 'lost man' who is 'consumed . . . by inner disgust'[39] – describes the Romantic Hamlet more generally, and a clear line of influence extends from this characterisation to later accounts of Hamlet in the works of Friedrich Nietzsche, Walter Benjamin and Theodor Adorno, among others.[40] This is precisely the view of Hamlet against which Margreta de Grazia takes aim, arguing that the tradition of reading the melancholy prince as modernity's first 'man of thought' is largely the projection of the late eighteenth- and early nineteenth-century think-ers who proposed it.[41] Like de Grazia, I see little continu-ity between Shakespeare's text and the existential Hamlet of post-Enlightenment Germany. However, I do see a continuity between Shakespeare's depiction of Cynic melancholy and the postures adopted by the string of intellectuals – from Herder and Schlegel to Hegel and Marx – who made the philosophy of history a cornerstone of post-Enlightenment thought. I hope to show that these thinkers, especially Hegel and Marx, formulate philosophies of history that afford meaningful contrasts with Hamlet's speculative philosophy, both in the theories that they espouse and in terms of the stances that they adopt, each in their turn, as the foremost conceiver of historical process.

The first link between the philosophy of history and Ger-many's wholesale adoption of Shakespeare was forged by Herder, who could not have written his seminal *This, too, a Philosophy of History* (1774)[42] had he not first written his essay 'Shakespeare' only a year before. Boldly included as the opening chapter of his *Sturm und Drang* manifesto, *Of Ger-man Character and Art*, this essay argues that Shakespeare deviates from the dramatic norms of ancient Greece because the expression of artistic genius is historically contingent.[43] If Shakespeare's art differs so thoroughly from that of Sophocles, it is because he lived in a different time, one that required its own artistic ideals to fully capture that moment's social consciousness. In this influential essay, Herder does not offer a developmental account of history so much as adopt a position of socio-historical relativity. However, crit-ics have understood this essay to lay a crucial foundation for Herder's later intuition that history names the cumulative process by which 'human nature' – what Hegel will later call 'World Spirit' – advances itself. No longer of the opinion that the people of each epoch express a truth unto themselves, Herder now insists that the civilisations of subsequent eras

inevitably build upon the foundation of their forebears: 'the
Egyptians could not be what they were without the people of
the Morn [Phoenicians], the Greek stood upon the shoulders
of the Egyptian, and the Roman mounted the saddle of the
entire world'.[44] This formulation makes it sound as if Herder
subscribes to a linear model of historical accumulation, but
elsewhere in the essay he more clearly envisions a dialectical
process of historical development:

> If human nature, in reference to the good, is not *an auton-
> omous divinity*, it must *learn* everything, it must be cul-
> tivated in progressive steps, in a *gradual struggle* it must
> advance ever further; if that is so, it will be shaped *most
> importantly*, or even *exclusively*, by those dimensions
> which move it toward virtue, struggle, and progress.[45]

Herder's premise that human nature is not god-like – that it
is not timeless and does not have an a priori form and
content – should recall us to the secular bent of Hamlet's
speculative philosophy. But whereas Hamlet understands
historical development to be mediated through a range of
inhuman natural forces, Herder proposes that humanity collectively functions as the vehicle for its own change and progress. According to Herder, this is the case precisely because
human nature discovers its fullest capacities through a process of learning, a developmental triptych of 'virtue, struggle,
and progress' that largely anticipates the arrival, some thirty
years later, of the Hegelian dialectic, a philosophy of history in which humanity's constant movement through thesis,
antithesis and synthesis brings World Spirit ever closer to the
attainment of Absolute Knowledge.

For the purposes of this chapter, it will suffice to say
that Hegel solves the problem of agency in more-or-less the
same way that Herder does: each thinker locates a form of
dialectically progressive rationality within the aggregation
of human experience across time. What Herder and Hegel

share, here, is an important insight into the mediating role
of collective human agency that Hamlet clearly omits from
his own account of historical development. Shakespeare
would, I think, largely agree with this insight, which he withholds from Hamlet in order to expose the prince's intellectual posture to critical scrutiny. That being said, I believe the
object of Shakespeare's scrutiny also extends to an aspect of
Hamlet's Cynic melancholy that Hegel can be said to uncriti-
cally adopt: a sense of self-importance and essential privilege
in being the practitioner of intellection who has made himself
into the foremost conceiver of historical process. Building on
Herder, Hegel ostensibly holds to the view that individual
genius is the manifestation of a given society's Spirit in its
current highest state of development, meaning that an individual's maximum potential is, and always will be, historically situated. But what of the person whose faculty of reason
finds its bearings in the rationality of history itself? What
of the person whose intellectual posture presumes to tran-
scend history, or, at least, to encompass it? What of Hegel,
or of Hamlet before him? Hegel, like Hamlet, places himself
above all others by contemplatively disjoining himself from
his given time in order to conceptually merge with time in its
larger historical flow.

My interest in this parallel resides in the very fact that
Hegel resists it, and, moreover, that his resistance is at its
most symptomatic when he comments upon Hamlet's ('infe-
rior') personal connection to Spirit. We see this on display,
for example, when Hegel explains Hamlet's overall stunt-
edness by pointing to the prince's melancholy disposition,
'which keeps its energy of soul pent up like the spark in the
flint', and which therefore 'remains exposed to the grim contradiction of having no skill, no bridge to reconcile its heart
with reality and so to ward off external circumstances'.[46]
Hegel understands Hamlet to manifest a troubled interiority, a state of inward conflict that is itself a fairly advanced

manifestation of spirit, but that ultimately figures as a mere steppingstone along a much greater path. By this view, Hamlet's inability to reconcile his 'heart' with 'reality' figures as a thesis and antithesis that he fails to sublate into a synthesis. Lacking the higher order of comprehension that could have sustained, and so withstood, the incommensurability of his heart and reality, Hamlet is thus presumed unable to think his way beyond the challenges posed by 'external circumstances'. For Hegel, it is this failure of thought, more than anything else, that dooms Hamlet to the endless purgatory of a 'grim contradiction'.

The irony of this assessment becomes clear when we set it alongside another moment of commentary, one in which Hegel invokes the ghost of Old Hamlet (who actually is doomed to purgatory) as a figure for World Spirit in the midst of its historical development:

> Spirit often seems to have forgotten and lost itself, but inwardly opposed to itself, it is inwardly working ever forward (as when Hamlet says of the ghost of his father, 'Well said, old mole! canst work i' the ground so fast?') until grown strong in itself it bursts asunder the crust of earth which divided it from the sun, its Notion, so that the earth crumbles away.[47]

Hegel's description of the ghost allows it to work perfectly well as a figure for World Spirit. That being said, it is telling that Hegel parenthetically appropriates Hamlet's remark concerning the ghost's progress. The irony, here, is quite rich, for when Hegel wants to comment upon World Spirit's forward advancement, all he has to do is put himself in Hamlet's place. Indeed, this irony is still further compounded in light of Hegel's claim (in the *Aesthetics*) that 'the appearance of the ghost in *Hamlet* is treated as just an objective form of Hamlet's inner presentiment'.[48] If we integrate this pronouncement with Hegel's more overt rumination on the philosophy of history, something Hegel himself would surely never do, then we end up with a proposition that locates the historical dialectic within the interior landscape of Hamlet's speculative philosophy. This is not to suggest that Hamlet manifests Absolute Knowledge through his conception of historical process; rather it is to suggest that Hamlet adopts the same posture that Hegel claims for himself: that of the foremost conceiver of history.

Hegel does not see the resemblance between Hamlet's posture and his own, and this is by no means surprising; by diagnosing Hamlet's inability to comprehend a larger, more meaningful horizon of possibility, Hegel presents himself as the one who is able to sustain this larger perspective. This becomes apparent when, near the end of the *Aesthetics*, Hegel returns to a discussion of Hamlet in order to establish an implicit distinction between himself and the melancholy Dane:

> Looked at from the outside, Hamlet's death seems to be brought about accidentally owing to the fight with Laertes and the exchange of rapiers. But death lay from the beginning in the background of Hamlet's mind. The sands of time do not content him. In his melancholy and weakness, his worry, his disgust at all the affairs of life, we sense from the start that in all his terrible surroundings he is a lost man, almost consumed already by inner disgust before death comes to him from the outside.[49]

Much of Hegel's assessment is accurate. Hamlet is disgusted by 'all the affairs of life', and death does always linger in the background of his mind. However, Hamlet is not an entirely 'lost man' (at least, he does not feel himself to be one), and this is the case precisely because Hamlet, like Hegel, does find a degree of contentment in the sands of time. Indeed, the chief difference between Hegel's and Hamlet's contemplative

postures is that Hamlet literally contents himself by speculating upon the material life of sand, dust, earth and loam
as they transubstantiate over time. As we know, one consequence of this difference is that Hegel arrives at a sounder
philosophy of history, one that more plausibly accounts
for humanity's participation in its own development. But
this is not the whole of the story, for the contrast between
Hamlet and Hegel cuts both ways. Though Hamlet's speculative philosophy falls short of Hegel's in the long run, his
imaginative fixation upon the sheer materiality of existence
anticipates one of the key insights that allows Marx to invert
the Hegelian dialectic, thereby supplanting it with historical
materialism.

Notably, Marx's turn to materialism provides him with a
philosophy of history that is able to comprehend the inevitability of a future in which his ideals will accord with reality.
In this respect, he resembles Hamlet much more than Hegel
does. Yet this resemblance, too, has its limits, for Marx,
like Hegel before him, manages to account for humanity's
collective agency in a way that Hamlet does not. Whereas
Hamlet never successfully thinks beyond a circular (and thus
ultimately static) human/nature binary, Marx achieves an
understanding of historical development in which humanity
creates its own growing room through its increasing dominion over nature. What's more, Marx comprehends that the
very means by which humanity strengthens its dominion over
nature – changes to its systems of labour – itself constitutes
humanity's growth.

In Marx's philosophy of history, it is labour that connects
humanity both to itself and to the natural world. Moreover,
it is only through deliberate attentiveness toward relations of
labour – what Marx calls the 'social relations of production' –
that he envisions our ever reaching the developmental end-
point of communism, a way of organising society that comes

remarkably close to Hamlet' kingless ideal. In this respect, at least, Hamlet falls tragically short of Marx, for even as Hamlet's speculative materialism shines a kingless future brightly in his mind's eye, he remains largely blind to the relations of production that everywhere surround him, relations that ensure him access to the world of thought precisely because others are more bound than he to the world of labour.

It would be disingenuous (and anachronistic) to credit Shakespeare with the production of a Marxian critique. Nevertheless, I hope to show, by way of conclusion, that Shakespeare begins to unravel the assembled networks of 'spectatorship and shared experience' that attach us to Hamlet's Cynic melancholy precisely by drawing our attention to the prince's unself-knowing complicity with the kinds of naturalised social imbalances that Marx, too, works to expose.[50] At the same time, however, I hope to show that Shakespeare's proto-Marxist unveiling of Hamlet's Cynic melancholy exposes to our view something inherent to this posture that has remained naturalised for Marx (and Hegel) as well: the assumption that an ethics of intellection remains grounded more in the world of lived experience than in the world of forms and ideals.

A King of Infinite Space, or, Hamlet's Bad Dream

Hamlet's posture of Cynic melancholy depends on one premise above all others: that he differs from Claudius just as much as Diogenes differs from Alexander. However, Shakespeare is throughout at pains to subvert this premise, to show that Hamlet's philosophical posturing does not distinguish him from Claudius nearly as much as he would like. This is especially true of the scene in which Hamlet first encounters Rosencrantz and Guildenstern, the two aspiring courtiers who have been tasked by Claudius to discover the heart of Hamlet's mystery. In the witty exchange that follows, Rosencrantz and Guildenstern try to coax Hamlet into admitting that he holds his own ambition for the throne, that he is, in other words, Claudius's like-minded competitor. Hamlet predictably rejects this notion, and, in so doing, identifies himself as a melancholy Cynic in particularly explicit terms. As we will see, however, Shakespeare uses this encounter as a means of foregrounding the general myopia inherent in Hamlet's Cynic self-identification.

The terms of this exchange begin with Hamlet's declaration that 'Denmark's a prison', an assertion of general discontentment that Rosencrantz takes as an occasion for needling Hamlet: 'Why then, your ambition makes it one. 'Tis too narrow for your mind' (II, ii, 239, 250–2). Hamlet in turn rejects the imputation of worldly ambition, and he does so in a way that instantly alerts us to the operations of his Cynic melancholy: 'Oh, god, I could be bounded in a nutshell and count myself a king of infinite space, were it not that I had bad dreams' (II, ii, 255–7). Here, we see Hamlet placing himself within a miniaturised (subjective) reworking of Diogenes' tub, and the suggestion seems to be that Hamlet's ethics of melancholy rumination grants him dominion over an incorporeal, cosmic and divine plane of existence. To be 'king of infinite space', then, is to invert the critical mission that prompts Diogenes' to become a 'citizen of the cosmos'[51]; it is to look inward in such a way that one's mind expands outward; it is to maximise one's powers of observation. However, Hamlet has no sooner identified himself with Cynic inwardness than he cites 'bad dreams' as an obstacle to the realisation of his cosmic kingliness. I would like to suggest that, for Shakespeare, Hamlet's 'bad dreams' are a figure for the more pervasive instability that plagues his critical vision whenever he believes himself to be most holding true to his posture of unworldly rational detachment. To see this about Hamlet is to undo the melancholy assemblage that ties us to him, and, as the verbal sparring between Rosencrantz,

Guildenstern, and Hamlet carries on, Shakespeare seems intent on helping viewers to this insight.

Never one to give up on a good probing, Guildenstern tries to replicate Rosencrantz's opening gambit, suggesting that Hamlet's 'bad dreams' are synonymous with his worldly ambition: 'Which dreams indeed are ambition' (II, ii, 251). But in a playful turn, Guildenstern then inverts and amplifies his proposed equation, not simply suggesting that ambition is itself as immaterial as a dream, but also that 'the very substance of the ambitious is merely the shadow of a dream' (II, ii, 251–2). I summarise their witty banter at such length in order to give context to the discussion's climax, in which Hamlet takes up the idea of an ambitious person's shadowy immateriality in order to imaginatively enact a Cynic revaluation of beggars and monarchs: 'Then are our beggars bodies, and our monarchs and outstretched heroes the beggar's shadows. Shall we to th' court? For by my fay, I cannot reason' (II, ii, 256–8).[52] Hamlet deploys the conceit of a body and its larger-but-less-substantial shadow in order to suggest that a beggar obtains a more solid and meaningful presence in the world than does a king. Here then, we have a reiteration of the Diogenes/Alexander paradigm, and Hamlet wastes no time in emphasising his placement within this context: 'Beggar that I am, I am even poor in thanks' (II, ii, 265).

Hamlet's announcement that he 'cannot reason' produces an effect similar to that of his first melancholy aside. It validates the special bond between Hamlet and an audience that shares in the 'private' knowledge that he is 'but mad in craft' (III, iv, 195). Thus, Hamlet's feigned madness further encourages our participation in a melancholy assemblage that has Hamlet's Cynic ruminations at its gravitational core. I wish to note, however, that this assemblage starts to unravel once viewers begin to recognise the truth behind Hamlet's claim that he 'cannot reason'. Hamlet's Cynic melancholy, which promises so much, ultimately dooms him to the shifting terrain of a bad dream. One moment, Hamlet sees himself as the disembodied king of 'infinite space', and the next moment he finds solidity in the body of a beggar, as if his Cynic stance imbues him with a kind of variable density that can alter the physics of personal cause and worldly effect. Hamlet's bad dream thus begins with fantasies of having it all, and the versatility that such a fantasy requires of Hamlet is precisely what leads to his critical disorientation. Having claimed for himself the solid body of a beggar, Hamlet's 'king of infinite space' now resembles the ambitious monarch that Guilden-stern likens to an immaterial shadow. In properly nightmar-ish fashion, this formal correspondence blurs the distinction between physical and metaphysical categories of power, and this is chiefly the case because Hamlet is never as absolute as he thinks in his rejection of the one and embrace of the other.

Ironically, this blurring of categories is nowhere more evident than in the graveyard scene, wherein Hamlet satis-fies his antagonism toward Claudius by speculating upon the natural processes by which the body of Alexander might one day be added to the structure of Diogenes' tub. The force of this cosmically mediated critique requires that Hamlet be firmly aligned with Diogenes, a Cynic affiliation that Hamlet confidently assumes for himself. Yet all this while, another diogenical figure continues to busily dig a grave. I would call it Ophelia's grave, but the gravedigger might disagree: 'it is mine', he insists, calling it a house that 'lasts till doomsday' (V, ii, 123; V, ii, 59).[53] The gravedigger's likeness to Diogenes and his tub is clear, as is the parallel between Alexander and Hamlet, who first decides to engage the gravedigger in con-versation. 'I'll speak to this fellow', Hamlet announces, like the prince he really is (V, i, 117). As this reversal makes plain, Hamlet's posture of Cynic melancholy has from the start been propped up by his condition of worldly comfort and privilege, meaning that Hamlet can contemplatively reject the world in which he lives only because that very world

constitutes the enabling condition for his contemplative posture's existence.

Earlier, I suggested that Hamlet's ruminations over Yorick's skull marked the zenith of the play's valorised depiction
of Cynic melancholy, but this is true only in part, for Shakespeare is trying to manage two competing perspectives in his
staging of this scene. On the one hand, Shakespeare presents
the graveyard scene as the culmination of his viewers' participation in Hamlet's melancholy assemblage, their coordi-
nation with and through the modern subjective experience
of Cynic melancholy. This is a vantage from which one per-
ceives Hamlet's ethics of intellection to be precisely that, an
ethics, a cultivated way of life that obtains for its practitioner a certain privileged access to the world's governing rationality, and hence to its essential truths. On the other hand,
Shakespeare's staging of this scene discloses to his viewers
the structural resistance of Cynic character, for the tableau
of Hamlet standing over the Gravedigger prompts viewers to
adopt a dramatic perspective rather than a subjective one. It
therefore serves to remind us that our engagement with ethical postures is always routed through formal and aesthetic
contingencies; it reminds us that the cultivation of character
carries with it a certain risk, for it sometimes allows us to feel
like we are grounding ourselves in the realm of the political
precisely when we are most immersed in the realm of the
aesthetic.

In the character of Hamlet, Shakespeare depicts an impossible critical orientation with which playgoers and readers
can nevertheless form an ethical identification. Shakespeare
demonstrates his insight into the figure of Diogenes by repro-
ducing in Hamlet the same aspirational dynamic that drives
certain thinkers to admire an extreme posture of Cynic melancholy. Having done so, however, Shakespeare works to
expose us to the error we commit in taking Hamlet's critical
orientation as a model for our own. The easy reversibility

with which Shakespeare can align Hamlet first with Diogenes and then with Alexander serves as a bracing reminder that, in practice, Hamlet falls far short of his own ethical ideal, and, moreover, that he lacks self-awareness precisely because of his relation to this ideal. Finally, then, Shakespeare shares his insight into the figure of Diogenes by prompting his audience to recognise that they have been caught in Hamlet's bad dream, his unstable relation to the fantasy of critical transcendence.

Notes

1. Nietzsche, *Beyond Good and Evil*.
2. De Grazia, *Hamlet without Hamlet*.
3. Shakespeare, *The Tragedy of Hamlet, Prince of Denmark* in *The Norton Shakespeare*, IV, iii, 31–2; V, i, 188–9. Further citations will be to this edition and in-text.
4. The emphasis I place on politics, here, might suggest that this formulation is more Marxian than Hegelian. However, I would argue that Hegel understands the process by which humanity gets closer to the attainment of Absolute Knowledge to index, among other things, progressive developments in the political organisation of human society.
5. See Strier, *Resistant Structures*, esp. pp. 1–9.
6. For an excellent account of intellectual melancholy in the early modern period, see Trevor, *The Poetics of Melancholy in Early Modern England*.
7. Walkington, *The optick glasse of humors*, 40^v.
8. Mazella, *The Making of Modern Cynicism*, p. 49.
9. *Problemata*, cited in Anon., *The Works of Aristotle*, vol. 7, p. 29, 954b21–27.
10. Ficino, *Three Books on Life*, p. 115.
11. As Trevor explains, Burton's understanding of melancholy is not confined to the Galenic model, for he 'goes out of his way to suggest that social ills contribute to one's dispositional tendencies'. According to Trevor, one of the social ills that particularly concerns Burton is the system of patronage by

which graduates of Oxford and Cambridge secure Church vacancies, a system that was increasingly overburdened by a surplus of Oxbridge degree-holders, and which had therefore begun to favour those young men whose dispositional qualities and social graces were not like those of a true intellectual. Consequently, Burton used *The Anatomy of Melancholy* as a ruminative vehicle for 'vent[ing] his frustrations over a patronage system that, in his eyes, is stubbornly bent on rewarding only ill-deserving pseudo-scholars'. See Trevor, *The Poetics of Melancholy in Early Modern England*, pp. 118, 120. For an account of the problems posed by the period's surplus of Oxbridge degree holders, see Curtis, 'The Alienated Intellectuals of Early Stuart England'.

12. Burton, *The Anatomy of Melancholy*, p. 4.

13. Burton, *The Anatomy of Melancholy*, p. 10.

14. Burton, *The Anatomy of Melancholy*, p. 4.

15. 'observe, v.'. *OED Online*. March 2013. Oxford University Press. http://www.oed.com/view/Entry/129893?rskey=1QGu dH&result=2 (last accessed 2 April 2013). Francis Bacon is one of the earliest best known proponents of scientific observation: 'And as for the footesteps of diseases, & their deuastations of the inward parts, . . . they ought to haue beene exactly obserued by multitude of Anatomies.' See Bacon, *Of the Proficience and Aduancement of Learning*, II sig. Ll2.

16. 'observe, v.'. *OED Online*. Not coincidentally, the *OED* also lists Bacon as the first recorded example of 'observe' being used in this way: 'Your Maiestie doth excellently well obserue, that Witch-craft is the height of Idolatry.' See Bacon, *Of the Proficience and Aduancement of Learning*, II. sig. Ggg4^v.

17. Erasmus, *Apophthegmes*, M5^r-M5^v. For another influential version of this story, see Plutarch, *The Lives of the Noble Grecians and Romanes*, p. 728.

18. See Wilson, *Arte of Rhetorique*, sig. Ddii^v; and Lyly, *Campaspe*.

19. Drew Daniel offers a useful summary of this editorial dispute in his chapter on *Hamlet* in *The Melancholy Assemblage*, esp. pp. 135–9.

20. Wilson, *Arte of Rhetorique,* sig. Ddii^v.

21. Daniel, *The Melancholy Assemblage*, p. 137.

22. To speak of cosmic action as opposed to cosmic process is, in this instance, simply a matter of perspective. My contention is that Hamlet's intellectual consolation rests on his holding to the perspective by which cosmic forces can be understood in terms that parallel the category of action that he cannot claim for himself.

23. For a detailed account of the relationship between fools and the memento mori topos in Shakespeare's England, see Shickman, 'The Fool and Death in Shakespeare'. Marjorie Garber also notes this link, specifically as Shakespeare handles it, in 'Remember Me'.

24. We should be reminded, here, of Jaques's first encounter with Touchstone, in *As You Like It*. As Jaques relates their first meeting, Touchstone pulls out a timepiece and discourses on the fact that everything comes to an end. Jaques uses this example as the chief justification for his own ambition for a motley coat.

25. Foucault, *Le courage de la vérité*, p. 258. My translation.

26. We should be reminded of Claudius's effort to grant Hamlet a sense of perspective with respect to the loss of his father: 'But you must know your father lost a father; / That father lost, lost his' (I, ii, 89–90).

27. De Grazia, *Hamlet without Hamlet*, p. 48.

28. Leroy, *Of the Interchangeable Course, or Variety of Things*, for example, understood history in terms of a perpetual waxing and waning of successive empires. Quoted in de Grazia, *Hamlet without Hamlet*, p. 49.

29. As Norman Cohn has established, the promise of a fifth, heavenly kingdom held a particular appeal for certain seventeenth-century millennial sects, for whom it figured as their 'central phantasy of revolutionary eschatology'. See Cohn, *The Pursuit of the Millennium*, p. 21. Quoted in de Grazia, *Hamlet without Hamlet*, p. 49.

30. Downing, *Christ and the Cynics*.

31. For a useful survey of this scholarship, see Eddy, 'Jesus as Diogenes?'.

32. Hegel, *The Philosophy of Right*, p. 20.

33. Interestingly, Hamlet seems to share this view of historical recurrence when he first enters the graveyard and finds himself reflecting upon an anonymous skull: 'Here's fine revolution, an we the trick to see't' (V, i, 82–3). It is only later, when he holds before him a *memento moriae*, instead of a memento mori, that Hamlet speculates upon nature's ability to provide humanity with a new kind of revolution: 'To what base uses we may return, Horatio! Why may not imagination trace the noble dust of Alexander till a find it stopping a bung-hole?' (V, i, 187–9).

34. For a general account of the French neoclassical assessment of Shakespeare, see Haines, *Shakespeare in France*.

35. Roger Paulin outlines the German reception of Shakespeare, with unparalleled detail, in *The Critical Reception of Shakespeare in Germany* 1682–1914.

36. Müller, 'Fragmente über William Shakespear', 78f, quoted in and translated by Paulin, *The Critical Reception of Shakespeare in Germany*, p. 442.

37. Quoted in Paulin, *The Critical Reception of Shakespeare in Germany*, p. 443.

38. It is in this context that, in 1844, the poet Ferdinand Freiligrath famously summed up the German zeitgeist with the assertion that 'Deutschland ist Hamlet'.

39. Hegel, *Aesthetics*, vol. 2, p. 1226; vol. 2, pp. 1231–2.

40. Nietzsche, *The Birth of Tragedy*; Benjamin, *The Origin of German Tragic Drama*, pp. 157–8; Adorno, *Negative Dialectics*, p. 228.

41. de Grazia, *Hamlet without Hamlet*.

42. Herder, *On World History*.

43. Herder, *Selected Writings on Aesthetics*, pp. 456–81.

44. Herder, *On World History*, p. 42.

45. Herder, *On World History*, p. 38.

46. Hegel, *Aesthetics*, vol. 1, p. 583.

47. Hegel, *Lectures on the Philosophy of History*, vol. 3, pp. 546–7.

48. Hegel, *Aesthetics*, vol. 1, p. 231.

49. Hegel, *Aesthetics*, vol. 2, pp. 1231–2.
50. Daniel, *The Melancholy Assemblage*, p. 134.
51. Laertius, *Lives of Eminent Philosophers*, 6.63.
52. It is noteworthy that Foucault arrives at a very similar formulation: 'The Cynic himself is a king; he is even the only king. Crowned sovereigns, visible sovereigns, as it were, are only the shadow of the true monarchy. The Cynic is the only true king.' See Foucault, *Courage of Truth*, p. 275.
53. This claim of structural permanence should, I think, be read alongside Hamlet's speculation that Diogenes' tub will persist long after the body of Alexander has disintegrated.

CHAPTER 5

CASH IS KING: TIMON, DIOGENES AND THE SEARCH FOR SOVEREIGN FREEDOM

Timon: Earth, yield me roots.
    [*He digs*]
Who seeks for better of thee, sauce his palate
With thy most operant poison.
    [*He finds gold*]

Shakespeare, Timon of Athens¹

The interpretative tradition that understands Diogenes to be a social critic takes its cue from Diogenes Laertius, who begins his chapter on Diogenes with three origin stories, the first of which concerns Diogenes' expulsion from Sinope and his subsequent conversion to the life of a philosopher:

> Diocles relates that he went into exile because his father was entrusted with the money of the state and adulterated the coinage. But Eubulous in his book on Diogenes says that Diogenes himself actually confesses in his *Pordalus* that he adulterated the coinage. Some say that having been appointed to superintend the workmen he was persuaded by them, and that he went to Delphi or to the Delian oracle in his own city and inquired of Apollo whether he should do what he was urged to do. When the god gave him permission to alter the political currency, not understanding what

this meant, he adulterated the state coinage, and when he was detected, according to some he was banished, while according to others he voluntarily quitted the city for fear of consequences. One version is that his father entrusted him with the money and that he debased it, in consequence of which the father was imprisoned and died, while the son fled, came to Delphi, and inquired, not whether he should falsify the coinage, but what he should do to gain the greatest reputation; and that then it was that he received the oracle.[2]

This story concerns the inception of Diogenes' critical mission to deface or alter 'the political currency'. In it, Diogenes begins by counterfeiting the tender of Sinope and ends by successfully exposing the fraud run rampant in Greek life, defacing not the currency, but the current: the unquestioned drift of politics. Consequently, this story has been read alongside another anecdote in which Diogenes privileges *parrhêsia*, or free and fearless speech, above all other things: 'Being asked what was the most beautiful thing in the world, he replied, "Freedom of speech" [*parrhêsia*].'[3]

Throughout this book, I have attended to a valorised reception of Diogenes that points back to this first origin story and to the collection of critique-oriented anecdotes that cohere around it, and so it is worth noting that this first account of Diogenes' philosophical beginnings has generally not been understood, in its later reception, to reference Cynic *askēsis* and the benefits of embracing a life of extreme asceticism. Instead, early modern thinkers found this latter aspect of Cynicism in the subsequent origin story wherein Diogenes learns from the ethical example set by a mouse:

Through watching a mouse running about, . . . not looking for a place to lie down in, not afraid of the dark, not seeking any of the things which are considered dainties, [Diogenes] discovered the means of adapting himself to circumstances. He was the first, say some, to fold his cloak because he was obliged to sleep in it as well, and he carried a wallet to hold his victuals, and he used any place for any purpose, for breakfasting, sleeping, or conversing.[4]

In the context of Cynicism's reception history, this alternative creation myth has worked at cross-purposes with the first origin story, for it omits any mention of Diogenes' critical orientation and instead dilates upon his determination to become indifferent to life's accidents, his proto-Stoic discovery that an abstemious way of life constitutes the best and only 'means of adapting himself to circumstances'. As we've seen in Chapter 3, Shakespeare draws attention to these competing interpretations of Cynicism's guiding purpose – to facilitate radically effective truth-telling, on the one hand, and to attain peace of mind, on the other – when he contrasts Lear's Fool to the 'unaccommodated man' Lear supposes Edgar to be. This contrast serves to register the mistake Lear makes in preferring Edgar's private ethical project over that of the Fool's public one. In dramatising this distinction, Shakespeare effectively captures an assumption that subtends the cleavage between these two teleological visions for Cynic practice: an ascetic way of life is presumed to underwrite the project of proto-Stoic indifference rather than serving as the enabling basis for outwardly directed critique.

This is not to say that no relationship has been understood to exist between Diogenes' freedom of speech and his rejection of worldly goods, but thinkers in the sixteenth century and beyond tended to downplay this aspect of the Cynic way of life, pragmatically relegating asceticism to the conventionally Aristotelean status of a virtuous mean-state – in which case abstemiousness ceases to be virtuous (and hence politically efficacious) when taken too far. Instead, early modern thinkers who formed an aspirational attachment to Diogenes imagined that the unique veridical powers of Cynic

truth-telling – which Foucault links to a virtue ('the courage of truth') that inheres not in moderation but rather in
ethical extremism – derived from other aspects of the Cynic
way of life. When Thomas Wilson cites accounts of Diogenes
confronting Alexander the Great to idealise the argumentative potency of Cynic outspokenness, he understands Cynic
critical agency to be achieved through an unwavering commitment to the parrhesiastic principle of saying exactly what
one thinks.[5] Alternatively, when Robert Burton likens himself to Diogenes in order to lay claim to a specifically Cynic
form of thoughtful sadness – one that posits contemplative
self-enclosure as public activism's final frontier – his conviction in this sublimated form of critical agency is based on the
notion that extreme dedication to an ethics of melancholy
rumination will enable him to satisfy his yearning for individual agency through communion with the vast and impersonal agency of the cosmos.

But while Diogenes' early modern admirers tended not to
draw a causal connection between Cynic *parrhêsia* and an
ascetic way of life, Shakespeare and Middleton's collaborative depiction of Timon suggests their sensitivity to seeing
precisely such a connection in the story of Diogenes misunderstanding the oracular pronouncement that he should alter
the currency.[6] That is, there is an implicit point being made
when Diogenes first corrupts the Sinopean coinage before
realising that his true purpose is to alter the political currency, one that Shakespeare and Middleton grasp far better
than many of their contemporaries: in order for Diogenes'
critical mission to succeed, he must leave the world of money
behind. He must operate, that is to say, entirely outside of
money's influence.

As I argued at the conclusion of Chapter 4, Shakespeare
draws upon precisely this insight when he undercuts Hamlet's
posture of Cynic melancholy by exposing its material underpinnings. It is in the graveyard scene that Hamlet most fully

inhabits an intellectualised critical stance, reflecting on the natural processes by which the body of Alexander the Great might eventually be incorporated into the structure of a dio-genical barrel in order to imagine a broader historical process by which the politics of kingship (for which he is not fit) will eventually be supplanted by a new, more ideal formation of the political. Yet this same scene is also the occasion for Shakespeare's contrasting of Hamlet with the gravedigger, an encounter that cuts against Hamlet's identificatory deployment of the Diogenes/Alexander binary by calling to our attention Hamlet's decidedly Alexander-like condescension in visiting a lowly subject. As this reversal makes plain, Hamlet's posture of Cynic melancholy has from the start been propped up by his condition of worldly comfort and privilege, meaning that Hamlet can contemplatively reject the world in which he lives only because those very comforts and privileges constitute the enabling (and debasing) condition for his contemplative posture's existence.

In their Cynic depiction of Timon, Shakespeare and Middleton invert Shakespeare's previous treatment of Hamlet in two key respects. First, they move from negatively applying the oracle's implied axiom to testing its positive account: can Timon leave the world of money well and truly behind and, in doing so, succeed where Hamlet failed? Second, they reverse the procedure of collapsing Alexander and Diogenes together (as is the case with Hamlet), instead presenting Timon as modelling himself first after the one and then after the other. In doing so, Shakespeare and Middleton deploy the Alexander/Diogenes diptych in a new way, using it as an occasion to test not one but two fantasies of sovereign freedom, both of which hinge on the possibility of existing beyond the reach of money's influence. In both his philanthropic and misanthropic modes, Timon attempts to free himself from the requirements of an otherwise moneyed world. Both attempts meet with failure, but these failures serve to diagnose two distinct fantasies of sovereign freedom that emerge in symptomatic response to a world in which cash is king.[7]

Over the past few decades, Shakespeare's canon has emerged as a privileged object of analysis within the domain of literary studies we now call 'the new economic criticism', and *Timon of Athens*, a play at the margins of traditional Shakespeare studies, has attained a position of considerable prominence in this developing subfield. Where Michael Chorost looks to the deployment of biological metaphors that grapple with money's apparent reproductive ability in interest-bearing loans, Derek Cohen attends to scenes that dramatise the destabilisation of both wealth and poverty as markers of social identity in England's increasingly debt-based economy. Amanda Bailey, focusing on a different aspect of early capitalism's socio-economic impact, tracks the play's engagement with the problem of the penal debt bond, a sixteenth-century legal practice that sought to anchor the value of credited money in the very person of the borrower. Grasping that the play moralises Timon's failure to understand – and successfully operate within – a cash and credit economy, Chorost, Cohen and Bailey all seek to learn from those characters who negotiate their economic conditions of existence with greater success. However, such an emphasis works at cross-purposes with the play as a whole, which consistently focuses on Timon's individualism and which mounts a clear indictment against those who eagerly participate in the monetised world of Athens. Unlike these critics, Shakespeare and Middleton are not primarily interested in tracking the effect that changing economic structures have on social bonds; rather, they are chiefly concerned with the effect these changes have on idealised notions of sovereignty's exceptional relation to the social and the political, especially with respect to money.[8]

When Shakespeare and Middleton have Timon undertake a project of ascetic extremism in the play's second half,
they put to the test an approach to Cynic critical activity
premised on overcoming the alienating effects of a cash and
credit economy. In doing so, they turn their diagnostic eye
toward a fantasy of sovereign freedom specific to the person
who, having perceived the alienating effects of mankind's
monetisation, seeks to reclaim his sovereign ability in order
to restore the world to its 'true values'. With their characterisation of a misanthropic Timon, Shakespeare and Middleton
shift away from the question of how best to speak truth to
power and toward the question of how best to speak truth to
monetised power, a critical venture in which freedom from
money's influence provides the sovereign basis both for fully
perceiving money's corrupting influence and for communicating the truth of that corrupting influence with incorrupt-
ible authority. In disclosing the political inefficacy of this
ethical undertaking, Shakespeare and Middleton anticipate
later developments in Diogenes' reception history that take
shape only in the eighteenth century and beyond.[9] By way
of conclusion, I will turn to this later reception history in
order to argue that Shakespeare and Middleton's portrayal
of a misanthropic Timon mounts an intervention that is even
more relevant now, in the era of late capitalism, than it was
at the play's writing.

In Acts I and II, Shakespeare and Middleton use their
portrayal of a philanthropic and Alexander-like Timon
both to disclose and to challenge a monarchical fantasy of
sovereign frankness that emerges, in early modernity, as a
compensatory response to the development of a cash and
credit economy. From this point of view, sovereign freedom
names the condition of a person thought to enjoy unrivalled
command over performative speech, a person who – like
a worldly embodiment of the unquenchable sun – has the
unique ability to speak new value into being. Following the

1579 translation of Marco Polo's *Travels*, which describes Genghis Khan's implementation of fiat money (currency whose value inheres solely in a ruler's edict), the possibility of such sovereign frankness was a live issue in England.[10] Indeed, at the time that Shakespeare and Middleton were writing *Timon*, James I's seemingly unsustainable scaling-up of royal patronage – combined with his absolutist interpretation of the crown's sovereign powers – meant that the monarchical fantasy of sovereign frankness was more topical than ever.[11] By disclosing the impossibility of this fantasy, Shakespeare and Middleton mount an intervention that is more pertinent to their own historical moment than it had ever been before and has ever been since, and it is therefore unsurprising that this more urgent anxiety serves as the focus of the play's opening half.

The Frank Sovereign and the Sovereign Franc

During his period of extravagant generosity, Timon insists that he has no interest in placing himself above anyone else, professing that his are the acts not of a patron, but of a true friend. However, even as Timon claims to act from within a relationship of mutual equivalence and absolute reciprocity, a relationship in which the interests and needs of his friends are indivisible from his own, Timon consistently seeks to further the imbalance between himself and the recipients of his largesse.[12] This is disclosed when Timon, who first displays his liberality by paying to free Ventidius from debtors' prison, refuses to accept any repayment once Ventidius has come into an inheritance. As many critics have noted, Timon's insistence upon a linear, rather than a circular, economy of gift-giving is analogous to the 'Big Man' systems of many non-Western cultures, wherein a truly great man gives unilaterally until his wealth is completely depleted.[13] The assumption is that other great men will give in turn, thus

restoring a depleted 'Big Man' to his original state of material splendour, and Timon, much in keeping with the 'Big
Man' system, tries to invoke this larger form of reciprocity
during his time of greatest need.

This analogy has proven to be highly persuasive, and yet,
in certain key respects, it has also been misleading. Though it
is true that Timon eventually resorts to the logic of a depleted
'Big Man', it does not follow that he has always understood
himself to be operating under this system's ultimately reciprocal terms. Indeed, I would argue that Timon's initial motiva-
tion for gift-giving rests on another logic entirely, one that is
native to the monarchical context of early modern England
and is therefore occluded from our view by readings that
hinge upon an anthropological analogy. This is made most
evident when Timon, reflecting on the scale of his own beneficence, rhetorically positions himself as a king of kings, as a
man of the same stature as Alexander the Great: 'Methinks
I could deal kingdoms to my friends, / And ne'er be weary'
(I, ii, 215–16). In a manner akin to that of a 'Big Man', Timon's
assertion of friendship is belied by the unidirectionality of his
gift-giving. But whereas even a 'Big Man' must eventually rely
upon the generosity of others, Timon expresses a desire to give
endlessly, to be, as the Poet puts it, a 'magic of bounty' (I, i, 6).

Of course, Timon possesses nothing like the generative
powers that he imagines. As his loyal steward, Flavius, despair-
ingly reveals to a fellow servant,

> [Timon's] promises fly so beyond his state
> That what he speaks is all in debt, he owes
> For every word. (I, ii, 192–4)

In pursuing his frank ideal, Timon has in fact been borrowing large sums of money – at interest – from the very
lords who benefit most from his one-way generosity. Thus,
quite ironically, Timon's attempt to instantiate boundless

generativity results in his instead embodying a condition of endlessly accelerating debt. In this respect, Timon is little different from England's King James I, and, as several critics have observed, Shakespeare and Middleton seem to have written *Timon* with a clear eye for establishing this parallel.[14] Like Timon, James borrowed unprecedented sums in order to finance his vast expenditures and lavish displays of patronage, and, as Coppelia Kahn's particularly insightful reading of the play makes clear, James was similarly taken with the idea that he could create value out of thin air, the idea that 'his power to give, at least on occasion, [w]as magical'.[15] For Kahn, Timon's and James's magical thinking can best be explained through a feminist psychoanalytic lens, one in which the symbolic order stems from a perceived lack in male, rather than female, genitalia. By this view, each man's fantasy of inexhaustible giving is symptomatic of masculinity's effort to prove its independence from female reproductive generativity. This is a powerful idea, one that fits well with the general misogyny expressed in *Timon*, yet the very aptness of this reading has obscured from our view the more immediate, monetary cause of Timon's and James's anxiety. This is to suggest that their magical thinking is primarily symptomatic of an early modern king's anxiety over his unexceptional relationship to expense. Faced with the rapidly changing landscape of early-stage capitalism, both Timon and James I find themselves struggling to reconcile the ideal of frank sovereignty to the reality of money's cost.

In framing the problem quite this way, I am myself indebted to W. H. Bizley's (tantalisingly brief) claim that *Timon* is informed by an under-recognised history of sovereign frankness:

What sort of history is it, let us ask, that lies behind the possibility that 'Charlemagne', say, was sufficiently illustrious to call such and such men Franks, to 'frankly' grant them title, to 'frank' the seals that granted the title, to 'enfranchise' those who were not yet Franks, and all with such royal backing and 'assurance' as had as yet no need of monetary 'francs,' the national exchange that the word now signifies?[16]

According to the *OED*, the word 'frank' first appears in the English language alongside its Germanic cognate in the medieval expression 'frank and free', a phrase used to describe the emerging status of a Franklin, a man who is 'free in condition; not in serfdom or slavery'.[17] But as Bizley astutely notes, a serf could not initiate his own entrance into a condition of freedom, and, consequently, he implies that we ought to engage in a form of speculative philology that aims to unearth and further theorise the sovereign source from which such individual freedoms are thought to proceed.[18] Bizley's momentary digression into philological conjecture suggests that the quality of frankness inheres first in the person of the king – he who is more 'frank and free' than anyone else – and that this quality can only then be extended to others through an act of performative speech.[19] According to this view, sovereign frankness names the personal state of exception that entitles a monarch to inaugurate other states of exception at no cost to himself, to enfranchise this or that serf as a Franklin, or to elevate this or that soldier to a newly created position among the landed gentry.[20]

From the outset, Timon ingenuously acts the part of the frank sovereign. Upon learning that Ventidius is being held in debtor's prison, Timon agrees to 'pay his debt and free him', a change in circumstances that amounts, in Timon's words, to 'being enfranchised' (I, i, 108). And later, when Timon discovers that his servant, Lucilius, has won the love of a wealthy man's daughter, he decides to enable the match by elevating Lucilius to a position of property:

Give him thy daughter.
What you bestow in him I'll counterpoise,
And make him weigh with her. (I, i, 148–50)

To be sure, neither of these instances involves Timon speaking new value into being, and, as Timon is himself willing to admit, he must 'strain a little' in order to 'build [Lucilius's] fortune'. Nevertheless, Shakespeare and Middleton are at pains to alert us to the sovereign nature of Timon's frank ideal, as is clear from the dip into exposition just before Timon's first entrance:

All those which were [Timon's] fellows but of late,
Some better than his value, on the moment
Follow his strides, his lobbies fill with tendance,
Rain sacrificial whisperings in his ear,
Make sacred even his stirrup, and through him
Drink the free air. (I, i, 79–84)

Spoken by the character known as the Poet, who is at least nominally an avatar for Shakespeare and Middleton as authors, this account of Timon's obsequious followers seems to be cast in a decidedly sardonic mould, one that prompts readers to inhabit the doubled perspective of those men who flatter Timon in order to take advantage of his generosity, men who share an inside joke when they enjoy certain commodities for free only because Timon incurs all the cost. However, much of this passage's force requires that we recognise Timon's quite singular point of view, a perspective from which the Poet's hyperbolic conclusion suddenly reads as a simple statement of fact. Timon, who believes himself to possess an infinite supply of freedom, genuinely accepts the notion that he can give freely unto others at no final cost to himself.

Timon's belief that he could 'deal kingdoms to [his] friends, / And ne'er be weary' (I, ii, 215–16) – much like

James' belief that he possesses some kind of magical generativity – is motivated by the fantasy of sovereign freedom. But
whereas the truly frank sovereign 'had as yet no need of monetary "francs"' in order to speak value into being, Timon and
James both live in a world wherein the power of money has
largely eclipsed the power of sovereign frankness. Nevertheless, the idea of sovereign frankness held just enough sway, in
Shakespeare's time, to generate a sustained tension between
these two modalities of value. As Bizley puts it,

> his is a time when there is still – even if only in memory –
> an observable connection between language and currency,
> between the speaking of a word and the guaranteeing of
> a coin, and *Timon*, we believe, is of particular interest
> because of the way it senses drama in that very fact.[21]

Here, the connection is revealed to be one of conflict, or, as
Bizley puts it, 'drama', for the very notion that a monarch
can 'guarantee' a coin's value runs counter to the emerging
notion that the value of a coin derives from the rates of its
circulation and exchange.[22]

Bizley is right to say that a memory of the conflict between
language and currency continued to linger in sixteenth-
century England, but in order to understand why this is the
case, we must re-examine certain events that transpired a
century and a half before. In 1356, during the Battle of
Poitiers, France's King Jean II was captured by English forces
and taken under protection. It was a momentous historical
event for both countries, and it ultimately resulted in Jean's
agreeing to purchase his freedom for three million crowns,
a truly massive sum. In order to facilitate his payment to
England, Jean needed to create a stable currency – something
that the French crown could no longer claim to be – and so,
in 1360, he issued an ordinance decreeing the minting of the
franc.[23] The irony of this situation inheres in the new coin's

name, which served both to commemorate Jean's newly regained freedom and also to reassert the fact of his perpetual sovereign freedom, a contradiction that Jean seeks to minimise by laying his emphasis on the latter: 'we have been liberated from prison and are free and at liberty forever [*franc et delivré à touzjours*]'.[24] On the one hand, Jean seeks to stabilise the value of his new currency by reminding its users of that value's truest source: not the material substance of which the coin is made, but rather the act of sovereign freedom by which the coin is made, that presumably immutable state of being that lends immediate validity to a monarch's performative speech-acts. On the other hand, the particular circumstances of the franc's creation undermine exactly this understanding of where value comes from: though Jean seeks to create the franc in the image of his own sovereign freedom, he is only in a position to do so because he has agreed to set the price of that freedom at the material worth of twelve-and-a-half tons of gold. This brings us back to the irony of the franc, which is also the irony of the frank sovereign's monetised degradation. I'd like to suggest that the idea of the frank sovereign, combined with the history of this figure's monetary debasement, informs the use of the word 'frank', at least as early as the fifteenth century, to describe a person who, like Timon, is 'liberal, bounteous, generous, lavish, [especially] in dealing with money'.[25]

Timon's Plain Dealing

The Timon that viewers first encounter in Shakespeare and Middleton's play fails to understand the true nature of his circumstances, the fact that he speaks from the same compromised position as France's Jean II and England's James I. However, compared to both Jean and James, Timon's aspiration for sovereign frankness turns out to be remarkably uncompromising, and, in the face of initial failure, it therefore drives him to pursue sovereign freedom through radically alternative means. The comparison between Timon's first and second attempts at sovereign freedom provides the play with its organising principle, and the authors drive this point home by presenting Timon with a Cynic foil in the play's opening scene.[26] The key moment occurs when Timon tries to turn the tables on Apemantus and his biting critiques by presenting the philosopher with a rich jewel, one meant to stand synecdochally for all of Timon's wealth and privilege: 'How dost thou like this jewel, Apemantus?' (I, i, 211). To which the philosopher quickly replies: 'Not so well as plain dealing, which will not cost a man a doit' (I, i, 212–13). The force of Apemantus's rejoinder lies in the implication that he, and not Timon, engages in an authentic form of frank speech – what he calls 'plain dealing' – and he offers as proof the simple fact that he is able to critique others frankly at no cost to himself, the fact that he only needs the protection of his ethical fortitude in order to cut a person to the quick with no fear of reprisal.[27]

That Timon initially fails to recognise the force of this critique is due to his latent belief that he already embodies sovereign frankness, in which case his acts of magnanimity are not instances of reckless expenditure because they are more properly the result of his kingly plain dealing, which does not cost him a doit, and of which he claims never to weary. Of course, at a certain level, Timon always understands that his gifts do cost him money – as he admits to Lucilius, he must 'strain a little' to build this young man's fortune – but he consistently operates under the assumption that he manifests an innate form of value that is both separable from and superior to his monetary value. Thus, when confronted with the true state of his crumbling finances, Timon comforts his distraught steward, Flavius, by insisting that his essential worth in the eyes of others means that he will always have money when he needs it:

Why dost thou weep? Canst thou the conscience lack
To think I shall lack friends? Secure thy heart.
If I would broach the vessels of my love
And try the argument of hearts by borrowing,
Men and men's fortunes could I frankly use
As I can bid thee speak. (II, ii, 170–5)

It is at this moment, in his time of greatest need, that Timon seems most to act the part of a depleted 'Big Man', one who is willing to receive the magnanimity, or friendship, of others. And yet, even here, Timon subscribes to the fantasy of the frank sovereign. This possibility subtends Timon's claim that he can 'frankly use' not only men's fortunes, but also the men themselves; and while he initially posits this frank use within the terms of friendship, these friendly terms are quickly belied by Timon's comparison to the power he holds over Flavius, a subordinate whom he freely commands.

When Timon discovers that he cannot 'frankly use' the fortunes that he had previously bestowed upon others, his sense of betrayal and disillusionment has more to do with the failure of his frankness than it does with the failure of his friends. Timon is shattered by the knowledge that he has not been manifesting an inherent value that dictates the value of money – the knowledge, to paraphrase Marx, that he is alienated from his sovereign ability, which now resides in money alone. It is at this point that Timon begins to understand something about Apemantus's axiom that even the churlish philosopher does not fully comprehend. Though it is accurate to say that an act of truly frank speech would incur no monetary cost, the greater truth lies in the inversion of this claim: in the presence of money there can be no acts of truly frank speech.

In the play's second half, the authors have Timon undertake a decidedly diogenical programme of ethical self-fashioning in order to manifest precisely this critique-oriented condition of sovereign freedom, a condition that would enable him to annihilate, not inaugurate, the value of money. Passing beyond the outskirts of the city, Timon begins the process of acquiring his critical sovereignty by crossing beyond a second, more significant threshold, one that marks the outer boundaries of civilised humanity itself – he takes off his clothes:

> Nothing I'll bear from thee
> But my nakedness, thou detestable town;
> . . . Timon will to the woods, where he shall find
> Th'unkindest beast more kinder than mankind. (IV, i, 32–6)

One way to understand Timon's rejection of clothing would be to say that he embraces a state of poverty more profound than his new financial circumstances actually require, but I think it more precise to say that his act of disrobing signals a movement beyond the category of poverty itself. Whereas an impoverished man feels driven to maintain such presumably bare necessities as the shirt on his back, and is therefore always bound by a relation of need to the world of money and commodified objects, Timon discards his clothing in order to renounce the very terms of that world's self-alienating forms of relation.[28]

This is not a trivial distinction, for Timon's refusal to find freedom in poverty encodes Shakespeare and Middleton's engagement with their period's Diogenes-inspired fantasy of critical sovereignty, a form of sovereign freedom that should not be confused with the less militant species of Cynic self-enfranchisement espoused by Crates (a pupil of Diogenes who in turn mentored Zeno, the founder of Stoicism).[29] Unlike Diogenes, whose ethics of radical austerity served to advance his critical mission, Crates practiced a less antagonistic brand of Cynicism focused exclusively on acquiring peace of mind through the embrace of poverty. The difference is teleological: for Crates, one achieves sovereign freedom the moment an ethics of voluntary impoverishment subjectively ensures one's sense of personal autonomy, one's sense that nothing beyond one's own control is needed to acquire happiness; for Diogenes (or, more precisely, for certain admirers of Diogenes), one achieves sovereign freedom only when one's sovereignty over the self is so absolute that it manifests as a condition of argumentative sovereignty over others.[30]

Observing Shakespeare and Middleton's distinction between radical and moderate Cynicisms allows us to understand Timon's misanthropic turn as a form of social engagement rather than solipsistic withdrawal. James Kuzner takes the latter view when he argues that a forest-dwelling Timon exemplifies the condition of sovereignty as theorised by George Bataille, who, Crates-like, understands sovereign freedom to involve the inner relation of man to the objects of his desire. By this view, 'the experience of sovereignty offers [Timon] a therapeutic exit from the world of precious things easily lost, freedom from the anguish that is anticipation – of what we do not have, of what we are not yet'.[31] And yet, if Timon seeks a therapy, it is one that operates on a global scale, one that requires Timon to maintain a political, future-oriented stance that cannot be reconciled with Bataille's account of sovereignty as the experience of objectless immediacy.

Following in Diogenes' footsteps, Timon aspires to the same model of sovereign frankness that captures Michel Foucault's imagination some 400 years later. As we saw in Chapter 1, Foucault turns to Diogenes in order to envision the means by which a truly militant philosopher and social critic might disrupt, indeed, utterly dismantle, the instrumentalised world in which we currently find ourselves:

> The Cynic is someone who, taking up the traditional themes of the true life in ancient philosophy, transposes them and turns them round into the demand and assertion

of the need for an *other* life. And then, through the image
and figure of the king of poverty [*roi de misère*], he trans-
poses anew the idea of *an other* life into the theme of a life
whose otherness must lead to the change of the world. An
other life for an *other* world.[32]

Graham Burchell's decision to translate '*misère*' as 'poverty' is
unfortunate, for it obscures Foucault's effort to tie Diogenes'
sovereignty to his defamiliarising ethical project, which
simultaneously subscribes to all the conventional principles
of Hellenistic philosophy and also produces out of them a
disorientingly unique and radical way of life. For Foucault,
there is a certain banality to the connections Cynicism draws
between the repudiation of social values founded on custom,
on the one hand, and the importance of disciplining oneself
into a state of self-mastery and self-reliance, on the other.[33]
Diogenes stands apart from this larger philosophic tradition
because of his relation to ethics, which leads him to undertake an indefinite process of adapting his way of life so as
to manifest these attributes as completely as possible. Both
familiar and strange, Cynicism shows the Greek world that
its own ethical propositions, if taken seriously, necessitate an
entirely different way of life, a way of life that acquires a
militant function in relation to society. By this view, an intem-
perate relation to these established ethical values constitutes
the most revolutionary *ethos* imaginable precisely because it
moves the practitioner beyond a condition of mere poverty.[34]
     For Shakespeare and Middleton, the difference between
embracing poverty and transcending it is figured in the difference between their own portrayal of Timon and the version of Timon set forward by Lucian, the second-century
satirist – and self-ascribed Cynic – whose dialogue, 'Timon
the Misanthrope', is acknowledged by scholars to be one
of the authors' principle sources for the play. In Lucian's
account, Timon responds to his bankruptcy and betrayal by

abandoning an urbane and mendacious Athens in favour of a country farm and the life of a paid farmhand: 'These indignities have made mee betake my selfe to this solitary place, to cloth my selfe in this lether garment, and labour in the earth for foure half-pence a day, here practising Philosophie, with solitarinesse and my mattocke.'[35] Here, Timon is understood to practice philosophy not only through the meditative practices of solitude and physical exertion, but also through the embrace of poverty: Timon must learn to be content with life's bare necessities, which he manages to meet on only 'foure half-pence a day'. Indeed, Lucian considers the embrace of poverty to be so central to Timon's philosophical training that he fashions it into an allegorical character: it is quite literally Poverty that strengthens and disciplines Timon after he has been mistreated and abandoned by Plutus, the god of gold:

> [Plutus] hath beene the meanes of the infinite miseries that have betide unto mee, betrayed mee into the hands of flatterers, delivered mee up to those that lay in wait for mee, stirred up hatred against mee, undid mee with voluptuous pleasures, caused every man to envie mee, and at the last most treacherously and perfidiously forsook mee: whereas honest povertie exercised mee in manlike labours, brought mee acquainted with truth and plaine dealing, furnished mee with necessaries when I was sicklie, and taught mee to repose the hopes of my life onely in my selfe, and to contemne all other things. Shewed mee what riches I had by her meanes, which neither the flatterer by faire speeches, nor the sycophant by subornation, nor the people by their indignation, nor the judge by indirect sentence, nor the tyrant by all his trecheries and pollicies are able to deprive mee of. Wherefore beeing enabled by labour, I dig in this plot of ground with a love to my worke, and out of sight of those vilanies that are practised in the citie, my mattocke furnishing mee sufficiently with food to my content.

In this account, Timon learns a number of good Cynic lessons from poverty. He becomes devoted to 'plaine dealing' and he discovers strength in *autarkia* (self-sufficiency), which he describes as a kind of wealth, as an inherent, non-monetary source of value. And yet, if Timon makes it sound as if he has become truly self-sufficient, he manages this claim only by obscuring his continued dependence upon a commodified world. Though Lucian's Timon asserts that his 'mattocke furnish[es him] sufficiently with food', it would be more correct to say that his labouring with the mattock (a pick-like tool) furnishes him with a small amount of money that he then uses to purchase a sufficiency of food. This Timon does not dig for food, he digs for wages, and it is therefore wrong of him to claim that his new life has enabled him to remain 'out of sight of those vilanies that are practised in the citie'. By working as a day labourer who earns money to produce the food that feeds Athens, Timon remains an integral, even a foundational, part of the very villainies he detests, villainies that remain out of sight only because he metaphorically glosses over the role that monetary exchange still plays in his life.

For Lucian, Timon's primary ethical objective centres on the subjective experience of contentment, and so Timon's display of unthinking hypocrisy does not have the kind of invalidating effect that it would were he additionally to pursue a critical mission against 'those vilanies that are practiced in the citie'. In Shakespeare's version of events, Timon practices a form of Cynicism chiefly oriented toward the production of social critique. Accordingly, the bankrupt lord removes himself not to a farm but to a forest. The significance of this distinction cannot be stressed enough, for it takes Timon out of an agrarian, quasi-pastoral setting – wherein the cultivation and commodification of nature is idealised – and instead places him in contact with nature in its purest, aneconomic form. Living in the forest, this Timon has no need for money, and so he literally digs for his food: 'Destruction fang mankind. Earth, yield me roots [*He digs*]' (IV, iii, 23).[36]

The full significance of this literalising move lies not in the contrast between Cynicism's proto-Stoic and critique-oriented teleologies, but rather in the distinction it generates between Timon's and Apemantus's methods for obtaining critical sovereignty. Shakespeare and Middleton present Timon as striving for the same kind of sovereign freedom that Foucault imagines, one that involves a radical and entirely immoderate pursuit of certain ethical ideals, and it is important to note that they make this choice against a discursive backdrop in which the question of moderation remained a live issue for many of Diogenes' admirers. In *Timon*, Shakespeare and Middleton distinguish between an understanding of Cynicism's critical mission in which the embrace of poverty serves as its enabling basis and one in which a condition beyond mere poverty must first be obtained. In this respect, Shakespeare and Middleton arguably find a resource in another of Lucian's dialogues. In Thomas Elyot's translation of *A Dialogue betwene Lucian and Diogenes* (1532), Lucian has himself come face to face with his greatest philosophical role model (Menippus notwithstanding), and the entire dialogue centres on a debate over the self-authenticating value of Lucian's temperate embrace of poverty, on the one hand, and Diogenes' more extreme renunciation of all worldly comforts and affordances, on the other.[37] In their exchange, Diogenes is quick to point out Lucian's fundamental hypocrisy: 'Sins thou lyue more temperately than the common sorte of men & them more wastfully: why than dooste thou blame me and not them?'[38] The force of this question lies in the implication that Lucian's stance is threatened by Diogenes' stauncher and more uncompromising rejection of material superfluities, the implication that Lucian ultimately proves himself to be a participant in – and defender of – the very society he presumes to critique.

Shakespeare and Middleton dramatise their own version of this debate when they have Apemantus and Timon speak to each other in Act IV, scene iii, an exchange in which the moderated and radicalised iterations of the Cynic critical stance are shown to correspond with the accommodation and adjuration of a moneyed world. In this scene, Apemantus accuses Timon of being a Cynic-come-lately, a convert whose enthusiasm for the cause leads him to overshoot the mark. By contrast, Timon denounces Apemantus for his reliance on the very system of commodity and excess he ostensibly seeks to critique. Whereas Timon digs for edible roots, Apemantus comes to the forest carrying a medlar, a pear that is picked too early and that therefore transitions almost immediately from unripe to rotten. Apemantus's willingness to eat this agricultural by-product demonstrates his ethical commitment to abstemiousness, but however unpretentious a medlar may be, it is still the product of a system in which money mediates between labour and consumption. This introduces a degree of hypocritical complicity for which Timon cannot stand. Consequently, when Apemantus sees Timon gnawing on a root and offers to 'mend [his] feast', Timon rejects the offer of a more 'civilised' repast, making quite clear his reasons for doing so: 'On what I hate I feed not' (IV, iii, 286; IV, iii, 305).

Ultimately, Shakespeare's purpose is not to privilege Timon over Apemantus. Rather, he uses their encounter to distinguish between two types of Cynic critical practice: one that fails to deliver world-changing critique because of its inherent hypocrisy (à la Lucian and Lyly), and one that fails precisely because it avoids that hypocrisy. Throughout Acts IV and V, Shakespeare and Middleton's depiction of Timon serves to illustrate the failure of this latter strategy, a strategy that might otherwise be viewed as a difficult but viable means of instantiating one's sovereign freedom and hence of delivering radical critique to world-changing effect.

An Earnest Man and an Honest Man

Timon transforms himself into a misanthrope in order to escape the corrupting influence of money. Yet Timon has no sooner achieved this goal than he is made to confront the greatest threat to its integrity. Digging for edible roots, Timon unearths a large quantity of gold:

> Destruction fang mankind. Earth, yield me roots.
>   [*He digs*]
> Who seeks for better of thee, sauce his palate
> With thy most operant poison.
>   [*He finds gold*]. (IV, iii, 23–5)

Timon's intention is literally to dig for his food, but the outcome, however absurdly, is that he literally digs for his wages. This second and decidedly illogical literalisation – technically, gold and money are not the same thing – is rendered still more problematic by the timing of Timon's discovery, for it raises the possibility that Timon has not absolutely renounced a commodified worldview, the possibility that he does want more money after all. As Timon digs, he apostrophises the earth, urging it to produce its 'most operant poison' for anyone who seeks more from it than basic subsistence, and it is at precisely this moment that Timon discovers the gold:[39]

>   What is here?
> Gold? Yellow, glittering, precious gold?
> . . . Thus much of this will make
> Black white, foul fair, wrong right,
> Base noble, old young, coward valiant.
> . . . This yellow slave
> Will knit and break religions, bless the accursed,
> Make the hoar leprosy adored, place thieves,
> And give them title, knee, and approbation
> With senators on the bench. (IV, iii, 25–38)

As it turns out, Timon instantly sees this glittering poison for what it is, suggesting that he really might be immune to its effects. Indeed, Marx points to this and another of Timon's misanthropic soliloquies to argue that Shakespeare correctly understands money's true nature to be the 'alienated ability of mankind', to be, in other words, a medium of exchange-value that enables its possessor to purchase the use of another person's attributes.[40] To paraphrase both Timon and Marx, a foul man who is rich enough to attract the fairest of women is not foul, nor is a man of base origins truly base if he buys the trappings of nobility, nor, again, is a coward who pays for courageous guards particularly cowardly, for he possesses the valour of others.[41] These examples show that money affords its possessor a wonderful degree of freedom. Yet it becomes clear the moment one's money runs out that freedom in this arrangement has become the functional property of money itself; it has become the 'alienated ability of mankind'.

In the figure of Timon, Shakespeare and Middleton take up the question of whether such a moment of clarity and critical insight can ever translate into an individual's articulation of world-changing critique, an articulation that would acquire its argumentative force from an individual's ability to entirely free himself from money's alienating effects. The authors go about answering this question in two stages, beginning with Timon's decision against spurning the unasked-for treasure:

> Ha, a drum! Thou'rt quick;
> But yet I'll bury thee.
>> [*He buries gold*]
>> Thou'lt go, strong thief,
> When gouty keepers of thee cannot stand.
>> [*He keeps some gold*]
> Nay, stay thou out for earnest. (IV, iii, 45–8)

Hearing the approach of interlopers, Timon's initial response is to carry on burying the gold, but at the last instant, he decides to retain some of the precious metal 'for earnest'. Given Timon's commitment to living the honest life of a Cynic, a life free from the constraints of money, it is puzzling to hear him speak of using money as 'earnest', that is to say, using it as his down payment, his pledge, his skin in the game. These metaphorical claims to immediacy (as if money were an extension of the self) are grounded in the same self-alienating logic that prompts Lucian's Timon to say that his 'mattocke furnish[es him] sufficiently with food'. But unlike his Lucianic predecessor, who never aspires to a condition of critical sovereignty, this Timon subjects himself to the crushing irony that he needs money to be earnest, and therefore can never be frank.

Timon's decision to keep some gold 'for earnest' must be understood as a tragic concession, for it suggests that he advances the critical component of his Cynic teleology only by deploying his sovereign ability in its alienated form. Knowing that gold is the earth's 'most operant poison', Timon spends the majority of Act IV handing out treasure to people whose use of it will most likely bring harm to Athens (e.g. Alcibiades, the prostitutes Phyrnia and Timandra, and a gang of thieves), and in this respect his retention and distribution of gold constitutes a form of critical activity. Yet Timon's use of money to dismantle the money-based society of Athens comes at a cost, for he can wield gold's poison against others only by succumbing to that poison himself. Timon's monetised approximation of Cynic free speech thus discloses the inherent irony of attempts to alter a world in which cash is king, a world in which even the fiercest opponents of mankind's monetisation inevitably concede that, at the end of the day, money talks.

Shakespeare and Middleton's two-part response thus begins with the disclosure that Timon falls categorically short of actualising true self-sovereignty, a disclosure that would seem to provide a clear-cut answer to the question of Cynicism's viability. It is at this point, however, that Shakespeare and Middleton go on to address Timon's lingering, secondary aspiration with respect to his critical mission: the hope that his own efforts, though monetarily compromised, might still play a crucial intermediary role in facilitating someone else's critical enfranchisement. This is precisely how Timon relates to Flavius, who alone demonstrates such a degree of compassion and solidarity with his erstwhile lord that Timon is compelled to revise his previously absolute judgment against humanity:

> Forgive my general and exceptless rashness,
> You perpetual sober gods! I do proclaim
> One honest man – mistake me not, but one,
> No more. (IV, iii, 487–90)

Here, Shakespeare and Middleton pointedly revise the story of Diogenes roaming the streets in broad daylight, lantern in hand, explaining to passers-by that he is looking for a single honest man.[42] In early modernity, this anecdote was understood to enact a critique of Athenian society, for Diogenes' redundant lantern broadcasts his conviction that the search he undertakes is pointless, that society is too corrupt for an honest man ever to be found. At the same time, however, Diogenes' ongoing performance of this unfulfillable search came to represent the perpetual, self-disciplining hardship that authenticates Diogenes himself as the world's single honest man, the only man able to speak honestly about the fact that no one else is honest. In Shakespeare and Middleton's repackaging of this anecdote, Timon's use of money for 'earnest' means that he can never truly be honest, and with the erasure of this one example of sovereign authenticity, the authors displace the ontological stakes of the story onto their revised ending of it.

Understood in this context, Timon's response to the discovery of 'one honest man' is as perplexing as it is telling. Just as he has done with the people he chooses to curse, Timon gives Flavius gold, but in this instance his instructions differ from that of the others. Rather than encouraging his old steward to spend his windfall, he urges Flavius to refuse any and all requests for monetary assistance. In other words, Timon enjoins Flavius to do the one thing that he himself could not:

> Go, live rich and happy,
> But thus conditioned; thou shalt build from men,
> Hate all, curse all, show charity to none,
> But let the famished flesh slide from the bone
> Ere thou relieve the beggar. Give to dogs
> What thou deniest to men. Let prisons swallow 'em,
> Debts wither 'em to nothing; be men like blasted woods,
> And may diseases lick up their false blood.
> And so farewell, and thrive. (IV, iii, 517–24)

Whereas Timon's retention of gold in 'earnest' inevitably ropes him back into the monetised world of alienated freedom, an honest man has the capacity to maintain a non-monetary relationship with his gold, to serve as the custodian of gold that he will never, ever use as money. For Timon, the prospect of Flavius's non-monetary custodianship is encoded in the injunction that he 'build from men', an edict that Timon would have Flavius carry to its logical extreme. To build away from all other men is, necessarily, to make one's home in the world without the purchased labour of others; it is to live in a way that makes it impossible for gold to be valued as money; it is to be rich only by virtue of nature's increase.

Timon imagines that an honest man will have no monetary use for gold, and it is in this context that he concentrates on warning Flavius against charitable spending, an attitude toward money that would merely replicate Timon's earlier belief that he could give away his wealth at no final cost to himself. Now steeped in his Cynic misanthropy, Timon sees the tragic flaw in his ostensibly sovereign posture, for he finally understands that exclusively charitable spending incurs the greatest cost of all: it requires the monetarily liberated benefactor to spend, in alienated form, the very sovereign frankness that he means to keep for himself. This is of course a lesson that Timon learns most fully in the second half of the play, not, that is, when he subscribes to the mere illusion of being free from money's constraints, but rather when he first enjoys and then relinquishes that freedom in order to retain some gold 'for earnest'. As Timon explains in his apostrophe to the gold he conserves: 'Thou'lt go, strong thief, / When gouty keepers of thee cannot stand [*He keeps some gold*]' (IV, iii, 46–7). Ironically, it is precisely with this decision to preserve a remainder of gold that Timon proves himself to be too 'gouty' – too tied to the world of commodities and consumption – to keep his horde honest. Saving the gold with an eye for its critique-oriented expenditure, Timon allows this newly monetised substance to rob him of the very sovereign freedom that he has given everything up to this point to obtain. Thus Timon discovers in Flavius an alternative to his own entrapment by gold, the 'operant poison' that he turns into a tool of critique by allowing himself to become money's instrument (IV, iii, 25). According to Timon, Flavius has the power to chart a different path, for it is only in the hands of an honest man that gold will itself become honest; only then will it be gold and nothing else.

The problem with this vision is its utter bleakness. Timon's account of an honest man's conduct articulates a misanthropic cosmology that is more extreme and inhospitable than any other offered in the play. This is the impoverished world in

which Timon envisions Flavius cultivating his sovereign freedom, and so it is with great irony that Timon's critical ideal
must be understood to fail even in its hypothetical fulfilment.
Like the falling tree that (absent anyone or anything to hear
it) theoretically makes no sound, the honest man in this scenario achieves the full power of frankness at the ironic cost of
communicative action itself.[43]

Notes

1. Shakespeare, *The Life of Timon of Athens* in *The Norton
   Shakespeare*, IV, iii, 23–5. Further citations will be to this edition and in-text.
2. Laertius, *Lives of Eminent Philosophers*, 6.20.
3. Laertius, *Lives of Eminent Philosophers*, 6.69. Notably, D. R.
   Dudley resuscitated the tradition of linking the *parrhêsia* anecdote to the oracle story in his pioneering work on Cynicism.
   See Dudley, *A History of Cynicism*, p. 28.
4. Laertius, *Lives of Eminent Philosophers*, 6.22.
5. Wilson, *Arte of Rhetorique*.
6. Recent scholarship on the authorship question has established that Middleton most likely penned the exchanges
   between Timon and his steward, Flavius. Although some
   of these Middletonian scenes will be central to this chapter's analysis, I would argue that my reading of the play is
   compatible with the fact of its co-authorship, for Middleton
   displays his own history of engagement with the figure of
   Diogenes. See, for example, Middleton's *Micro-cynicon*. For
   a helpful review of *Timon*'s co-authorship, see Smith, 'The
   Authorship of *Timon of Athens*'.
7. Despite the fact that very few of the transactions depicted in
   Timon are 'cash transactions' in the way we normally think of
   them, many critics have followed Karl Marx in accepting that
   Shakespeare and Middleton's observations about the social
   value of money, gold and other forms of material wealth in
   their proto-capitalist moment enable them to articulate a

keen basic insight into the nature of the cash nexus. See Muir, 'Timon of Athens and the Cash Nexus', pp. 56–75; Cohen, 'The Politics of Wealth in *Timon of Athens*', esp. p. 151; and Grady, '*Timon of Athens*', esp. p. 432.

8. See Chorost, 'Biological Finance in Shakespeare's *Timon of Athens*'; Cohen, 'The Politics of Wealth in *Timon of Athens*'; and Bailey, '*Timon of Athens*, Forms of Payback, and the Genre of Debt'. For a discussion somewhat similar to Chorost's on the relation in *Timon* between usury and the natural/artificial reproductive dichotomy, see Fischer, 'Cut My Heart in Sums'.

9. For an account of this aspirational attachment to Diogenes in the eighteenth and twentieth centuries – especially among Jean D'Alembert, Denis Diderot, Peter Sloterdijk and Michel Foucault – see Shea, *The Cynic Enlightenment*.

10. See Polo, *The most noble and famous trauels of Marcus Paulus*, pp. 66–7.

11. See James I, *The true lawe of free monarchies*.

12. For recent scholarship on the early modern friendship tradition, see Lochman et al., *Discourses and Representations of Friendship in Early Modern Europe, 1500-1700*, and Shannon, *Sovereign Amity*.

13. In pursuing my analysis, I offer an alternative to the growing body of *Timon* criticism that explains Timon's generosity by resorting to anthropological accounts of the potlatch chief or the 'Big Man' system. For an anthropological account of this, see Mauss, *The Gift*. For an example of scholarship that suggests an analogy between the 'Big Man' system and the Jacobean patronage system, see Gundersheimer, 'Patronage in the Renaissance', p. 13.

14. Coppelia Kahn gives this argument its most sustained treatment, though Jonathan Goldberg also notes it in passing. David Bevington and David L. Smith, in a tangential response to Kahn, use *Timon of Athens* as a case study for 'determining whether it is possible to argue for a topical correlation between fiction and reality'. See Kahn, 'Magic of Bounty'; Goldberg, *James I and the Politics of Literature*,

p. 268 n. 22; Bevington and Smith, 'James I and *Timon of Athens*'.

15. Kahn, 'Magic of Bounty', p. 44.

16. Bizley, 'Language and Currency in *Timon of Athens*', p. 21.

17. 'frank, adj.2', definition 1a, *OED Online* (March 2013, Oxford University Press), http://www.oed.com.ezproxy. princeton.edu/view/Entry/74214?rskey=ovntB5&result=9# eid (last accessed 4 June 2015).

18. Bizley alerts us to the fact that he is constructing a speculative history by invoking Charlemagne only in scare quotes. Here, his interest has more to do with 'a Charlemagne' than it does with the Charlemagne ('Language and Currency in *Timon of Athens*', p. 22).

19. The role of performative speech, in such moments of granting, raises for Bizley the question of sufficiency: at what point does a ruler become so 'illustrious', powerful or commanding that his edicts on the conditions of others are assured to carry the force of material truth? This explains Bizley's example of Charlemagne, a ruler more-or-less equal in stature to Alexander the Great.

20. By using the term 'state of exception', I am of course invoking the work of Carl Schmitt and Giorgio Agamben. But whereas Schmitt and Agamben discuss the state of exception in the context of democratic government (which must occasionally institute exceptional negations of its own democratic principles), I discuss the state of exception in the context of monarchical sovereignty. Moreover, I differ from Schmitt and Agamben insofar as I attend to a state of exception that gives rights rather than taking them away, a state of exception that constitutes an act not of violence but of generative beneficence. See Schmitt, *The Crisis of Parliamentary Democracy*; Schmitt, *The Concept of the Political*; Agamben, *Homo Sacer*; and Agamben, *State of Exception*.

21. Bizley, 'Language and Currency in *Timon of Athens*', p. 21.

22. Writing in the early 1630s, Rice Vaughan makes precisely this point in *A discourse of coin and coinage* (published posthumously and edited by Henry Vaughan): 'I shall convince

hereafter an important and popular Error, by which many are persuaded, that Princes can give what value they list to Gold and Silver, by enhancing and letting fall their coins, whenas in truth Gold and Silver will retain the same proportion towards other things, which are valued by them, which the general consent of other Nations doth give unto them, if there be a Trade and Commerce with other Nations: by which inter-course it comes to pass, that if the price of Gold and Silver be raised, the price of all Commodities is raised, according to the raising of Gold and Silver; so as let any particular Prince or State raise the price of Gold and Silver as they list, yet they will still hold the same proportion towards other things val-ued by them, which the general consent of other Nations neer about them doth give unto them.' See Vaughan, *A discourse of coin and coinage*, pp. 7–8.

23. Here we see a clear parallel between the circumstances that form the backdrop for Jean's and Timon's attempts to exer-cise their sovereign freedom, for as Peter Holland notes, the value of a talent seems to undergo rapid inflation during the first two acts of *Timon*. See Holland, 'The Merchant of Venice and the Value of Money', pp. 13–14.

24. Jean II, 'Ordonnance qui establit une Ayde, qui fixe le prix des Monneyes, & qui contient des Reglements sur le prix des denrée & des salaires des Ouvriers, sur les Prevostez & Tabellionages, & sur les Sergents'. My translation.

25. 'frank, adj.2', definition 2a, *OED Online* (March 2013, Oxford University, Press) http://www.oed.com.ezproxy. princeton.edu/view/Entry/74214?rskey=ovntB5&result=9# eid (last accessed 4 June 2015).

26. In a series of allusions to Cynicism's etymology, Apemantus is either called a dog or self-identifies as one on seven differ-ent occasions: I, i, 204; I, i, 221; I, i, 271; II, ii, 81–2; IV, iii, 251; IV, iii, 314; and IV iii, 358. Similarly, Aristotle refers to Diogenes by way of his popular moniker rather than his proper name: 'and the Dog called Athenian taverns the messes of Attica' (Aristotle, *Art of Rhetoric*, p. 237). Various schol-arly editions of *Timon* have made note of the connection. See,

for example, Klein, 'Appendix: The Timon Legend' 201; and Shakespeare, *The Life of Timon of Athens*, in *The Norton Shakespeare*, I, i, 203 note 7.

27. This is the argument that Dio Chrysostom has Diogenes make in his *Fourth Discourse on Kingship*, a highly influential text for early modern conceptions of the Diogenes/Alexander paradigm. See Chrysostom, *Discourses* 1-11, pp. 199–203.

28. For an example of scholarship that evaluates Timon exclusively through the wealth/poverty binary, see Cohen, 'The Politics of Wealth in *Timon of Athens*'.

29. For a useful primer on Crates, see Dudley, *A History of Cynicism*, esp. pp. 42–53; as well as Navia, *Classical Cynicism*, esp. pp. 119–44.

30. Critics often link Timon's act of disrobing to Lear's similar effort to become a living example of 'unaccommodated man', and indeed the likeness is no accident, for the latter also occurs in a pointedly Cynic context. As F. G. Butler and R. A. Foakes have both noted, Lear's confused address of Tom o'Bedlam as a potential counsellor of variously Greek origin – 'Let me talk with this philosopher', 'I'll talk a word with this most learnèd Theban', 'Noble philosopher, your company', 'Come, good Athenian' (Q xi, 131, 134, 152, 157) – puts him at the crossroads of the model set out by Crates, a 'learned Theban', and the one set out by Diogenes, who is, at least in an adoptive sense, a 'good Athenian'. See Butler, 'Who Are King Lear's Philosophers?', esp. pp. 511–13; and Foakes, *King Lear*, III, iv, 153 note.

31. Kuzner, *Shakespeare as a Way of Life*.

32. Foucault, *Courage of Truth*, p. 287.

33. For Foucault's account of Cynicism's scandalous banality, see *Le Courage de la Vérité*, pp. 213–14.

34. Notably, Foucault's theorisation of Cynic critical sovereignty imagines the emancipatory power of Cynic truth-telling to inhere in the Cynic's inhabitation of his ethical practice, meaning that the 'speech-act' of sovereign frankness constantly emanates from the Cynic regardless of whether he

speaks or no. Something similar can be said of Shakespeare and Middleton's Cynic depiction of Timon.

35. Lucian, *Certaine select dialogues of Lucian together with his true historie*, p. 153.

36. Shakespeare and Middleton's decision to have Timon dig for roots may be drawn from accounts of Diogenes doing the same. In Thomas Lodge's *Diogenes in His Singularitie*, Diogenes reflects upon the general depravity of Athens and comes to the following conclusion: 'What should Diogenes then doo but be singular, to see the better sort so sensuall? I thinke it rather better to weare patches on my cloake, than to beare the patch on my head: & rather to feede on rootes, than to be defiled with royot.' Similarly, in *Ephemerides of Phialo*, Stephen Gosson notes that Diogenes 'fedde uppon rootes'. See Lodge, *Catharos. Diogenes in his singularitie* (1591), 1ᵛ; and Gosson, *Ephemerides of Phialo*, p. 28.

37. By my count, Menippus appears in twelve of Lucian's dialogues while Diogenes appears in nine.

38. Lucian, *A dialogue betwene Lucian and Diogenes of the life harde and sharpe, and of the lyfe tendre and delicate*, A2ʳ⁻ᵛ.

39. In Lucian's account, the earth contains gold by virtue of divine intervention. Zeus, taking pity on Timon, asks Plutus to visit the misanthrope and restore his wealth. Though Timon rejects Plutus's offer and sends the god away, Plutus decides, nevertheless, to place gold in the path of Timon's digging.

40. Marx, *Economic and Philosophic Manuscripts of 1844*, p. 168.

41. As Marx puts it, 'he who can buy bravery is brave, though he be a coward' (*Economic and Philosophic Manuscripts of 1844*, p. 169).

42. For an account of this anecdote's evolution from 'looking for a man' to 'looking for an honest man', see Sayre, *The Greek Cynics*, p. 68.

43. Michael Warner makes a similar point when he invokes the story of Diogenes masturbating in public to exemplify a mode of critical engagement that forecloses the possibility of social change. Whereas Diogenes figures the attempt to do away with a public/private distinction entirely, queer and feminist

theory find their deconstructive tendencies tempered by the desire that their critical disclosure have a world-making effect, specifically one that requires the category of the public within which a counterpublic might cohere. Diogenes' critical activity fails, in other words, because he does not present his audience with the prospect of a shareable world. See Warner, *Publics and Counterpublics*, esp. pp. 24–31.

CODA

In this book, I have tried to show that it is only with the rise of dramatic realism that the figure of the Cynic truth-teller begins to provoke sustained interpretive crisis, a crisis that takes shape in the sixteenth century and that goes on to drive key developments in our literary, philosophical and political history. Through my readings of Shakespeare's plays, I have also tried to show that literature – along with its academic offspring, literary criticism – is uniquely positioned to diagnose the interpretive errors that consequently underwrite philosophical and political ideas about the means of achieving extreme critical agency. What these two over-arching aims have in common is the critical methodology I develop in order to advance them, and I conclude this book by briefly commenting on the value this method holds for early modern studies in particular and for the discipline of literary studies in general.

Methodologically, my concern in this book has been the intersection between literary character and ethical character that occurs when realism and its attendant protocols of practical didacticism force the two realms of *ethos* together. Focusing on the figure of the Cynic truth-teller, I attend to a key instance in which this point of intersection becomes problematised, and I do so because it allows me to tell a kind of history in which literary form drives cultural formation. Telling this particular kind of intellectual history – the kind produced by our didactic relation to an (otherworldly) ethical ideal, our relation, in other words, to a literary possibility that is also a political impossibility – calls upon disciplinary expertise that is particular to the literary critic. It takes a great deal of close reading and formal analysis to unpack the representational and discursive cross-traffic between literary character and ethical character, and so the kind of history my critical methodology works to construct and consequently examine is one in which the field of literary criticism holds analytical priority over adjacent fields like history, philosophy and politics.

Jane Gallop has argued that disciplines rise and fall institutionally based not only on whether or not they have a discipline-specific method that justifies their existence, but also on whether or not other disciplines see value in that method and seek to make use of it.[1] By this way of thinking, literature departments are in the midst of a massive trade deficit. We use the interpretive tools of history, philosophy, political theory, cognitive science, sociology and so on to produce our work, and while we continue to deploy close reading and our own particular breed of formal analysis in conjunction with these imported methods, we are largely alone in doing so. There's nothing new in expressing the sentiment that scholars in other disciplines would do work that better advances the goals of their own fields were they only to take skills like close reading seriously, but our own views on the matter have failed to make much impact, even in the disciplines most adjacent to us (and upon which we have ourselves borrowed so heavily). Why is this? In large part, it is because we have not done a good enough job of identifying the range of scholarly undertakings that (1) fall clearly within the wheelhouses of these other disciplines and (2) simply cannot be tackled rigorously without recourse to literary-critical ways of seeing.[2] One way for us to do this is to draw out the histories of political and philosophical thought that cohere around certain literary and para-literary characterisations, particularly those that complicate people's efforts to learn practical wisdom from virtual examples, as happens to be the case with figurations of the radically effective truth-teller. Such work makes visible a history that historians are not in a position to recount without our help. Likewise, it makes visible a history of interpretive error in our philosophical and political thought that philosophers and political theorists are not in the best position to diagnose and resolve.

Above all, attending to the kind of vexed intersection between literary character and ethical character that indexes our reception of the Cynic critical ideal makes visible the relevance of literary criticism to every discipline that takes up the project of prudential deliberation in a sustained way. Scholars of history, philosophy and politics all use their disciplines as an opportunity to stage the vicarious exercise of practical wisdom. In various ways and to differing degrees, these efforts all make use of virtual examples that are either drawn directly from literature or that hew to realism's principles of probable causation, thereby producing the kind of characterisations that I have been calling 'para-literary'.[3] My point isn't that thinkers in these disciplines are wrong to be inventing their examples. As I have argued in this book, the realist turn happens precisely because virtual scenarios enable us to vicariously test our practical reason more thoroughly than ever before. Rather my point is that this dependence on the virtual, which is so tied up in the realist literary form, means that scholars in these disciplines are prone to making precisely the kind of mistakes that I, following Shakespeare, diagnose with respect to the figure of the Cynic truth-teller. When it comes to the prudential analysis of virtual examples, historians, philosophers and political theorists need the tools of literary criticism to do their job well, and literary critics can and should make plain the cross-disciplinary need for their methods by doing more of this kind of work themselves.

In *Shakespeare and the Truth-Teller*, I have illuminated Diogenes' reception history as it is produced by efforts to read figural representations of the radical truth-teller through the lens of practical didacticism. A great deal more work can be done in tracking the relationship between literature – both in the early modern period and beyond – and the very central role that Diogenes' reception plays in our intellectual history. Of course, the kind of reading I bring to bear on classical Cynicism can fruitfully examine the figuration of a range of characters that have made their way into our cultural formations, our political theories, our philosophical models. I encourage my readers to break out their lanterns and search after them.

Notes

1. Gallop, 'The Historicization of Literary Studies and the Fate of Close Reading'.
2. Jonathan Kramnick makes just this sort of argument with respect to cognitive scientists and the ways in which their work would be materially aided by a better understanding of fictionality's capacity to explore the workings of the mind. See Kramnick, *Paper Minds*.
3. In the context of history, the clearest example would be the work historians do when they appeal to counterfactual histories. See Gallagher, *Telling It Like It Wasn't*. Philosophers and political theorists draw on a wider range of virtual examples, from analysing literary characters to generating their own characters and scenarios to their engagement with loosely historical example.

BIBLIOGRAPHY

Anon. *Ad C. Herennium, de ratione dicendi (Rhetorica ad Herennium)*, trans. Harry Caplan. London: Heinemann, 1954.

Adorno, Theodor. *Negative Dialectics*, trans. E. B. Ashton. New York: Continuum, 1973.

Agamben, Giorgio. *Homo Sacer: Sovereign Power and Bare Life*, trans. Daniel Heller-Roazen. Stanford: Stanford University Press, 1998.

Agamben, Giorgio. *State of Exception*, trans. Kevin Attell. Chicago: University of Chicago Press, 2005.

Anon. *The Works of Aristotle*, trans. W. D. Ross and J. A. Smith, 12 vols. Oxford: Clarendon Press, 1927.

Anon. *Mankind*, in *Three Late Medieval Morality Plays*, ed. G. A. Lester. New York: W. W. Norton, [c.1470] 1981.

Aristotle. *Art of Rhetoric*, ed. Hugh Lawson-Tancred. New York: Penguin Classics, 1991.

Aristotle. *Prior Analytics*, trans. A. H. Jenkinson. In *The Works of Aristotle*, Vol. 1 ed. W. D. Ross. Oxford: Oxford University Press, 1928.

Aristotle. *The Ethics of Aristotle*, trans. D. P. Chase. New York: Dutton, 1950.

Aristotle. *Laches and Charmides*, trans. Rosamond Kent Sprague. Indianapolis: Hackett, 1992.

Augustine. *The City of God against the Pagans*, trans. George E. McCracken. Cambridge, MA: Harvard University Press, 1957.

Bacon, Francis. *Of the Proficience and Aduancement of Learning.* Oxford: Leon Lichfielf, 1605.

Bacon, Francis. *The Wisdome of the Ancients*, trans. Sir Arthur Gorges. London: John Bill, 1619.

Badiou, Alain. *Saint Paul: The Foundation of Universalism*, trans. Ray Brassier. Stanford: Stanford University Press, 2003.

Bailey, Amanda. *Of Bondage Debt Property and Personhood in Early Modern England.* Philadelphia: University of Pennsylvania Press, 2013.

Bale, John. *King Johan*, ed. Barry B. Adams. San Marino: The Huntington Library, [1539] 1969.

Benjamin, Walter. *The Origin of German Tragic Drama*, trans. John Osborne. London: Verso, 2009.

Betz, Hans Dieter. 'Jesus and the Cynics: A Survey and an Analysis'. *The Journal of Religion* 74, no. 4 (October 1994): 453–75.

Bevington, David, ed. *King Lear*. New York: Pearson Longman, 2007.

Bevington, David and David L. Smith. 'James I and *Timon of Athens*'. *Comparative Drama* 33, no.1 (Spring 1999): 56–87.

Bizley, W. H. 'Language and Currency in *Timon of Athens*'. *Theoria* 44 (May 1975): 21–42.

Blakemore Evans, G. et al. (eds), *The Tragedy of King Lear* in *The Riverside Shakespeare*. Boston: Houghton Mifflin, 1997.

Branham, R. Bracht. 'Nietzsche's Cynicism: Uppercase or Lowercase?' In *Nietzsche and Antiquity: His Reaction and Response to the Classical Tradition*, ed. Paul Bishop. Rochester: Campden House, 2004, 170–81.

Burckhardt, Jacob. *The Civilization of the Renaissance in Italy*, trans. S. G. C. Middlemore. London: Penguin, 1990.

Burton, Robert. *The Anatomy of Melancholy.* Oxford: John Lichfield, 1621.

Butler, F. G. 'Who Are King Lear's Philosophers? An Answer, With Some Help from Erasmus'. *English Studies* (1986): 511–24.

Cassirer, Ernst. *The Individual and the Cosmos in Renaissance Philosophy*, trans. Mario Domandi. New York: Barnes and Noble, 1963.

Cerano, Anthony. 'The Relation between Prudence and *Synderesis* to Happiness in Medieval Commentaries on Aristotle's *Ethics*'. In *The Reception of Aristotle's Ethics*, ed. Jon Miller. Cambridge: Cambridge University Press, 2012, 125–54.

Chabon, Michael. *The Yiddish Policemen's Union*. London: Harper Perennial, 2007.

Chapman, George. *Bussy D'Ambois*, ed. Nicholas Brooke. Manchester: Manchester University Press, 1999.

Chorost, Michael. 'Biological Finance in Shakespeare's *Timon of Athens*'. *English Literary Renaissance* 21 (1991): 349–70.

Chrysostom, Dio. *Fourth Discourse on Kingship*. In *Discourses 1–11*, trans. J. W. Cahoon. Cambridge, MA: Harvard University Press, 1932, 169–233.

Chrysostom, Dio. *Discourses 1–11*, trans. J. W. Cohoon. Cambridge, MA: Harvard University Press, 1971.

Cohen, Derek. 'The Politics of Wealth in *Timon of Athens*'. *Neophilologus* 77, no. 1 (January 1993): 149–60.

Cohn, Norman. *The Pursuit of the Millennium: Revolutionary Millenarians and Mystical Anarchists of the Middle Ages*. London: Pimlico, [1957] 1993.

Colclough, David. *Freedom of Speech in Early Stuart England*. New York: Cambridge University Press, 2005.

Curtis, Mark H. 'The Alienated Intellectuals of Early Stuart England'. In *Crisis in Europe, 1560–1660*, ed. Trevor Astin. New York: Basic Books, 1965, 295–316.

D'Alembert, 'An Essay upon the Alliance betwixt Learned Men, and the Great'. In *Miscellaneous Pieces in Literature, History, and Philosophy by Mr. D'Alembert*. London, 1764.

Daniel, Drew. *The Melancholy Assemblage: Affect and Epistemology in the English Renaissance*. New York: Fordham University Press, 2013.

Diderot. 'Essai sur les règnes de Claude et de Néron'. In *Œuvres completes*, ed. Roger Lewinter, 15 vols. Paris: Club Français du Livre, 1969–73.

Diderot. 'Mémoires sur différents sujets mathématique'. In *Œuvres completes*, ed. Herbert Dieckman, Jean Fabre and Jacques Proust. Paris: Hermann, 1975.

Diderot. 'Encyclopedia'. In *The Encyclopedia of Diderot & d'Alembert Collaborative Translation Project*, trans. Philip Stewart. Ann Arbor: Scholarly Publishing Office of the University of Michigan Library, 2002, http://hdl.handle.net/2027/spo.did2222.0000.004 (last accessed 22 February 2019).

Doloff, Steven. '"Let me talk with this philosopher": The Alexander/Diogenes Paradigm in *King Lear*'. *Huntington Library Quarterly* (1991): 253–5.

Donawerth, Jane. 'Diogenes the Cynic and Lear's Definition of Man, *King Lear* III.iv.101–109'. *English Language Notes* (1977): 10–14

Downing, F. Gerald. *Christ and the Cynics: Jesus and other Radicals in First-Century Tradition*. Sheffield: JSOT Press, 1988.

Downing, F. Gerald. *Cynics, Paul, and the Pauline Churches: Cynics and Christian Origins II*. New York: Routledge, 1998.

Dudley, Donald R. *A History of Cynicism: From Diogenes to the 6th Century A.D.* London: Methuen, 1937.

Dyrberg, Torben Bech. 'Foucault on *parrhesia*: The Autonomy of Politics and Democracy'. *Political Theory* 44, no. 2 (2016): 265–88

Eddy, Paul Rhodes. 'Jesus as Diogenes? Reflections on the Jesus Cynic Thesis'. *Journal of Biblical Literature* 115, no. 3 (Autumn 1996): 449–69.

Erasmus, Desiderius. *Apophthegmes*, trans. Udall, 1542.

Ficino, Marsilio. *Three Books on Life*, ed. and trans. Carol V. Kaske and John R. Clark, vol. 2. Binghamton, NY: Renaissance Society of America, 1989.

Fischer, Sandra K. '"Cut My Heart in Sums": Shakespeare's Economics and *Timon of Athens*'. In *Money: Lure, Lore, and Literature*, ed. John Louis DiGaetani. Westport: Greenwood Press, 1994, 187–95.

Flynn, Thomas. 'Foucault as Parrhesiast: His Last Course at the Collège de France (1984)'. In *The Final Foucault*, ed. James Bernauer and David Rasmussen. Cambridge, MA: MIT Press, 1987.

Foakes, R. A. ed. *King Lear*. London: Thomson Learning, 1997.

Folkers, Andreas. 'Daring the Truth: Foucault, Parrhesia and the Genealogy of Critique'. *Theory, Culture & Society* 33, no. 1 (2016): 3–28

Foucault, Michel. 'The Ethics of Care for the Self as a Practice of Freedom: An Interview with Michel Foucault on January 20, 1984' in *The Final Foucault*, trans. J. D. Gauthier, ed. James Bernauer and David Rasmussen. Cambridge, MA: The MIT Press, 1991, 1–20.

Foucault, Michel. *Fearless Speech*, ed. Joseph Pearson. Los Angeles: Semiotext(e), 2001.

Foucault, Michel. *Le Courage de la Vérité: Le gouvernement de Soi et des Autres II*. Paris: Gallimard, 2009.

Foucault, Michel. *The Government of Self and Others*. Lectures at the Collège de France, 1982-1983, ed. Fréderic Gros and trans. Graham Burchell. New York: Palgrave Macmillan, 2010.

Foucault, Michel. *The Courage of Truth: The Government of Self and Others II*. Lectures at the Collège de France, 1983–1984, trans. Graham Burchell. New York: Palgrave Macmillan, 2011.

Foucault, Michel. *On the Government of the Living*. Lectures at the Collège de France, 1979-1980, trans. Graham Burchell. New York: Palgrave Macmillan, 2012.

Fowler, Elizabeth. *Literary Character: The Human Figure in Early English Writing*. Ithaca: Cornell University Press, 2003.

Franek, Jakub. 'Philosophical Parrhesia as Aesthetics of Existence'. *Continental Philosophy Review* 39 (2006): 113–34.

Gallagher, Catherine. *Telling It Like It Wasn't: The Counterfactual Imagination in History and Fiction*. Chicago: University of Chicago Press, 2018.

Gallop, Jane. 'The Historicization of Literary Studies and the Fate of Close Reading'. *Profession* (2007): 181–6.

Garber, Marjorie. '"Remember Me": Memento Mori Figures in Shakespeare's Plays'. *Renaissance Drama* 12 (1981): 3–25.

Garver, Eugene. *Aristotle's Rhetoric: An Art of Character*. Chicago: University of Chicago Press, 1994.

Goddard, William. *A Satirycall Dialogue or a sharplye-invective conference, betweene Allexander the great, and that truelye woman-hater Diogynes*. George Waters, 1616.

Goldberg, Jonathan. *James I and the Politics of Literature*. Baltimore: Johns Hopkins University Press, 1983.

Gosson, Stephen. *Ephemerides of Phialo*. London: Thomas Dawson, 1579.

Grady, Hugh. '*Timon of Athens*: The Dialectic of Usury, Nihilism, and Art'. In *A Companion to Shakespeare's Works*, Volume 1, *The Tragedies*, ed. Richard Dutton and Jean E. Howard. Malden, MA: Blackwell, 2006, 431–51.

Graham, Kenneth. *The Performance of Conviction: Plainness and Rhetoric in the Early English Renaissance*. Ithaca: Cornell University Press, 1994.

de Grazia, Margreta. *Hamlet without Hamlet*. Cambridge: Cambridge University Press, 2007.

Gundersheimer, Werner. 'Patronage in the Renaissance: An Exploratory Approach'. In *Patronage in the Renaissance*, ed. Stephen K. Orgel and Guy Fitch Lytle. Princeton: Princeton University Press, 1981.

Hadot, Pierre. *Philosophy as a Way of Life: Spiritual Exercises from Socrates to Foucault*. New York: Blackwell, 1995.

Haines, C. M. *Shakespeare in France. Criticism. Voltaire to Victor Hugo*. London: Oxford University Press, 1925.

Hampshire, Stuart. *Innocence and Experience*. Cambridge, MA: Harvard University Press, 1989.

Hegel, G. W. F. *Lectures on the Philosophy of History*, trans. E. S. Haldane, 3 vols. London: Kegan Paul, 1896.

Hegel, G. W. F. *The Philosophy of Right*, trans. T. M. Knox. New York: Oxford University Press, 1952.

Hegel, G. W. F. *Aesthetics: Lectures on Fine Art*, trans. T. M. Knox, 2 volumes. Oxford: Oxford University Press, 1975.

Herder, Johann Gottfried. *On World History: An Anthology*, ed. Ernest A. Menze and trans. Michael Palma. Armonk: M. E. Sharpe, 1997.

Herder, Johann Gottfried. *Selected Writings on Aesthetics*, ed. and trans. Gregory Moore. Princeton: Princeton University Press, 2006.

Hirsh, James. 'The Origin of the Late Renaissance Dramatic Convention of Self-Addressed Speech'. *Shakespeare Survey* 68 (2015): 131–45.

Holinshed, Raphael. *The Chronicles of England, Scotland, and Ireland*. London, 1577.

Holland, Peter. 'The Merchant of Venice and the Value of Money'. *Cahiers Élizabéthains* 60 (2001): 13–30.

Hornback, Robert. 'The Fool in Quarto and Folio *King Lear*'. *English Literary Renaissance* 34, no. 3 (Autumn 2004): 95–132.

Hutson, Lorna. *The Invention of Suspicion: Law and Mimesis in Shakespeare and Renaissance Drama*. Oxford: Oxford University Press, 2007.

Hutson, Lorna. *Circumstantial Shakespeare*. Oxford: Oxford University Press, 2015.

James I. *The true lawe of free monarchies: or The reciprock and mutuall dutie betwixt a free king, and his natural subiecks*. Edinburgh, 1598.

Jean II. 'Ordonnance qui establit une Ayde, qui fixe le prix des Monneyes, & qui contient des Reglements sur le prix des denrée & des salaires des Ouvriers, sur les Prevostez & Tabellionages, & sur les Sergents' in *Ordonnances Des Roys De France De La Troisième Race*, Vol. 6. Paris, 1741.

Julian. *Orations 6–8*, trans. Wilmer Cave Wright. Cambridge, MA: Harvard University Press, 2014.

Kahn, Coppelia. '"Magic of Bounty": *Timon of Athens*, Jacobean Patronage, and Maternal Power'. *Shakespeare Quarterly* 38, no. 1 (Spring 1987): 34–57.

Kinney, Daniel. 'Heirs of the Dog: Cynic Selfhood in Medieval and Renaissance Culture'. In *The Cynics: The Cynic Movement in Antiquity and Its Legacy*, ed. R. Bracht Branham and Marie-Odile Goulet-Cazé. Berkeley: University of California Press, 2000, 294–328.

Klein, Karl. 'Appendix: The Timon Legend'. In *Timon of Athens*, ed. Karl Klein. New York: Cambridge University Press, 2001.

Knights, L. C. *How Many Children Had Lady Macbeth? An Essay in the Theory and Practice of Shakespeare Criticism*. Cambridge: The Minority Press, 1933.

Kramnick, Jonathan. *Paper Minds: Literature and the Ecology of Consciousness*. Chicago: University of Chicago Press, 2018.

Krueger, Derek. 'Diogenes the Cynic among the Fourth Century Fathers'. *Vigiliae Christianae* 47, no. 1 (1993): 29–49.

Kuzner, James. *Shakespeare as a Way of Life: Skeptical Practice and the Politics of Cognition*. New York: Fordham University Press, 2016.

Laertius, Diogenes. *Lives of Eminent Philosophers*, trans. R. D. Hicks. Cambridge, MA: Harvard University Press, 1972.

Lazzarato, Maurizio. *Signs and Machines: Capitalism and the Production of Subjectivity*, trans. Joshua David Jordan. South Pasadena: Semiotext(e), 2014.

Lemm, Vanessa. 'The Embodiment of Truth and the Politics of Community: Foucault and the Cynics'. In *The Government of Life: Foucault, Biopolitics, and Neoliberalism*. New York: Fordham University Press, 2014, 208–23.

Leroy, Luis. *Of the Interchangeable Course, or Variety of Things*, trans. Robert Ashley. London: Charles Yetsweirt, 1594.

Lievsay, John. 'Some Renaissance Views of Diogenes the Cynic'. *Joseph Quincy Adams Memorial Studies* (1948): 450.

Lochman, Daniel T., López, Maritere and Hutson, Lorna (eds), *Discourses and Representations of Friendship in Early Modern Europe, 1500–1700*. Farnham: Ashgate, 2011.

Lodge, Thomas. *Catharos. Diogenes in his Singularitie*. London: William Hoskins and John Danter, 1591.

Long, A. A. 'The Socratic Tradition: Diogenes, Crates, and Hellenistic Ethics'. In *The Cynics: The Cynic Movement in Antiquity and Its Legacy*, ed. R. Bracht Branham and Marie-Odile Goulet-Cazé. Berkeley: University of California Press, 1996, 28–46.

Lucian. *A dialogue betwene Lucian and Diogenes of the life harde and sharpe, and of the lyfe tendre and delicate*, trans. Thomas Elyot. London, 1532.

Lucian. *Certaine select dialogues of Lucian together with his true historie*, trans. Francis Hickes. Oxford, 1634.

Lyly, John. *Campaspe*, ed. G. K. Hunter. Manchester: Manchester University Press, [1584] 1991.

Machiavelli, Niccolò. *Machivael's [sic] discourses upon the first decade of T. Livius, translated out of the Italian. To which is added his Prince*, trans. Edward Dacres. London, 1663.

Martin, John Jeffries. *Myths of Renaissance Individualism*. Basingstoke: Palgrave Macmillan, 2004.

Marx, Karl. *Economic and Philosophic Manuscripts of 1844*, trans. Martin Milligan. New York: International Publishers, 1964.

Maus, Katherine Eisaman. *Inwardness and Theater in the English Renaissance*. Chicago: University of Chicago Press, 1995.

Mauss, Marcel. *The Gift: Forms and Functions of Exchange in Archaic Societies*. New York: Norton, 1967.

Mazella, David. *The Making of Modern Cynicism*. Charlottesville: University of Virginia Press, 2007.

Middleton, Thomas. *Micro-cynicon*. London: Thomas Creede, 1599.

Miller, Andrew H. *The Burdens of Perfection: On Ethics and Reading in Nineteenth-Century British Literature*. Ithaca: Cornell University Press, 2008.

Montaigne, Michel. *The Essayes or Morall, Politike and Millitarie Discourses*, trans. John Florio. London, 1603.

Muir, Kenneth ed. *King Lear*. London: Methuen, 1972.

Muir, Kenneth. 'Timon of Athens and the Cash Nexus'. In *The Singularity of Shakespeare, and Other Essays*. Liverpool: Liverpool University Press, 1977.

Muir, Kenneth. *The Singularity of Shakespeare, and Other Essays*. Liverpool: Liverpool University Press, 1977.

Muller, Adam. 'Fragmente über William Shakespear', *Phöbus. Ein Journal für die Kunst* (1808).

Navia, Luis E. *Classical Cynicism: A Critical Study*. Westport, CT: Greenwood Publishing Group, 1996.

Newsom, Robert. *A Likely Story: Probability and Play in Fiction*. New Brunswick, NJ: Rutgers University Press, 1988.

Niehues-Pröbsting, Heinrich. 'The Modern Reception of Cynicism: Diogenes in the Enlightenment'. In *The Cynics: The Cynic Movement in Antiquity and Its Legacy*, ed. R. Bracht Branham and Marie-Odile Goulet-Cazé. Berkeley: University of California Press, 1996.

Nietzsche. *The Birth of Tragedy: and The Case of Wagner*, trans. Walter Kaufmann. New York: Knopf Doubleday, 1967.

Nietzsche, Friedrich. *The Gay Science*, trans. Walter Kaufmann. New York: Vintage Books, 1974.

Nietzsche, Friedrich. *Beyond Good and Evil: Prelude to a Philosophy of the Future*, ed. and trans. Marion Faber. New York: Oxford University Press, 1998.

Parks, Joan. 'History, Tragedie, and Truth in Christopher Marlowe's *Edward II*'. *SEL Studies in English Literature, 1500–1900* 39, no. 2 (Spring 1999): 275–90.

Paulin, Roger. *The Critical Reception of Shakespeare in Germany 1682–1914: Native Literature and Foreign Genius*. Hildesheim: Georg Olms Verlag, 2003.

Plutarch, Lucius. *The Lives of the Noble Grecians and Romanes*, trans. Sir Thomas North. London: Thomas Vautruiller, 1579.

Polo, Marco. *The most noble and famous trauels of Marcus Paulus*. London, 1579.

Prozorov, Sergei. 'Foucault's Affirmative Biopolitics: Cynic Parrhesia and the Biopower of the Powerless'. *Political Theory* 45, no. 6 (2017): 801–23.

Rasmussen, Douglas B. 'Human Flourishing and the Appeal to Human Nature'. *Social Philosophy and Policy* 16, no. 1 (Winter 1999): 1–43.

Ribner, Irving. *The English History Play in the Age of Shakespeare*. New York: Octagon Books, 1979.

Rigolot, François. 'The Renaissance Fascination with Error: Mannerism and Early Modern Poetry'. *Renaissance Quarterly* 57 (2004), 1219–34.

Rowlands, Samuel. *Diogenes Lanthorne*. London: Edward Allde, 1608.

Sarkar, Debapriya. '*The Tempest*'s Other Plots'. *Shakespeare Studies* 45 (2017): 203–30.

Sayre, Farrand. *The Greek Cynics*. Baltimore: J. H. Furst, 1948.

Schmitt, Carl. *The Crisis of Parliamentary Democracy*, trans. Ellen Kennedy. Cambridge, MA: MIT Press, 1988.

Schmitt, Carl. *The Concept of the Political*, trans. George D. Schwab. Chicago: University of Chicago Press, 1996.

Scodel, Joshua. *Excess and the Mean in Early Modern English Literature*. Princeton: Princeton University Press, 2002.

Scott, Gary Alan. 'Games of Truth: Foucault's Analysis of the Transformation from Political to Ethical *Parrhêsia*'. *The Southern Journal of Philosophy* 34 (1996): 97–114.

Şenocak, Neslihan. *The Poor and the Perfect: The Rise of Learning in the Franciscan Order, 1209–1310*. Ithaca: Cornell University Press, 2012.

Shakespeare, William. *King Lear*, ed. Kenneth Muir. London: Methuen, 1972.

Shakespeare, William. *The Norton Shakespeare*, ed. Stephen Greenblatt, Walter Cohen, Jean E. Howard and Katharine Eisaman Maus. New York: Norton, 1997.

Shannon, Laurie. *Sovereign Amity: Figures of Friendship in Shakespearean Contexts*. Chicago: University of Chicago Press, 2002.

Shannon, Laurie. 'Poor, Bare, Forked: Animal Sovereignty, Human Negative Exceptionalism, and the Natural History of *King Lear*'. *Shakespeare Quarterly* 60, no. 2 (Summer 2009): 168–96.

Shea, Louisa. *The Cynic Enlightenment: Diogenes in the Salon*. Baltimore: Johns Hopkins University Press, 2010.

Shickman, Allan R. 'The Fool and Death in Shakespeare'. *Colby Quarterly* 34, no. 3 (1998): 201–25.

Skelton, John. *Magnificence*, ed. Paula Neuss. Manchester: Manchester University Press, [1519] 1980.

Skura, Meredith Anne. *Tudor Autobiography: Listening for Inwardness*. Chicago: University of Chicago Press, 2008.

Sloterdijk, Peter. *Critique of Cynical Reason*. Minneapolis: University of Minnesota Press, 1987.

Smith, M. W. A. 'The Authorship of *Timon of Athens*'. *Text: Transactions of the Society for Textual Scholarship* (1991): 195–240.

Stafford, Anthony. *Staffords Heavenly Dogge*. London: George Purslowe, 1615.

Stinton, T. C. W. '*Hamartia* in Aristotle and Greek Tragedy'. *The Classical Quarterly* 25, no. 2 (December 1975): 221–54.

Strier, Richard. *Resistant Structures: Particularity, Radicalism, and Renaissance Texts*. Berkeley: University of California Press, 1995.

Strier, Richard. *The Unrepentant Renaissance: From Petrarch to Shakespeare to Milton*. Chicago: University of Chicago Press, 2011.

Tamboukou, Maria. 'Truth Telling in Foucault and Arendt: Parrhesia, the Pariah and Academics in Dark Times'. *Journal of Education Policy* 27, no. 6 (November 2012): 849–65.

Tanke, Joseph J. 'Cynical Aesthetics: A Theme from Michel Foucault's 1984 Lectures at the Collège de France'. *Philosophy Today* 46, no. 2 (Summer 2002): 170–84.

Taylor, E. M. M. 'Lear's Philosopher'. *Shakespeare Quarterly* 6, no.3 (Summer 1955): 364–5.

Taylor, Gary. 'Monopolies, Show Trials, Disaster, and Invasion: *King Lear* and Censorship'. In *The Division of the Kingdoms: Shakespeare's Two Versions of King Lear*, ed. Gary Taylor and Michael Warren. New York: Oxford University Press, 1983.

Taylor, Gary and Warren, Michael (eds). *The Division of the Kingdoms: Shakespeare's Two Versions of King Lear*. New York: Oxford University Press, 1983.

Trevor, Douglas. *The Poetics of Melancholy in Early Modern England*. Cambridge: Cambridge University Press, 2004.

Urkowitz, Steven. *Shakespeare's Revision of King Lear*. Princeton: Princeton University Press, 1980.

Vaughan, Rice. *A discourse of coin and coinage*. London, 1675.

Walkington, Thomas. *The optick glasse of humors*. London: John Windet, 1607.

Warner, Michael. *Publics and Counterpublics*. New York: Zone Books, 2002.

Watt, Ian. *The Rise of the Novel: Studies in Defoe, Richardson, and Fielding*. London: Chatto and Windus, 1957.

Westlund, Joseph. 'The Theme of Tact in *Campaspe*'. *SEL Studies in English Literature, 1500–1900* 16, no. 2 (1976): 213–21.

Wiles, David. *Shakespeare's Clown: Actor and Text in the Elizabethan Playhouse*. Cambridge: Cambridge University Press, 1987.

Wilson, Thomas. *The Arte of Rhetorique*. London: Richard Grafton, 1553; repr. Gainesville: Scholars' Facsimiles and Reprints, 1962.

Zagan, Cristian. 'Foucault: On Parrhesia and Rhetoric'. *Hermeneia* 15 (2015): 98–105.

INDEX

Note: page references with 'n' indicate chapter notes.